Donated by
The Public Interest Institute
to The Heartland Institute
2016

Comparative Studies in
Local Economic Development

Recent Titles in
Contributions in Economics and Economic History

Rural Change in the Third World: Pakistan and the Aga Khan Rural Support Program
Mahmood Hasan Khan and Shoaib Sultan Khan

Soviet Political Economy in Transition: From Lenin to Gorbachev
A. F. Dowlah

The Diary of Rexford G. Tugwell: The New Deal, 1932–1935
Michael Vincent Namorato, editor

Making Markets: An Interdisciplinary Perspective on Economic Exchange
Robin Cantor, Stuart Henry, and Steve Rayner

Technology and U.S. Competitiveness: An Institutional Focus
W. Henry Lambright and Dianne Rahm, editors

The Development of the Greek Economy, 1950–1991
George A. Jouganatos

Business Finance in Less Developed Capital Markets
Klaus P. Fischer and George J. Papaioannou, editors

Logs for Capital: The Timber Industry and Capitalist Enterprise in the Nineteenth Century
Sing C. Chew

The American Pulp and Paper Industry, 1900–1940:
Mill Survival, Firm Structure, and Industry Relocation
Nancy Kane Ohanian

Aspirations and Realities: A Documentary History of Economic Development Policy in Ireland since 1922
James L. Wiles and Richard B. Finnegan

Multinational Culture: Social Impacts of a Global Economy
Cheryl R. Lehman and Russell M. Moore, editors

The Age of Giant Corporations: A Microeconomic History of American Business, 1914–1992, A Third Edition
Robert Sobel

Comparative Studies in Local Economic Development

PROBLEMS IN POLICY IMPLEMENTATION

Edited by
Peter B. Meyer

PREPARED UNDER THE AUSPICES OF THE
POLICY STUDIES ORGANIZATION

Stuart S. Nagel, *Publications Coordinator*

Contributions in Economics and
Economic History,
Number 144

GREENWOOD PRESS
Westport, Connecticut • London

Library of Congress Cataloging-in-Publication Data

Comparative studies in local economic development : problems in policy
  implementation / edited by Peter B. Meyer.
    p. cm. — (Contributions in economics and economic history,
  ISSN 0084-9235 ; no. 144)
  "Prepared under the auspices of the Policy Studies Organization,
  Stuart S. Nagel, publications coordinator."
  Includes bibliographical references and index.
  ISBN 0-313-28820-8 (alk. paper)
  1. Economic development projects—United States—Case studies.
  2. Economic development projects—Great Britain—Case studies.
  3. Community development—Government policy—United States—Case
  studies. 4. Community development—Government policy—Great
  Britain—Case studies. I. Meyer, Peter B. II. Policy Studies
  Organization. III. Series.
  HC110.E44C66 1993
  338.973—dc20   92-35599

British Library Cataloguing in Publication Data is available.

Copyright © 1993 by the Policy Studies Organization

All rights reserved. No portion of this book may be
reproduced, by any process or technique, without the
express written consent of the publisher.

Library of Congress Catalog Card Number: 92-35599
ISBN: 0-313-28820-8
ISSN: 0084-9235

First published in 1993

Greenwood Press, 88 Post Road West, Westport, CT 06881
An imprint of Greenwood Publishing Group, Inc.

Printed in the United States of America

The paper used in this book complies with the
Permanent Paper Standard issued by the National
Information Standards Organization (Z39.48-1984).

10 9 8 7 6 5 4 3 2 1

For Kristen

Contents

I. OVERVIEW

   1. Local Economic Policy and Its Implementation:
      Case Studies of Innovative Efforts
      Peter B. Meyer   3

   2. Putting Targeted Economic Development to Work: The Role of
      Targeted Marketing in an Economic Development Program
      C. Theodore Koebel and Cara L. Bailey   17

II. EXTERNAL AND ENVIRONMENTAL INFLUENCES
ON LOCAL IMPLEMENTATION

   Introduction   33

   3. Local Economic Development in a Traditional Industrial Area:
      The Case of the Ruhrgebiet
      Gerd Hennings and Klaus R. Kunzmann   35

   4. Employee Buyouts and Loans to Preserve Jobs:
      The South Bend Experience
      Charles Craypo and Jerry Paar   55

5. Policy Instruments in West Central Scotland
and Their Local Authority Context
William F. Lever   69

6. Regenerating Urban Neighborhoods: Local People as
Implementers of Economic Development Policies
Alan McGregor and Andrew A. McArthur   85

III. SPILLOVERS AND COMMUNITY RESPONSE:
LOCAL FORCES SHAPING ECONOMIC DEVELOPMENT
PROGRAM IMPLEMENTATION

Introduction   101

7. From Cannery Row to Gold Coast in Baltimore:
Is This Development?
Robert P. Giloth   103

8. Industrial Change and Conflict in Urban Redevelopment:
The Case of South Cardiff, Wales
Huw Thomas and Rob F. Imrie   119

9. Strategic Planning for the Port of New Orleans
Alma H. Young and Robert K. Whelan   131

IV. COMPARATIVE ANALYSIS: A CASE AND SOME LESSONS

10. A Tale of Two Cities: Revitalizing Corby, Northamptonshire,
and Youngstown, Ohio
Terry F. Buss   149

11. On the Possibility of Pro-Active Community Development
David Fasenfest   169

References   179

Index   193

About the Editor and Contributors   199

Part I

Overview

1

Local Economic Policy and Its Implementation: Case Studies of Innovative Efforts

Peter B. Meyer

> It must be remembered that there is nothing more difficult to plan, more doubtful of success, nor more dangerous to manage than the creation of a new system. For the initiator has the enmity of all who would profit by the preservation of the old institutions and merely lukewarm defenders in those who would gain by the new ones. The hesitation of the latter arises in part from the fear of their adversaries, who have the laws on their side, and in part from the general skepticism of mankind which does not really believe in an innovation until experience proves its value.
>
> Machiavelli 1947:15

WHY EXAMINE IMPLEMENTATION CASE STUDIES — AND HOW?

This volume, like many others dealing with public policy and its implementation, contains a series of case studies. The case study approach can be challenged for its limited capacity to contribute to generalizations about causality. Such generalizations, it is argued, lie at the core of advancing scientific understanding of observable phenomena and relationships. The dilemmas of case study work plague all forms of comparative analysis, regardless of the degree of statistical sophistication and capacity to identify causality associated with any comparison, since each situation is unique.

Each case involves different conditions, institutions, political and social values, and relationships that shape findings and generate biases. Researchers should recognize and, if possible, control for such factors in analysis. The research problem is compounded when we compare local situations in different nations, for then we have to address not only the comparisons of the cities but also variations in their national, institutional, and other contexts.

Yet crossnational comparisons abound. Nowhere is this more evident than in a growing array of comparisons between the United States and the United Kingdom, especially with respect to economic development strategies (Fasenfest 1992; Feagin 1990; Schwarz and Volgy 1988; Wolman and Goldsmith 1990). Such effort is driven by local economic development pressures: new ideas are constantly demanded by practitioners, and the pervasiveness of this activity draws scholars' attention. The absence of an overt language barrier appears to facilitate the search for innovations and insights from the other side of the Atlantic.

Despite extensive borrowing of tactics and techniques between the United States and the United Kingdom, the actual practice of local economic development varies substantially between the countries (Benington and Geddes 1990; Clavel 1983; Meyer and Boyle 1990; Meyer and Kraushaar 1989). Major differences, moreover, exist in the criteria brought to bear in evaluation of economic revitalization efforts (Fasenfest 1992; Feagin 1990; Meyer 1992).

The roots of these differences may lie in the background, training, attitudes, and perceptions of the people who are active in local economic development. Alternatively, the divergent experiences may be due to the legal and cultural constraints on the processes of implementation of what are fundamentally similar economic development policies. Examination of the details of different policy implementation efforts may help identify some of the causes of successes and failures, as well as the general patterns of forces that impede the changes pursued by economic development programs.

Unfortunately, much of the literature on local economic development efforts has focused on either the formulation and content of policies and plans or their impacts in the community and marketplace. The link between a policy and its outcomes is the implementation process itself. To the extent that this process is treated as a black box, any efforts at policy transfer or program replication may be doomed to failure since the forces that shape particular implementations, thus affecting their success, are ignored.

This problem is the rationale for our focus on implementation in this volume. The broader scope of this collection of cases that spans the Atlantic is grounded in the recognition that massive variation exists in law, custom, and the effective powers of the state — even within a single country. A focus on a single nation-state could overlook such variety, while the lessons from particular cases in one nation could be directly relevant to a setting in another country, because they face similar local "implementation-shaping" conditions.

The fact remains that the number and extent of different conditions in any comparison of cases is so great that we cannot fully control for variation. This is evident even in the very popular bilateral comparison of the United States and the United Kingdom. Our ability to understand the roles played by the institutional, cultural, and legal differences between the two countries is enhanced by a detailed case from another country, Germany. Policy implementation in the Ruhrgebiet, the traditional heart of steel and coal production in Germany, provides a case example of a "middle ground" between U.S. and U.K. national contexts for local and regional economic development efforts. Chapter 3, which examines this experience, begins the collection of in-depth implementation discussions and offers a platform from which to address the British and American cases.

This chapter introduces and sets a context for the cases that follow. First, we summarize differences in the national contexts of the cases presented. Next, we examine the "implementation problem" in greater detail, considering the conflict that inevitably accompanies change and offering a systematic means for examining divergent priorities, policy orientations, and expectation for program outcomes. Third, the implementation problem in each case is presented in the context of the policy analysis space we construct. We conclude with some observations on reading cases and the analytical effort required to extract lessons for action or hypotheses for further research.

DIFFERENCES IN NATIONAL IMPLEMENTATION CONTEXTS

We need to set the context for implementation efforts in the three countries from which the cases are drawn, since all assume some knowledge of cultural, political, and legal factors shaping local efforts. The starkest differences are between the United States and the United Kingdom; Germany serves as a middle ground. Thus, we examine first the differences between the U.S. and U.K. contexts, and then we discuss how the German situation fits into the overall context.

Differences between the United States and United Kingdom lie in two critical dimensions: (1) political/institutional, and (2) legal. We examine each in turn for clarity, although they clearly overlap.

Political/institutional differences are obvious in the nature of the state: unitary in Britain and federal in the United States; parliamentary in Britain and presidential in the United States; geographically compact in Britain and dispersed in the United States. Differences also arise in politics: party discipline is tight in Britain, and adherence to political party manifestos minimizes the need for compromises with other parties; however, compromise across the board is inherent in the United States. Ideological postures (including an overtly "socialist" agenda) and actions driven by them are accepted in Britain, but ideologically driven policies in the United States must be rationalized with a social good or ideologically neutral argument. Finally, local governments in Britain encompass significantly larger populations than are the norm for local ("minor") civil divisions in the United States.

In implementing policies, relatively large local jurisdictions rarely need to bargain and compromise with other small units to achieve policy consistency across a meaningful space. The unitary state centralizes underlying public power far more than is possible in the federal system. The combination of ideological politics and strict party discipline in Britain then weakens the pressures, so evident in U.S. policy debates, for detailed economic rationales (and cost-benefit analyses) of public policies; they can be pursued because they are ideologically correct, even if not demonstrably most efficient or effective (and, in any case, "effectiveness" is defined by the currently dominant ideology).

Legal differences center on the powers of the state, especially the local state. The myriad multipurpose governmental units in the United States appear to have "general government powers," the legal right to do whatever they wish with the funds they decide to raise for themselves, subject to very broad constraints. The effective operational constraints on U.S. local governments derive from their limited revenue-generating powers. In Britain, by contrast, local governments have limited "statutory powers" and are not permitted to spend more than the proceeds of a 20 mil assessment on local property for all other discretionary functions (including economic development until very recently). The level of taxes local governments can levy has been reduced by the national state in the United Kingdom, as have central government cash grants for local public purposes, which in the past exceeded 50 percent of the revenues of many local governments.

The very proliferation of small local units in the United States reflects its reliance on competitive behavior (emulating for-profit firms) as its policy implementation mechanism. Individual municipalities are forced to rely on their own internal resources, most commonly real estate taxation, for operating revenues. This enforced municipal self-reliance is evidence of the continued acceptance of the so-called Tiebout hypothesis extolling the virtues of intermunicipal diversity and competition, a perspective that reflects the U.S. individualist ethos and distinguishes it from the European democracies (Tiebout 1972).

The upshot of these variations in legal empowerment is simply that the *capacity* of the local state to act independently in the United States far exceeds that of its counterpart institutions in the United Kingdom. Although the U.K. local state, being larger on average, may have more resources and a larger local economy to address and influence, and its agents may have more status in attempting to wield such influence, the greater independent taxing and spending powers of the U.S. local state create the capacity for a more proactive response to perceived policy problems. By contrast, the ideological individualism accompanying the proliferation and relative independence of the U.S. local state produces local revenue-generation problems that inhibit its *willingness* to act, especially in the face of private sector pressures for freedom from control and local taxation (Newton 1975:247–249).

Germany provides a context for local action that blends the U.S. and U.K. conditions. The nation is organized federally, with significant autonomy for the states (*Laender*) and, below them, for local political jurisdictions. Local government units are generally larger than those in the United States, and national and state funds augment local tax revenues in providing resources for intervention, in much the same way as central government grants do in Britain. The grants are, in fact, revenue equalizing, sharing resources from more affluent regions with impoverished areas. Ideology affects political interactions, but splits along industry lines within the private sector are more visible than in either the United States or United Kingdom. The absence of a cohesive private sector "line," combined with the autonomy and size of the local state, should permit more extensive local intervention and more freedom to implement focused policies in pursuit of local economic and social interests than would be plausible in either the United States or Britain.

THE IMPLEMENTATION PROBLEM: DIMENSIONS OF CONFLICT

Implementation of a new policy is never fully assured. A policy is a set of principles or a statement of objectives. It must be translated into a program, which is a course of action expected to generate desired results. The implementation problem arises from the fact that the program is based on expectations, and these forecasts — of reactions on the part of public or private sector entities; environmental factors in world, national, or regional economies; and the capacity of program personnel to take intended actions — may be faulty.

The very fact that the policy is new means that it will induce change. If no change from what would otherwise occur is expected, then there is no reason to create a program that does not already exist. Change, by itself, always generates conflict at some level, as the quote from Machiavelli that opened this chapter makes clear. Conflicts may emerge at several levels and between different organizations and individuals acting on the local economic scene. On the state level, there may be conflicts over local, regional, and national objectives. The public and private sectors are recognized to have different perspectives, and the conflict may emerge from the different rates of return to the different sectors from the new policies. Clearly, there is no reason to assume unanimity on the part of the private sector itself, as business interests may conflict with those of workers or community groups and landowners, and different industrial sectors themselves may disagree on the expected impacts (and thus the desirability) of proposed programs.

We can characterize this conflict in terms of divergent objectives or goals on the part of the parties involved in a local economic development effort. Disagreement may, of course, derive from different perceptions or predictions of impacts as well (Meyer 1992). Whatever the source of disagreement, it is likely to be manifest in differences in choices made among action alternatives.

Even before action programs are determined, policy selection is inevitably a matter of choice. A range of action alternatives and program emphases always exists. Implicit or explicit criteria for "success" shape the actions taken, regardless of rhetorical rationales or ideological postures. (Accounting processes inherent in selection of success criteria require that certain outputs be generated and measured while other outputs are, by definition of the accounting systems, ignored, even though they may arguably have economic value.)

A multidimensional decision-space for selection of economic development program orientations can be represented in the form of choices for positions along a series of discrete axes. Previous work on local economic policy choices in Britain measured such program decisions in terms of choices between extreme alternative emphases on nine scales. The nine choices, presented in Table 1.1, were found to be orthogonal; they may be interpreted as fully defining a nine-dimensional policy space (Meyer 1991b).

Local economic development officials, for example, may stress wealth creation in order to generate capital to sustain new investment, but they may find that workers' demands for current incomes force a shift during the implementation process toward greater emphasis on job creation. Attraction of non-local business and investment is a common priority, but implementation of such programs may produce conflicts with those concerned about local businesses and the value of local investments in homes. Long-established businesses may promote a specialization strategy that strengthens their competitive position in world markets, while new entrepreneurs may expect their efforts to be complemented by local programs to stimulate economic diversification. Reliance on market forces to stimulate new investments may run afoul of citizen demands for more immediate proactive efforts by the local public sector. The conflicts may not be between one pole and another on any of the nine dimensions in Table 1.1, but over position on the scale — the degree of emphasis on generating income, for example, relative to that on creating jobs at any pay level. But conflicts will inevitably emerge in the implementation process.

The chapters in this volume examine a variety of implementation efforts or actions to pursue, in the words of Machiavelli, "the creation of a new system." At the most basic level, all the innovations described involve some increase in community control over local economic conditions and prospects. Those who would profit under the old system and thus resist change may be local economic actors ("sunset" industries, for example) or non-local organizations that benefit from competition between communities wanting to attract new branch plants and offices. The potential beneficiaries of the new system may be workers, homeowners, local businesses, or other local people and institutions. Neither group is homogenous, and both may be severely divided over desired ends — and means for change.

In Chapter 2, Theodore Koebel and Cara Bailey examine three alternative approaches to asserting local control through targeted marketing to non-local businesses. They provide an example of the systemic constraints on action by very activist-oriented local governments and development groups. With no conflict over heavy emphases on growth and on new business recruitment, local efforts may be stymied by data constraints and other non-local information factors. Thus, the creation of a new system can be seen to be inherently difficult simply because another system is in place, even in the absence of visible conflict over the new approaches.

Part II of this volume turns to more specific external, non-local forces that constrain local implementation alternatives. The institutional political environment may be characterized as generally passive. However, this passivity and the institutional structures and beliefs fostering quantitative growth, not local control or development, can result

Table 1.1
Local Economic Development Policy Choices

1. WEALTH CREATION AND THEN JOBS or DIRECT JOB CREATION
   The relative importance of direct or indirect provision of paid work incomes to unemployed people is a key element in choice of strategy or approach toward economic development.

2. NUMBER OF JOBS or TOTAL WORK INCOMES
   The two are not simultaneous, and there may be a need to choose between a small number of higher paid positions and a larger number of lower paid jobs.

3. FOR-PROFIT SECTOR EXPANSION or INCREASED ECONOMIC ACTIVITY
   The extent to which emphasis is placed on private for-profit enterprises or other forms of economic activity can vary.

4. GENERAL PROGRAMS or EFFORTS TARGETED AT SPECIAL GROUPS
   The extent to which economic development is targeted on groups with special needs or problems — youth, minorities, women, disabled, etc. — should reflect a conscious decision.

5. ECONOMIC GROWTH or COMMUNITY ECONOMIC DEVELOPMENT
   Growth is simply an increase in levels of economic activity. Development implies some increase in local control — and thus in local economic stability. Different strategies are associated with the two approaches.

6. SECTORAL SPECIALIZATION or ECONOMIC DIVERSIFICATION
   Specialization, drawing on local comparative advantage, characterized all development efforts through the 1970s, but it is not always the best approach. The need for diversification varies with local economies.

7. ECONOMIC DEVELOPMENT or INDUSTRIAL (MANUFACTURING) DEVELOPMENT
   Economic activity includes mining, agriculture, etc., distribution of goods and provisions of services, as well as manufacture of products; the emphasis on manufacture, that is, industrial activity, varies in different local economies.

8. LOCAL ENTERPRISE DEVELOPMENT or NON-LOCAL BUSINESS RECRUITMENT
   Some mix is generally chosen on the basis of local economic capacities, including entrepreneurship and the ability of the area to generate its own capital for investment as well as resources for export.

9. PASSIVE PUBLIC INCENTIVES or ACTIVE PUBLIC INVESTMENT
   The decision about how active the public sector is to be as a leading agent is critical to overall strategy choices. In general, policies have tended toward reactive rather than proactive approaches.

Case Studies of Innovative Efforts

in apparently active constraints and real conflicts over directions of local efforts. This is all the more probable when non-local forces and institutions interact with local economic actors who are resistant to the proposed innovations.

Klaus Kunzmann and Gerd Hennings vividly describe the conservative forces challenging diversification of the Ruhrgebiet, promoting continued emphasis on manufacturing and denigrating the prospects for local indigenous development. Notwithstanding the potential of local and regional governments within the German federal system and acceptance of high levels of public sector activism, regional private elites continue to dominate the local economic agenda and challenge a variety of innovative efforts. The result is that innovation is led by the same forces that contributed, by their actions at the local level, to the very conditions they are proposing to correct.

Charles Craypo and Jerry Paar's discussion of an employee ownership case illustrates that even overt institutional change does not necessarily alter the emphasis of programs or permit implementation of innovations. Despite putative ownership change, the conflict over wealth creation relative to job creation remained in the South Bend Lathe case, and management's growth emphasis clearly conflicted with worker and community interest in development and assertion of more local control. The question of the appropriate balance of general relative to targeted programs lay at the core of the policy debates over the directions of the revolving loan fund established in South Bend, overlaying questions of emphasis on business attraction relative to nurturance of local firms.

William Lever provides a further example of the passive resistance to change and the importance of the supra-local state in his discussion of west central Scotland. While the local state pressed social criteria such as control, job creation, targeted efforts, and total labor incomes, the regional and national state emphasized profit criteria and thus growth, wealth creation, general programs, and total jobs. Regardless of local efforts to innovate and increasing state activism, the national state and its Scottish agencies, as critical funding sources for local public and nonprofit agency efforts, restrained implementation of such agendas by constraining the flow of funds. Given this financial stranglehold, the eventual attack on the legal powers of the local state seem to have been overkill.

Continuing our examination of the Scottish experience, Alan McGregor and Andrew McArthur chronicle the emergence of new organizations as the implementors of innovations. As neighborhood responses to rising and continuing economic distress, community businesses combine a set of objectives and priorities that older development organizations seem to have ignored as a possibility. They definitely are or intend to be for-profit organizations, but they complement activist local government and may rely on such activism in their formative years. Unlike most firms, they are geographically targeted and may consciously limit their markets to serve narrow clienteles, both with goods and services and with social returns (which are pursued alongside profits). The supra-local state and traditional local economic promotion agency responses to the community business movement highlight once again the growth-development and control choice issue and that of local reinvestment versus non-local business attraction.

Part III of this volume examines a trio of local conflicts that share a common cause: a focus on some form of waterfront development. The implementation conflicts in these three cases derive not from external actors but from divisions within a local community (admittedly, of course, those divisions may have non-local roots). The common thread across these cases is a concentrated focus on a geographic subarea in a city or region that results in failure to adequately address the broader local economic situation and potential negative spillovers immediately outside the area. Given the boundary offered by a river, harbor, or other waterfront, the spillover into the water is not relevant; unfortunately, it appears that the spillovers inland are often ignored as well, and conflicts thus arise.

The city of Baltimore highlights the conflict between local control of development and pursuit of growth alone. Robert Giloth's case involves workers' and residents' concerns with traditional land value maximization efforts. Conflict arises not from different business development efforts but over the neglected negative effects of traditional economic development. In effect, the case involves a challenge to public sector action undertaken for its own sake, one that takes a too narrowly economic orientation. In raising the question of "growth for whom?" the neighborhood groups whose efforts Giloth chronicles challenge the degree of emphasis on wealth creation, for-profit firms, and diversification without regard for its impact on the different groups of people that make up a city or metropolitan area.

The south Cardiff, Wales, case described by Huw Thomas and Rob Imrie involves a similar conflict between existing land uses and occupants and the forces seeking to transform land uses and values to maximize economic activity, profits, and diversification through public intervention. However, the negative effects and potential resistance in this case involve existing businesses rather than workers and residents. The parallels between the two cases are striking. The apparent inability of small businesses in Cardiff to defend their interests, for all that they may have more legitimacy as creators of wealth and jobs, underscores the need for organization in the pursuit of any innovations in development. The Cardiff small businesses that maintain a highly individualist orientation to the pursuit of their ends seem less well equipped to challenge potentially damaging policies than workers and community groups that have long since learned that their only chance of success lies in common efforts and organization.

Alma Young and Robert Whelan provide another dimension of local conflict over waterfront development, tracing the interactions of two public sector bodies attempting to maximize benefits of waterfront development in New Orleans. Unlike the other two cases, this one involves relatively equal power on both sides of the conflict, and thus a tendency toward stagnation and inaction in the face of external pressures that should induce change. Questions of local control, diversification, sectoral reorientations of the economy, and the distribution of benefits of change (wealth versus jobs; total jobs versus total earnings) underscore a conflictual relationship that appears to be as much about political and economic turf as about development itself.

LEARNING FROM — AND BUILDING ON — CASE STUDIES OF IMPLEMENTATION

The two chapters in Part IV engage in direct comparison of cases, which is the first step to the generalization needed to make such examples useful to future policy formation and implementation. Both chapters provide insights that can be drawn from this collection and suggest agendas for further research and reflection.

A direct comparison of revitalization in two depressed steel centers in Britain and the United States serves to elaborate the findings on the importance of local implementation organizations from the cases described in Part III. Terry Buss's examination of Corby and Youngstown focuses on the use of very traditional tools for economic stimulus — business subsidies — in the face of mass local unemployment. Critical to the greater success reported for Corby were its recognition of the need for immediate diversification, its acceptance of the realities of the external factors acting on the local economy, its efforts to mix nurture of existing businesses with attraction of new firms, and above all, its recognition and acceptance of the essential leadership role to be played by a local activist state. These principles could have been articulated in a case examination of the one city alone, but the argument is made immeasurably stronger through a direct comparison to a city under analogous economic pressures that failed to act in a manner appropriate to the conditions it faced. Buss then takes case study examination to its logical next step: the selection of different cases in which interlocality and intercommunity variation is limited and controlled. His approach permits detailed examination of the specific implementation strategies that affect levels of success in pursuit of local economic development objectives.

David Fasenfest concludes the volume with a reflection on the common findings suggested by the entire collection of case studies. By way of introduction, we have dwelled here on the conflicts and sources of division that inhibit implementation of local economic strategies. Fasenfest reviews the case descriptions and extracts critical lessons and principles that can form the foundation for any effort to assert increased local control over the national and world system forces that act on peoples' local choices and economic opportunities.

Lessons for action derive neatly from these two chapters. First, following Buss's example, implementers or intervenors in implementation processes in any one setting can look to one of these cases (or others in print) to compare to their own situation. The objective is to find one or more cases that permit critical variables in the situation to be held constant. (In Buss's case, for example, the historical sectoral reliance on steel and the shock of plant closings provide a common set of local economic conditions, from capital stock to worker qualifications.) In Part III, all three cases share a common focus on maximizing waterfront land values in a development effort led by wealth creation. The cases thus identified would permit examination of remaining variables to determine specific local forces and factors shaping implementation processes. Such an examination could in turn enable interested innovators to modify or improve their approaches in order to permit implementation of desired programs.

Second, on the research front, additional work needs to be done to identify and examine in depth pairs or series of parallel cases. Some beginnings in this regard are indicated by the introduction to Part III and by Buss's chapter in Part IV. Ideally, groups of cases can be gathered that control for different types of variation in the implementation environment. International comparisons may be critical to finding cases with parallel economic conditions, but comparative case studies within single countries are essential to the study of impacts of varying external economic forces on communities with similar internal legal, political, and cultural institutions and values that experience common external political and institutional constraints.

In the case of federally structured countries such as the United States, domestic comparative case studies may need to be limited to single states, since each of the fifty states exhibits different economic development policies and institutional settings. As we have noted, the existing comparative literature addressing single countries tends to emphasize statistical methodologies, examining economic conditions before and after some set of interventions. Such studies are more easily accomplished given sophisticated computer data bases, but they do not contribute to an improved understanding of the forces shaping the implementation of particular programs and the impacts those innovations actually have on local economies.

The argument for the case study in this arena is strong indeed. Without many more in-depth cases, especially of successful innovations, it is difficult to see how implementation bodies can overcome the "general skepticism of mankind" that Machiavelli argues impedes support for change. Cases that people consider to be applicable to their local conditions may well constitute the experience that Machiavelli claims is needed before people can accept the value of an innovation. Only if the idea is deemed valuable will there be a strong potential for broad-based public support of the implementation effort, and any innovation needs such support.

Finally, only evidence of successful experiences presented in terms the citizenry at large can understand will ever enable people to overcome the "fear of their adversaries," which are often unknown and unidentifiable national and world market processes that adversely affect local economies. Statistical proofs of the utility of particular intervention efforts can never have the impact on public opinion that descriptive demonstrations can attain. If Machiavelli is right, then the fear of attempting innovation must be overcome, and attaining that objective requires more, and more detailed, case study analysis.

2

Putting Targeted Economic Development to Work: The Role of Targeted Marketing in an Economic Development Program

C. Theodore Koebel
Cara L. Bailey

Local economic development has recently been described as "a relatively untargeted intermunicipal sales or marketing competition" (Levy 1990:158). Marketing dominates local professional practice and the development of rational planning techniques is of much lower priority. Communities try out the latest fad, promote themselves to the entirety of economic sectors and industries, and wait for a call from a suitor — all without much regard to their own economic structure and foreseeable potential for business development. The economic development game thus resembles a lottery in which the players might not have high expectations but where the fear of leaving the game is a more important motivation than the potential for winning.

Is it possible to remove some of the blind randomness from the economic development game? Input-output methodologies have been available for some time, and the development of non-survey tables has received substantial research attention (see Bruckner, Hastings, and Latham 1987; Stevens, Treyz, and Lahr 1988). However, the input-output technique has been used primarily for impact analysis and not for prescriptive planning. Advances in economic development research have not filtered down to local economic development policy implementation in part because of the complexity of the techniques and the lack of "off-the-shelf" comprehensive models that communities can use without much research expertise. The need for more comprehensive analytical models was well stated by Glen Pulver in 1984 and remains true today:

Up to this point, there is no well-defined system of comprehensive community economic analysis. No major effort has been made to combine the many individual tools into a collective set which can be used in diagnosing local problems and opportunities. There is no mechanism to tie together the total economic reality of a specific community's circumstances with all options for community economic development. Consequently, individual tools are used to look at single problems and local, state, and national policy makers continue to implement development strategies based on panaceas and/or shared ignorance. (p. 25)

If it is to improve implementation, such community economic analysis should be specific and pragmatic enough to permit identification of marketing targets that have a relatively high potential for success. This selectivity, according to David Sweet (1986:1), "concentrates energy, money and research in the area of greatest payoff: it is aimed at the kind of development a community wants and needs, and it targets industries whose needs can realistically be met by a specific community." Targeting industries is most effective when community leaders from all sectors develop a pragmatic implementation strategy to deal effectively with the political and economic domains of the *process* of change (McGahey 1990). Utilization of targeted marketing models as part of an economic development implementation strategy is demonstrated in our case analyses that follow.

Targeted marketing concentrates development efforts on those industries needing labor, markets, and suppliers that best match what the community has to offer (Thompson and Thompson 1987). The approach could be applied to identifying targets for relocation, retention, expansion, or indigenous start-ups across all sectors, including services and retail trade (Huskey 1985; Ahlbrandt and DeAngelis 1987). Further, the results of targeting efforts can facilitate future discussion concerning community economic development strategy (McGahey 1990).

A recent survey of local economic development directors indicated that 78 percent of them claimed to target industries for marketing efforts (the method of targeting was not included in the survey). However, most agencies conducted their targeting at only the one-digit and two-digit Standard Industrial Classification (SIC) levels ("manufacturing" is at the one-digit level and "food processing" is at the two-digit level), which is of minimal utility. Only 10 percent of the directors surveyed indicated they targeted at more specific levels of industrial classification or manufacturers of specific products (Levy 1990).

The limited use of targeted marketing, despite its logical appeal, is due to several factors: (1) There are risks associated with the economic analyses used in identifying appropriate targets; (2) Errors in the specification or calibration of models could divert efforts and lead to frustration and failure; (3) The data required for targeted marketing might be dated or at too aggregate a level to permit the identification of firm-level marketing targets. Moreover, a community's economic development program is often influenced more by interorganizational rivalries and the perceptions of powerful community leaders than by empirical analysis (Vogel 1990). Nonetheless, targeting models that are methodologically sound can assist economic developers in better understanding the economy of their communities and in their communications with local leaders.

This chapter provides insight into the use of rational targeted marketing models as an element of a local economic development strategy. This is done by (1) briefly reviewing the concept of interindustry linkage as it relates to targeted marketing; (2) examining the use of three targeted marketing models that illustrate the potential and the pitfalls of the implementation tool; and (3) identifying improvements for future applications of targeted marketing.

INTERINDUSTRY LINKAGE AND TARGETED MARKETING

Central to targeted marketing is the concept of linkages. Business establishments are linked economically and spatially to their suppliers, labor, and customers (Markusen 1985; Webber 1984; King 1984; Beavon 1977; Berry 1967). Links to suppliers ("backward linkages") involve purchases of raw materials or intermediate goods or links to labor for local personnel (Thompson and Thompson 1985; 1987). Links to customers ("forward linkages") can represent intermediate or producers' goods and sales to final demand by consumers.

Interindustry and spatial linkages with important locational implications for firms were identified by William Beyers (1981). Businesses engaged in producing products for final consumption have high forward linkages and low backward linkages, with a tendency to locate relative to the geographic distribution of final demand. Primary producers for final demand (commodities or services) have low forward and low backward linkages, with strong value-added characteristics. Intermediate producers with high forward and backward linkages would necessarily be concerned about the availability of supplies (but not necessarily local suppliers) and access to customers (again, not necessarily local).

Differences in the magnitude of forward and backward linkages are only one dimension of spatial linkage. Beyers (1981) elaborates the analysis to identify eight different patterns, based on extent of spatial links (local, regional, and broader). A. Markusen (1985) traces how these patterns shift over the product life cycle and the dynamics of interindustry linkages. Expanding on the original product life cycle theory, which argues that the locational requirements of an industry shift as the industry grows, stagnates, and ultimately declines, Markusen expands the product life cycle to include a "profit cycle." The evolution of production within a firm inherently affects profitability conditions, which in turn shape spatial linkages. The regional economy is redefined over time as its firms evolve through the profit cycle, shifting between Beyers's eight interindustry linkage categories. Relocation of a firm will occur if the geographical system of economic linkage does not meet the market requirements of the firm.

The issues of access to final demand, intermediate demand, or suppliers are generic to most location decisions and entrepreneurial start-ups. Essentially, what a targeted marketing approach attempts to provide is ready access to information about the economic linkages existing within a community and a broader region, along with information on labor, transport, and other cost factors influencing the location decision. By analyzing these linkages, the targeted marketing approach attempts to identify where opportunities exist for import substitution, serving undersupplied markets or meeting the needs of a company relative to markets, suppliers, and labor.

THREE TARGETED MARKETING MODELS

The implementation of three targeted marketing models reviewed herein provides a range of classification techniques and user experiences. The three models are (1) the Small Business Development System (SBDS) developed by the Council for Economic Action (CEA) (1982a; 1982b; 1983; 1984; 1989a; 1989b; 1990); (2) the Regional Growth Potential (RGP) model developed by David Sweet (1980; 1986); and (3) the Tennessee-Tombigbee (Tenn-Tom) model developed by Robert Bohm and his colleagues (1983) for the U.S. Army Corps of Engineers. The SBDS program is primarily oriented to neighborhood development and relies on a location quotient method for identifying development opportunities. The RGP relies on input-output techniques coupled with industry growth potential, market area delineation, and industry requirements for transportation, labor, utilities, or ports to identify targeted sectors and firms. The Tenn-Tom model expands the input-output approach with a gravity industrial location model and a calculation of potential profitability in each development location (i.e., county).

The Small Business Development System Model

The SBDS model (CEA 1984) was designed to improve the survival rate of business start-ups and to generate new job opportunities (CEA 1989a). The SBDS model was originally designed for use with community-based organizations for the purpose of neighborhood development. However, the SBDS model can be applied on a community-wide basis involving a broader group of participants.

The SBDS model has five components, the first of which, *Market Identification,* is a prerequisite for any effort to pursue business opportunities. The others (*Community Outreach* to locate would-be entrepreneurs, *Management Education* for them, assistance with *Capital Access,* and *Technical Assistance* to business start-ups) are essential to success but rely on good targeting of new business creation efforts (CEA 1989a).

Industry identification and targeting should be the first critical, path-setting step toward developing an economic development strategy (Blakely 1989). The market identification process developed by CEA requires prescreening of industries by a local client, such as a city or county economic development office, and by CEA to identify the sectors that have the management, capital, and neighborhood characteristics that meet the client's development objectives (CEA 1990a). In Boston (CEA 1982a:4), the prescreening limits the analysis to "five major industry clusters containing a total of 551 industries," concentrated in light manufacturing, trade, and services. The selected industries are then classified as undersupplied, oversupplied, or in equilibrium in the local market area. CEA's research has shown that 70 to 80 percent of the industries in an urban area are typically classified as being in equilibrium, 10 to 15 percent are oversupplied, and the remaining 10 to 15 percent are undersupplied in the local economy. This classification is based on an urban hierarchy approach that assumes the equilibrium number of establishments in these industries to be similar among cities of similar size, economic conditions, and socioeconomic characteristics.

The target community can be defined as a neighborhood, town, city, county, or metropolitan statistical area (MSA) (CEA 1990). The target community's commercial composition is compared to the commercial composition of approximately a half dozen other communities having "highly similar economies," based on twenty indicators such as "demographic mixes, social and economic conditions, transportation networks, and spatial characteristics" (CEA 1982a:4). CEA then applies the location quotient method to determine in which industries the target community is undersupplied relative to its comparison group.

The market identification process then uses a comprehensive field analysis to confirm the existence of undersupplied business functions. Field visits enable data to be collected on a large sample of businesses in the targeted industry to confirm a pattern of undersupply. Such field checks are mostly valuable in confirming the number of businesses within the market area. However, verifying undersupply is not an easy task. For example, unprofitable businesses, business failures, and other indicators of oversupply might reflect problems with the intrametropolitan distribution of supply (i.e., declining and expanding submarkets within the metropolitan area). This would be the case with local consumer-oriented businesses, for which the market area might be substantially smaller than the MSA. In the Boston SBDS model, for example, of the 62 industries initially classified as undersupplied, only 49 (79%) had that status confirmed by the detailed field work (CEA 1982a).

Since the primary purpose of the market identification process is to identify potential industries for local business start-ups or expansions, the next step in the process is to examine the competition in the market area. Using firm-level data on the undersupplied industries,[1] the market identification process further classifies the identified undersupplied industries into markets that are "competitive," "concentrated," or "served through imports." Undersupplied industries in competitive markets, which have limited access to capital and management expertise, are considered the most likely for successful business start-ups or expansions under the SBDS programs.

The last step in the market identification process is to classify the undersupplied industries according to their recent and projected growth trends; the greatest success potential is attributed to undersupplied industries that have been expanding. About one-third of the forty-nine undersupplied industries in the Boston area were identified as "significant targets of opportunity for start-up and/or expansion" (CEA 1982a).

The SBDS model, a comprehensive economic development strategy, has been successfully implemented, according to CEA, after adoption in nineteen cities in the United States (CEA 1989a). Successful implementation is based upon the net growth in the number of business establishments in undersupplied industries. Between 1984 and 1989 the number of business establishments in undersupplied industries in communities assisted by the SBDS model increased by five new businesses per year

The Role of Targeted Marketing

per neighborhood assisted. The long-term impacts of the SBDS model are not yet evident because of the relatively short time period in which the model has been operating. CEA is currently implementing a tracking system to document the progress of SBDS business start-ups. The data collected will be useful in evaluating the success and failure rates of business start-ups assisted by the SBDS model.

The Regional Growth Potential Model

While the urban hierarchy approach of the market identification component of the SBDS model is probably best suited to retail trade and local or community market services, the Regional Growth Potential (RGP) model concentrates on regional-level interindustry linkages that identify industries in which there are significant backward linkages to nonlocal suppliers or important forward linkages to local intermediate or final demand markets (Sweet 1986). The use of an input-output methodology is a sophisticated means of identifying these linkages and the level of interregional imports and exports; it is best used as a beginning step in a comprehensive economic development program.

The interindustry linkages approach of the RGP model can be used to identify several different types of industries for targeting. Exports to other regions indicate sectors with competitive advantages; agglomeration benefits of locating like industries together can be identified with a focus on sectors with exports of intermediate goods; and sectors with high imports of intermediate goods or raw materials suggest candidates for an import substitution strategy. The RGP model was intended to incorporate an analysis of interindustry linkages within a strategic economic development program that follows the identification of local economic development goals and the screening of targeted industries based on industry growth potential, sources of materials and supplies, market area served by the industry, transportation requirements, labor supply, energy and utility requirements, and port orientation. The output of the model was a mailing list of targeted businesses for future marketing.

One of the attractions of the RGP model is its specification of market areas, which is done for each target industry for sales to intermediate and final demand (Sweet n.d.:3). "The RGP calculates the unique market area within which 75 percent of sales are made for each target industry.... [M]ost inter-industry purchases and sales will occur within a 1,000 mile market radius." The model then computes "the total dollar value of the target industry's market and the dollar value of markets served by existing industries (competitors) in that area, and then reports the resulting dollar value of the net market potential with the market area analyzed." Local and regional resources and suppliers for the targeted market are also identified, based on "the distance at which the industry normally acquires that type of product or service."

In an application of the RGP model to the Louisville, Kentucky, area, seventy-two industries (at the four-digit SIC level) were preliminarily identified as targets. These industries were further screened and reduced to ten on the basis of local development goals, each industry's growth potential, and locational requirements of the industries. The ten industries were oriented to intermediate products, and they readily illustrate the differences in objectives and output of the manufacturing-oriented RGP model and the retail service–oriented SBDS model. Examples of products from the ten industries include corrugated and solid fiber boxes, miscellaneous plastic products, motors and generators, and industrial controls.

The initial intention in the use of the RGP by the Louisville Metropolitan Chamber of Commerce was to identify firms to be targeted in a direct mail promotion campaign. The Chamber had been recently restructured to lead the community's economic development and business recruitment effort (Vogel 1990), and targeted marketing was to be a central element of its approach. Although a list of firms was generated, the users did not feel that the supporting data on local advantages were detailed enough for marketing directly to the identified firms. Instead, the local development agencies used the model results in the preparation of "industry opportunity studies" that were used in marketing at trade shows and in other sector-specific communications (Linares 1990).

The difficulties of following an analytical approach to targeted economic development are well highlighted by the Louisville case. Although they were ostensibly committed to targeting, the local development agencies failed to establish a clear link between analysis and marketing. The agenda was much more likely to be set by interorganizational rivalries and the perceptions of powerful community leaders about the direction of the economic development effort (Vogel 1990). The community's most prominent recent development efforts (recruitment of the Presbyterian Church, USA, national headquarters and expansion of the regional airport) were generated from the shared visions of a small group of business and elected leaders and were unrelated to any analytical framework for integrated economic development. Despite millions of dollars spent on strategic formation efforts, the Louisville effort was effectively dictated by its local "growth machine" (Logan and Molotch 1987).

The Tennessee-Tombigbee Corridor Model

The Tennessee-Tombigbee (Tenn-Tom) model is very similar in intent to the RGP model, but it incorporates additional analytical techniques. The Tenn-Tom model has three broad steps:

(1) . . . a general gravity-potential type industrial location model which permits an unconstrained ranking of industries on the basis of potential profitability for each Corridor County, (2) to constrain the selection process on the basis of three "industrial development strategies," and (3) to permit modification of the selection process in the field on the basis of a matching of industry and county characteristics. (Bohm, Herzog, and Schrottmann 1983:28)

The Tenn-Tom model improves upon the conceptual design of other models in several ways: it ranks potential profitability of industries at the four-digit SIC code level; it incorporates final and intermediate demand; it includes the relative attraction of firms toward clients or suppliers; and it estimates demand potential, reflecting the size of markets and the distance to those markets for both final and intermediate demand. The results of the model can be adjusted depending on the economic development strategy to be implemented. Three such strategies are explicitly recognized: the attraction of high wage industries (relative to local wages), import substitution, and the attraction of industries with high employment growth potential. The results can be further refined by matching the industry and the community in terms of transportation, energy, water, and local supply requirements; relative wage levels; education resources; number of similar firms in the area; public services; and local development incentives offered by the community.

Unfortunately, the conceptual superiority of the Tenn-Tom model was empirically supported by data and research that were about a decade old at the time of its implementation a decade ago, and they have not been updated. The relative locational pull of clients and suppliers was based on a survey of industrial location factors conducted in 1973 (U.S. Department of Commerce 1973). Distance decay coefficients were based on a study of interregional commodity flows published by William Black in 1972. Even more critical, the model could not incorporate the impact on location decisions of the single most important attraction being introduced — the creation of the Tennessee-Tombigbee waterway itself.

The Tenn-Tom model's data problems and inability to consider the development of a new transportation resource led to its abandonment by the U.S. Army Corps of Engineers and the Tenn-Tom Waterway

Development Authority (Birindelli 1990; Walden 1990). It was logically and analytically superior to the SBDS and RGP models, but it serves to illustrate the limitations of analytical rigor in an ever-changing environment: extremely heavy data requirements doom sophisticated models in the absence of heavy investment in rapid information-updating techniques; since surveys of location factors are few and far between, no model based on such data can retain current utility over time.

The Tenn-Tom Waterway Authority has turned to a comparative analysis approach as an alternative to an economic model (Walden 1990). The authority commissioned a study to examine waterway industries and found that industries locating on water routes tended to be heavy manufacturers. The study further examined manufacturing processes of the identified industries to discern what resources the Tenn-Tom Corridor could provide to a waterway industry. Targeted industries are those that can be supported by area resources and available sites and can fulfill criteria established by the county in which the industry will locate (i.e., employment generation). Once industries are identified for targeting, sites for potential development are determined. Recruiting efforts are geared toward media promotions, such as advertising in industrial trade and site development publications. The site-by-site approach enables the economic development planners to meet the specific goals of the counties within the region while planning at a regional level because of the "bottom-up" nature of the approach. Presently, the Authority is satisfied with the results of this approach and reports that targeting industries with specific needs for access to waterways has resulted in private investment of approximately $2 billion within a four-year period (Walden 1990).

IMPLICATIONS FOR IMPLEMENTATION

There are two stages to the implementation of a targeted marketing strategy: the implementation of analytical method, and the implementation of the economic development strategy based on the results of the analysis. Problems can arise in both stages. Those encountered in the first stage are mostly technical issues of modeling and analysis, while the problems encountered in the second stage center on the political commitment to targeting, the logical and political persuasiveness of the analytical method, and the model's accommodation of special features of the local situation. It is important for planners, analysts, and development specialists to question each other on the accuracy, logic, and utility of the overall targeted marketing program.

The predominant methodological issue concerning the use of economic models for targeted marketing is that of obtaining locally relevant interindustry and comparison data. Any approach that uses average measures derived from comparison areas, such as similar sized communities or the nation, assumes that local production functions and inputs are similar in the target community and all comparison communities. Even if there are similar proportional levels of supply in the comparison communities, the average number of firms for these communities could be an imprecise estimate of the equilibrium level for the target community. The output of the target community's local economy might be influenced by specialization in a particular industry or a single establishment that serves national or international markets.

The comparative estimation technique also can be influenced by more than gross income and population size, while the supply of firms or employment might reflect differences in production, business organization, and the propensity to import from neighboring communities. Supply, which relates to the output of firms, would be estimated most accurately by production data, followed by employment, and the number of firms would be the least accurate surrogate measure.

Another implementation problem faced by any approach using secondary data is the periodicity of updates. Often data from secondary sources are two or more years out of date when they become available for use. The problem of outdated data was especially critical in the user's decision to abandon the Tenn-Tom model. Updates of the Economic Development Administration survey on industry location factors and Black's study on interregional commodity flows are essential for current application of this model, but they are not available. However, current data from the Unemployment Insurance Administration files (or ES202 reporting forms) can be obtained by local governments and universities (White et al. 1990).

The second key methodological issue is the need for local field verification of secondary source data. Collecting regional purchase-and-supply data is essential to improving the accuracy, reliability, and use of targeted marketing. The need for a local survey is especially important among large, dominant industries in the local market (Bruckner and Hastings 1983). The survey need not cover large numbers of firms and can be limited to interviews with major local suppliers or purchasers in order to obtain data on local markets. Additional interviews with prospective economic development targets or with major firms entering the local market could help establish the probable location of their purchases, as was discovered in the Tenn-Tom case. Any expectation of significant local multiplier effects should be "reality checked" to determine the degree to which supplies will be imported from other regions.

In addition to these problems, it is important that the delineation of the local region properly capture the supply areas of the inputs to the industries under examination (Cartwright, Beemiller, and Gustely 1981:59). A too narrowly defined local region might exclude important suppliers that already are located in the market area. In addition, concentration of suppliers in other regions should be examined, particularly if the regions have important locational characteristics that continue to benefit these establishments or are in close proximity to the subject community.

Targeted marketing models are useful only if their results are applicable to specific marketing activities. The analysts and the economic developers need to chart a clear course from the results of the analysis to the implementation of marketing strategies. The obvious result of a targeted marketing analysis is the identification of a targeted sector, which then needs to be linked to individual firms (with addresses and names of the chief executive officers) through several private data bases (such as Dun and Bradstreet's). The targeted marketing program should also generate output that could serve as a preliminary market analysis for prospective firms and should be sufficiently credible and persuasive to influence venture capital investors, commercial lenders, and agencies offering government grants or financing.

Targeted marketing models that have been integrated into a comprehensive economic development strategy and have been verified with field observations appear to be the most effective to implement. The SBDS model's success may be due in part to its integration with an implementation strategy vested in a single agency, the Council for Economic Action. By contrast, the RGP and the Tenn-Tom models were not successfully applied to targeted marketing in large part because they were not integrated into local development agencies' comprehensive strategies.

CONCLUSION

The experience with the three targeted marketing models discussed in this chapter provides important suggestions for a community's use of this approach. The design and implementation of a targeted marketing program should be an interactive process between the users and the builders of the model. For successful targeted implementation of *any* strategy, the research and sales portions of the targeted marketing team need to ask the following questions about the model, its results, and the sales strategy it will influence:

- What is the local community's overall marketing strategy? How will targeted marketing fit into that strategy?
- How will the output of the model be used in marketing, and at what level of detail (e.g., three- or four-digit SIC code or individual establishments)?
- How does the model identify potential targets? What assumptions does it make about the local community? How are these assumptions justified?
- How do labor, energy, and other inputs factor into the analysis and into the marketing program?
- How recent are the data being used to identify targets?
- What local testing of model outputs will be done? How will potential markets be verified?

Targeted marketing can remove some of the randomness in economic development and thus focus local resources for economic promotion, but practitioners should be aware of the shortcomings of the economic method employed in the market analysis. There is limited evidence of the ability of targeting to actually increase the successful development of entrepreneurial start-ups or recruitment of businesses to a community, since targeting is one part of a program that has other elements. The successful implementation of targeted marketing may thus be due to its integration into an ongoing economic development implementation strategy and the quality of other development resources brought to bear. Targeting does not produce development, but it may make implementations more resource efficient.

NOTE

1. A reliable source of U.S. firm-level data is Dun and Bradstreet's Dun's Market Identifier (DMI) file. The DMI file includes data on approximately five million firms per year in all U.S. economic sectors at two-year intervals from 1976 to 1986. Data in the DMI file is collected primarily for credit information (Kraushaar and Feldman 1987).

Part II

External and Environmental Influences on Local Implementation

Local economic development efforts cannot be assessed or evaluated in isolation. The increasing internationalization of production and the emergence of new patterns of world economic integration require that non-local factors be considered in the course of development policy formation and, even more important, in the implementation of policies and programs.

Policies and programs tailored to local conditions may fail to address the problems caused by external forces over which local planners and developers have little control. The broader economic environment can also change in unanticipated manners, undermining or rendering inappropriate efforts that were previously viable.

Charles Craypo and Jerry Paar provide an example of a well-intentioned effort that failed to address non-local market forces at the outset and that changed in response to a shifting environment over time. Local conflict stemmed from different perceptions of the environment in which programs were implemented. This experience underscores the importance of such external influences, real and perceived, on the success of local efforts.

William Lever, examining local efforts in west central Scotland, and Gerd Hennings and Klaus Kunzmann, discussing regeneration efforts in Germany's traditional steel and coal region, the Ruhrgebiet, both provide evidence on the importance of the external, supra-local structures of the state as influences on local policy implementation. Regardless of the specific private market environments in which local efforts are generated, the political and bureaucratic structures of the state shape local public sector efforts. Those legal and cultural factors also influence the local state's relationship to local private development efforts. Although the settings and the ultimately prominent local economic development agents are vastly different in the two cases, the lessons they offer run in tandem.

The Scottish and German experiences recounted by Lever, Hennings, and Kunzmann demonstrate that policy implementations must be designed with careful attention to the supra-local state structures within which they have to operate. In effect, the cases present a serious lesson for American development efforts in which local initiatives have been emulated between communities across the fifty states. Program failures experienced in the United States may have been less a matter of poor policy than inadequate implementations that failed to consider state-to-state variations in the political and bureaucratic environments for local economic development efforts.

Finally, Alan McGregor and Andrew McArthur bring the role of such external influences down to the neighborhood level, discussing the range of action options and potential contribution of highly geographically specific programs. Their finding suggests that implementation efforts must devote careful attention to the dangers of conflicting, or at least differing, goals, which can characterize even different neighborhoods within a single municipality.

3

Local Economic Development in a Traditional Industrial Area: The Case of the Ruhrgebiet

Gerd Hennings
Klaus R. Kunzmann

With five million inhabitants, the Ruhrgebiet is Europe's largest industrial agglomeration. Including the cities of Duisburg, Essen, Bochum, and Dortmund, it is by far the largest urbanized area of Germany, surpassing united Berlin. It is a typical old industrial agglomeration, once based on coal and steel, and suffering as the decline of those sectors has dragged down the entire regional economy. Since the early 1970s, the region has experienced a considerable loss of jobs and, subsequently, of its populace.

In 1987, despite some signs of successful restructuring, the economic climate in the region had reached a historical low with yet another round of closures of coal pits and steelworks. The subsequent militant actions of the steel workers in Duisburg against the closure of their steel mill in Rheinhausen (such as the blocking of a strategic motorway bridge over the Rhine and the week-long squatting at the works) received nationwide attention in the German mass media. This event peaked the generally negative external image of the Ruhrgebiet among the public as that of a perishing industrial region.

However, this was an isolated dip. With the overall positive macroeconomic development of Western Europe, stimulated in part by the announcement of the Single European Market 1992, the industrial region has experienced steady job growth through most of the 1980s. Consequently, soon after 1987, a new optimism spread across regional enterprises. This development was paralleled by considerable migration flows of German ethnics from the East (from the former Soviet Union,

Poland, East Germany, Romania) to the urban communities of the Ruhrgebiet, a phenomenon that turned population decline into an unexpected new population growth. Surprisingly, and despite the unexpected immigration, unemployment rates fell from a high of 15 percent in 1982 to 11.3 in 1991. Though this rate is still above the national average (6.5 percent), the decrease represents an unexpected success for the region.

However, numerous problems remain and the magnitude of these problems has sparked new efforts to revitalize the region. The objective of this chapter is to describe and preliminarily assess three special initiatives that have been launched. To understand the background of these approaches, the underlying regional economic conditions in the Ruhrgebiet will first be sketched. By way of preface, however, it may be useful to explain a few specific features of regional economic policy in the German context related to its strong federal system and to the country's economic doctrine, the *Soziale Marktwirtschaft* (socially oriented market economy). This background is important for two reasons: First, familiar labels and catchwords — some not even translated into German (e.g., "public-private partnership") — have to be seen in their explicit German sociopolitical context and the even more unique policy conditions of the Ruhrgebiet. Second, the peculiar Anglo-American debate on the conflicts between national and local state and political priorities is absent in Germany. Consequently, despite linguistic similarities of problems, labels, and approaches, many of these questions in Anglo-American analyses are not even raised in Germany.

There is a paucity of literature on local economic development in Germany. The relationships of local and national tiers are not of much concern in Germany, as has been the case in the United States in the period of Reaganomics and in Great Britain under Thatcherism. Moreover, local economic policy has not been a priority of policy analysis research. Successes and failures of local economic development are rarely assessed, and the need for such evaluation is rarely argued. There are no significant debates on growth or non-growth coalitions, except occasionally in local politics, and the leverage of local economic policy is rarely an issue. Nevertheless, in Germany, local economic development has gained policy importance during the last two decades (Bennet, Krebs, and Zimmermann 1990).

ECONOMIC DEVELOPMENT IN THE RUHRGEBIET: EMPLOYMENT CHANGE FROM 1970 TO 1987

The loss of 110,000 jobs in the Ruhrgebiet between 1970 and 1987 was considerable. In relative terms this decline amounted to only 5.2 percent of over two million jobs. However, compared with the average 8 percent job *growth* in the entire Federal Republic of Germany, this figure constitutes an exceptionally high relative loss of employment in the Ruhrgebiet.

The general deindustrialization process in the traditional industrial countries of the western hemisphere cost the Ruhrgebiet 397,000 manufacturing jobs, a decline of over 32 percent between 1970 and 1987. On the other hand, the services sector generated 285,000 new jobs in the region, a figure that is impressive even though it is still below the national average rate of service job increase. The Ruhrgebiet has become a region in which the service sector, with its 60 percent share in total employment, has become the lead employer.

The decline in manufacturing and the rise of the service sector is attributable to the following factors:

- The previously dominant coal and steel sectors lost much of their former economic importance for the region. At the end of the 1950s, 63 percent of all manufacturing jobs and 40 percent of the total employment in the region was still in these two sectors; by 1987 these figures were 30 percent and 11 percent, respectively.

- Moreover, for an extended period of time, the other manufacturing sectors in the Ruhrgebiet suffered from comparatively higher job losses than in other regions of West Germany. Only since 1985 have some local manufacturing sectors, particularly mechanical engineering and plastics processing, showed revitalization and new job growth.

While production-oriented services have mushroomed in the region, growth in private consumer-oriented sectors has been retarded by the continuous decline of the traditional regional industries, and thus loss of local purchasing power.

In the last decade of the twentieth century, the economic structure of the Ruhrgebiet as a whole is, undoubtedly, much more diversified and less vulnerable to the anticipatable decline of the coal and steel sector than it was twenty years ago. However, economic diversification needs to be accelerated to further modernize the regional economic base.

THE INSTITUTIONAL AND SOCIOPOLITICAL BACKGROUND OF LOCAL ECONOMIC DEVELOPMENT IN GERMANY

To understand the new policy approaches to regional restructuring in the Ruhrgebiet and to be able to compare the complex mechanisms of policy implementation with those in the United States or in Great Britain, it is useful to briefly sketch key facets of the institutional and sociopolitical background of local economic development in Germany (Ardagh 1991). The three factors shaping the institutional and sociopolitical context of local economic development in Germany are (1) the strong vertical division of power, the three-tier system, and the subsidiarity principle; (2) the influence of political parties; and (3) the traditional role of the unions. These contextual facets are briefly examined in the following sections.

The Vertical Division of Power: The Three-Tier System and the Subsidiarity Principle

Centralism, as in France or Great Britain, has no tradition in Germany. As constituted in the *Grundgesetz* (basic law), Germany is a structured three-tier system with a clear division of power and competence between the federal level (the Bund), the state level (sixteen *Laender*), and the local level (communes), each tier with its own legislature. The *Freie Reichstadte* (free cities) of the Middle Ages, the various *Kleinstaaten* of the seventeenth, eighteenth, and nineteenth centuries, and the first unified state of Germany (established only in 1870) are the essential roots of Germany's federal system, a system reinforced by the Allied forces after 1945.

Following the subsidiarity principle, the federal government has no power over the communes. Their control lies exclusively with the state governments. Article 28 of the Basic Law guarantees the communes the right to regulate all the affairs of the local community. This power of *Kommunale Selbstvenwaltung* (communal self-government) is a key to understanding local politics in the country. The communes have mandated tasks, such as energy and water supply provision, urban land use planning and zoning, and social welfare, and discretionary tasks, which include culture and local economic development.

Local governments in Germany have independent powers to raise taxes. The budget of the average commune in the 1980s consisted of 30 percent locally raised taxes, 25 percent *Zuweisungen* (general grants) from the state government, 23 percent local tariffs and charges, and 22 percent other sources, mainly credits. Two facets of this system are of particular importance: land taxes and the intercommunal solidarity mechanism.

Land taxes play a negligible role in Germany. The significant revenue sources are the local share of the income tax and the share of the local industry tax, levied on profits and capital, the rate of which is set by the commune. Hence, local urban revenues are closely linked to the ups and downs of the local economy. This dependence explains the importance of local economic development policy.

However, there is an intercommunal solidarity mechanism, the *Kommunaler Finanzausgleich* (intercommunal equalization of tax potential), which implies that communes experiencing economic decline quasi-automatically receive bigger shares of state grants (Bennet 1983). A consequence of this equalization mechanism is that although communes are forced to cut their expenses when they incur economic decline, they are able to continue most of their mandatory and voluntary functions at more or less the same quality level.

Various rounds of local government consolidation in Germany over the last one hundred years (the last such "functional reform" took place in 1975) have created rather large and efficient local governments. Suburbanization repeatedly has resulted in the extension of the core city's administrative boundary, assuring a metropolitan area policy. The system leaves little room for the federal government to intervene in local urban and economic development. Rather, the local state plays an important role in this field.

The national political change in the early 1980s from the Social Democrats to the Conservatives could not alter this context. Although the change from a Keynesian to a more free market–oriented economic policy made slogans like "more market orientation," "deregulation," "flexibility," or "privatization" more popular, the local level was hardly touched by this change. Despite some efforts to introduce entrepreneurial zones, to promote the entrepreneurial city, and to deregulate the comprehensive planning and environmental legislation, little changed. Thus, there was no reason for the communes to challenge national economic policy, so the policy conflicts that arose in Britain or in the United States did not emerge in Germany.

The System of Political Parties

The German democratic system is very much a permanent party democracy, based as a rule on four dominant political parties. The resulting implications for local economic development are described as follows.

The well-established political party system in Germany follows the three-tier system of government. Political careers at regional or national levels depend to a large extent on their power bases in the local constituency. Hence, members of the federal and state parliaments are permanently involved in local politics and local development.

Election campaigns in Germany are almost exclusively financed out of the federal government's budget on a per vote basis. This system guarantees the relative independence of parties from vested economic interests and lobbies. It helps assure that, as a rule, political and economic careers are not interlinked, at least not at the local level. Hence, politicians in Germany are tied less to the private economic sector than is the case in other countries.

Despite this clear division of labor, economic development policies play a key role at all tiers. By and large, there is consensus for an economic growth policy across all parties. Even Die Grunen (the Greens), following the more pragmatic Social Democrats, recognize that considerable financial means are necessary to achieve their ecological and social goals. Obviously, however, the Social Democrats favor a more redistributive policy than their conservative counterparts. This is also true for the various unions that cut through all political parties from the Left to the Right.

These facts have prevented the established system from experiencing any radical changes following the government change in the early 1980s. Various reforms have been initiated and implemented (e.g., tax reforms have widened the gap between entrepreneurial profits and labor wages; the unions could not protect members from flexible wage schemes in industrial enterprises; and social benefits for underprivileged sections of the population have been cut). However, the well-established and successful welfare state has not been altered. Given the fact that Germany in the 1980s had experienced a long period of unprecedented economic growth despite relatively high unemployment rates (7 to 9 percent), major ideological conflicts in economic policy did not occur. Consequently, the new focus on private entrepreneurship did not bring about a "new privatism," as has been the case in the United States or in Great Britain (Barnekov, Boyle, and Rich 1989).

The Moderate Role of the Unions

The limited federal government push for a free market results from the power and influence of unions in the country. The unions and their co-determination rights are well anchored in the legal system of Germany.

The negotiability of contracts between unions and employers' associations is constitutionally guaranteed; the right to organize is assured for employees in enterprises with more than five employees; and in publicly held corporations, one-third of the board members have to be representatives of the employees. In larger coal and steel corporations, such co-determination rules and regulations (e.g., social concerns, security aspects, or hiring and dismissal procedures) are even more comprehensive and protective. The well-established mechanism of social cushioning, called *Sozialplan*, has proven to be very successful. Obviously, all such rules and regulations evoke continuous conflicts within enterprises, but they link the unions closely to management decisions.

Given such traditions, the unions by and large support public and corporate growth and modernization strategies. Their main concern is for the social cushioning of those employees who are affected by such changes. Social stabilization is a major priority, and despite the fact that 41 percent of all employees in Germany are union members, the number of days lost in labor strikes prior to 1992 has been minimal. The unions have supported modernization, demanding only moderate wage increases during the 1980s. In exchange for their support, regional wage differences were abandoned and three million new jobs were created. Hence, in contrast to the United States, a considerable proportion of the national labor force profited from structural change. Losers were the poorly qualified male and female (and disproportionally foreign) workers. (There are five million foreigners living in Germany, about 6.5 percent of the total population.)

Worker adjustment has generally been eased by an array of special programs aimed at reintegrating the long-term unemployed into local and regional economies, combining employment initiatives with retraining. Youth unemployment is being attacked through the traditional German dual-training scheme, which combines on-the-job experience with classroom instruction.

THE INSTITUTIONAL AND SOCIOPOLITICAL BACKGROUND OF THE NEW REGIONAL INITIATIVES IN THE RUHRGEBIET

Employment decline in the Ruhrgebiet's coal and steel industries and their forward and backward linkages has led to (1) high long-term unemployment and selected outmigration of qualified labor, and (2) decreasing tax revenues while local government expenses for social welfare have exploded. Additional general grants of the state government to local governments, and special one-time grants for urban redevelopment (in Northrhine Westphalia up to 85 percent of local costs for such measures are taken over by the state government), have enabled local governments to maintain their urban management capability and engage in modernizing their urban infrastructure. Hence, there was no significant public disinvestment in the region. Although there is evidence of marginalization and poverty in the Ruhrgebiet, so far the social underclass has not become spatially concentrated into isolated areas in which crime, drug abuse, and vandalism accumulate, or in which urban riots take place. Though the larger and smaller communities in the Ruhrgebiet have numerous problems, compared with other cities in old industrial regions of Europe and the United States they are relatively well off.

The Sociopolitical Milieu of Local Economic Development

The relative well-being of the communes in the Ruhr is based on a well-balanced system of private entrepreneurship and partial public counter-power against excesses of early capitalism. This system is strongly rooted in traditions that reach back to the nineteenth century, when a so-called municipal socialism laid the foundations for a civic responsibility for providing public physical, social, and cultural infrastructure for local enterprises and citizens. Private market forces, public institutions, and an efficient system of urban planning jointly shape and guide the development of cities in Germany in a well-balanced interplay of forces. Thus, the concept of privatism is irrelevant in Germany.

Nevertheless, there *are* local growth coalitions in which the semipublic local chambers of trades and commerce, representing the entrepreneurial interests, are key actors. In the past, growth coalitions in the Ruhrgebiet successfully guaranteed the unprecedented economic growth of the industrial region. However, they neglected the particular interests of smaller and medium-sized enterprises. As a rule, the influential actors (including the Social Democrats and unions in such coalitions) were committed to the larger coal and steel corporations. Thus, the growth coalitions in the Ruhrgebiet differ from those in the United States: they are not "land based" (Molotch 1976). The traditional industries in the Ruhrgebiet owned and controlled the land they required for their functioning and possible extension. Profiting from low land and property taxes, they were never interested in raising land values.

In the late 1970s, the traditional growth coalitions reached their limits. They lost their economic power and influence because of a decline in the coal and steel industries. Their counterparts in political parties and unions, personally rooted in the traditional industries, turned more and more into lobbyists for public subsidies from federal and state governments. Subsequently the growth coalitions became forces *resisting* economic change. The region's local economic development departments have a record of successfully attracting new firms while providing industrial land for their local clientele. As is typical of such service departments, however, their style tended to be reactive, not innovative. Their inability to initiate innovative projects is due, at least in part, to the traditionalism of local opinion leaders. The local level, then, has not exhibited much economic development initiative.

Strategies for Regional Economic Development

No regional economic development strategy has been formulated for the Ruhrgebiet as a whole. This planning gap is due to the absence of a powerful regional economic promotion and development agency, and the traditional competition between major cities in the region. However, the patchwork of various state programs, strategic papers of the major cities, and projects already initiated or implemented can be identified as an implicit regional strategy.

The focus of this strategy is on the modernization of the industrial structure. Given the negative image of the region and recent disappointing results in attracting inward investment (mainly caused by the low mobility of German industries), the strategy emphasizes the development of regional endogenous potential. This potential consists mainly of (1) medium-sized enterprises that were formerly dependent on linkages to coal and steel industries, and (2) start-ups in high-technology sectors. A key to the development of this potential lies in the creative potential of the new technical universities established in the region during the 1960s and 1970s.

In contrast to most American cities, the cities of the Ruhrgebiet did not focus on office development, convention halls, high-income housing, or urban tourism. Rather, they focused on a reindustrialization strategy combining newly established high-tech firms with the expansion and diversification interests of traditional low-tech industries. Such a strategy reflects traditional attitudes of the regional elites; it also follows the national macro-economic industrial policy, which emphasizes industrial rather than financial capital as a basis for coping with global economic development trends. German research in this field stresses the need to reinforce the lead function that industrial development plays in promoting production-oriented services, a point overlooked in many other industrialized states.

The regional development actors in the Ruhrgebiet believe that such a strategy helps to overcome unemployment more than strategies focusing on services. New growth in the industrial sector, paralleled by a complementary growth of services, is certainly a strategic goal that, under the regional conditions in the Ruhrgebiet, is much better balanced than a policy of highlighting services.

However, innovative approaches are not easy to implement in the traditional coal- and steel-oriented regional milieu. Given the resistance to change, the new approaches for regional restructuring in the Ruhrgebiet have adopted slogans of American and British privatism policies, encouraging and stimulating innovative actors from "below" to form new growth coalitions and to join their forces for initiating and implementing new projects. Despite some linguistic similarities, the sociopolitical context of regional and local economic development in the Ruhrgebiet differs considerably from that in the United States or in Britain.

NEW APPROACHES TO REGIONAL RESTRUCTURING IN THE RUHRGEBIET

Three new approaches to regional restructuring in the Ruhrgebiet illustrate this point. They are:

- Zukunftsinitiative Montanregionen (Initiative for the Future of Coal and Steel Regions);

- Internationale Bauausstellung Emscher Park (EmscherPark International Building Exhibition); and

- Initiativkreis Ruhrgebiet (Initiative for the Ruhrgebiet, launched by chief executive officers of major companies).

All three initiatives were launched in the late 1980s to overcome particular constraints of regional restructuring. They clearly represent different ideological strands and perspectives and draw on divergent assessments of the shortcomings of previous public sector approaches to regional restructuring.

Sparking Endogenous Local Economic Development: The Zukunftsinitiative Montanregionen

Reacting to the regional crisis in 1987, the state government of Northrhine Westphalia established a new regional policy initiative under the imposing title of Zukunftsinitiative Montanregionen (ZIM) (MWMT

1987). Responding to the poor performance of previous policies, the state government did not seek to develop and establish another comprehensive, top-down regional development program. Instead, the state economics ministry invited the local actors in the coal and steel region to develop projects that aimed at stimulating new innovative approaches and industrial growth coalitions from the bottom up. The only guidelines the state government provided for the development of local projects were five very broadly defined action priority areas:

- Innovation and technology promotion;
- Promotion of future-oriented training of the labor force;
- Measures to create new or to secure existing jobs;
- Extension and modernization of physical infrastructure; and
- Environmental improvement and energy conservation.

The concise policy paper describing these action areas included an array of suggestions for appropriate projects, reflecting the present international state of the art of innovative regional policies. One of the most striking features of this initiative is the fact that the state government has finally abandoned structure-conserving measures designed to preserve the traditional industrial base of the Ruhrgebiet. Another change is the emphasis on new actors: local governments, other locally influential public or semi-public institutions (e.g., the universities or the local chambers of trade and commerce), and private enterprises are invited and encouraged to participate. They have been asked to consent and collaborate on innovative and future-oriented projects based on endogenous resources and potentials and to submit proposed projects to the state government for financing. Neither explicit guidelines for project support nor a financial ceiling for individual projects were defined. The funds for the projects came from the budget of the state government, from the Federal Republic, and from European Community funds channeled through the state government. They total around two billion deutschmarks ($1.2 billion).

The state government has promised to contribute to the financing of those projects and to ensure interministerial coordination where required. Three principles have been defined for such projects:

1. They are particularly innovative and capable of renewing the regional industrial structure (innovation principle);

2. They enhance public and private cooperation and co-financing by public and private investors (public-private partnership principle);

3. They have been developed and agreed to by more than one local government with a number of regional private, semi-public, and public actors, based on a roughly sketched regional action program (consensus principle).

The sociopolitical rationale behind these principles is obvious: mobilization of local public and private actors and the synergy of local know-how, local initiative, and local co-financing. The state government has attempted to trigger (1) the crossing of parochial boundaries of local government, and (2) cooperation between public institutions and private enterprises at the local or subregional level.

The response to the state government's unusual call for projects was impressive. Despite a rather short notice, the first round in 1987 saw 895 proposal submissions (MWMT 1987). Although there are no data on how many of the proposed projects have been or are being implemented, new developments in the administration of the ZIM suggest perceived success:

1. In 1989, the geographically limited initiative was spatially expanded to cover the entire state territory;

2. The state and local actors are continuing to bargain over approval for certain projects to which commitment remains high.

The record of applications for support shows the following:

1. The majority of projects submitted and funded were in the field of technology and industrial innovation (25 percent of all projects submitted under the program were initiated from private industrial enterprises and firms calling for assistance in research and development, or R&D, activities). This has contributed to a further growth of the young R&D complex of the Ruhrgebiet.

2. Another focus of institutional assistance is the funding for modernizing existing vocational (labor) training activities in the region.

3. Another group of supported projects combined reutilization of derelict industrial land with the development of new decontam-

ination and recycling technologies. These projects added further strength to the regional environmental industries, one of the most promising new economic sectors of the Ruhrgebiet (MURL 1989).

The Zukunftsinitiative Montanregionen has exhibited a series of implementation problems, despite good intentions and state-level institutional flexibility:

1. Quality and efficiency differences among local governments and subregional coalitions in submitting innovative projects have caused new disparities. In some local environments, relative failures in raising funds for submitted projects during the first round have caused the local actors to identify more innovative initiatives and projects.

2. The sheer volume of projects submitted under the programs taxed the absorptive management capacity of the administration of many local authorities. State-approved innovative and promising projects could not be implemented locally because of lack of management capacity, particularly in the smaller communities of the region.

3. The state government itself underestimated the need and pressure for accelerated interministerial coordination, which it had promised but could not deliver and sustain in all cases.

4. The creation of new, streamlined decision-making structures for project selection and approval at the state level was long resisted by forces objecting to an implementation process that bypassed local government policy committees.

Notwithstanding such implementation problems, the initiative may be said to be a success since it has stimulated two significant and promising institutional changes. First, it has made public sector–led private-public partnerships acceptable when they previously were rejected, especially by local governments. Second, it has produced new growth coalitions centered on small- and medium-sized high-tech firms, regional universities, and the more dynamic local government managers. Both innovations stand in stark contrast to the previous efforts to conserve the traditional coal and steel industries.

The Zukunftsinitiative Montanregionen has uncovered some of the weaknesses of local implementation machineries. Despite — or maybe because of — this disclosure, the initiative has been a success in generating new, locally driven, economic development efforts.

Cleaning and Greening an Industrial Townscape: The Socio-Ecological Efforts of the Internationale Bauausstellung Emscher Park

The Emscherzone is the backwater of the Ruhrgebiet. It is a large industrial belt reaching from Hamm to Duisburg. The area, 800 square kilometers in size and comprising seventeen communes with two million inhabitants in 1990, is by far the largest industrial complex in Germany. It was built on a foundation of coal mines, steel production factories, and coal power plants. The problems of the region include an obsolete infrastructure, heavy dependance upon jobs in the traditional coal and steel sectors, lack of usable open space, and hectares of derelict and contaminated land. Compared with other parts of the Ruhrgebiet, the average household is poorer and less educated, car ownership is lower, unemployment higher, the proportion of resident ethnic minorities higher, and housing standards lower. Visually, the area is dominated by the bulky skylines of industrial plants and numerous coal heaps and collieries, cut through with busy or obsolete railway tracks, open sewers, and shipping canals. Obviously, the quality of life is lower than in other parts of the Ruhrgebiet, so attracting investment to the area is very difficult.

In May 1988, the government of Northrhine Westphalia decided to stage the Internationale Bauausstellung Emscher Park (the Emscher Park International Building Exhibition, or the IBA-EmscherPark). The term "exhibition," however, is misleading. The IBA-EmscherPark is an ambitious ten-year project (MSWV 1988). As the prime minister of Northrhine Westphalia has officially stated, it will "provide business and professional organizations with an opportunity for long-term involvement in the comprehensive renewal of the Emscherzone." The IBA-EmscherPark is an ambitious regional effort to improve the environment and the physical appearance of the region by setting and enforcing new social, ecological, and aesthetic standards for innovative projects. It aims, as the official Memorandum on Content and Organization conveys, "to provide impulses of a conceptional, practical, political, financial and organizational nature for the future ecological, economic and social restructuring of the Emscher area," attempting to attract innovative investors and actors to the region and to remove its unfavorable image (MSWV 1988).

In an approach similar to that of the Zukunftsinitiative Montanregionen, the IBA-EmscherPark raised its ideas by a "call for projects" encouraging public and private actors in the region to submit ideas and projects for revitalizing the Emscherzone, promising both political and financial support. The guidelines for the kind of projects expected reflect the socio-ecological emphasis of the initiative, following a long tradition of socially motivated urban planning doctrines in Germany. The type of guideline projects that the IBA-EmscherPark Agency wishes to see implemented include:

- The ecological improvement of the Emscher River system, currently an artificial and regulated man-made drainage system;
- The reconversion of the Rhine-Herne Canal zone into a leisure area;
- The conservation of derelict industrial sites as monuments and reusable structures;
- The creation of attractive industrial parks;
- The promotion of new forms of owner-occupied housing; and
- The advancement of new approaches to social and cultural development at the neighborhood and local community level.

Apart from developing a comprehensive strategy for the physical reconversion of the region and for the promotion of the previously mentioned guideline projects, planning workshops and architectural competitions will be initiated and carried out by the Agency.

Economic development is clearly not the main objective of the IBA-EmscherPark, nor is it the support of regional or local economic growth coalitions. The initiative aims at supporting socially and ecologically oriented housing, protecting and conserving the industrial heritage, regenerating the heavily damaged regional ecosystem, and creating an attractive regional townscape. Thus, the IBA-EmscherPark raises the quality of soft location factors and prepares the ground for new economic investment in a long-term transformational approach.

The responsibility for all IBA activities has been assigned to a newly established (and 100 percent public) regional development agency with a highly competent professional staff. The only funding the organization receives is for its operations and planning efforts. No resources are distributed through the IBA-EmscherPark, since the objective of the agency is to generate local and regional, public and private, support for the types of efforts it endorses.

In effect, only those proposals that have the IBA approval stand any chance of state-level funding; such endorsement helps attract other public and private funds as well. The IBA management team also helps projects along by assisting with administrative and bureaucratic bottlenecks. The real regeneration contribution of the Agency is its contribution to changing the image of the Emscher area and its industrial landscape, altering public and private perceptions so that the built-up infrastructure and architecture are not seen as impediments to development, but as resources for adaptive reuse.

No formal assessment of this relatively new effort is possible yet. A preliminary review of its impacts suggests that (1) the mere existence of the project appears to have already drawn international attention to this backyard of the Ruhrgebiet, and (2) the IBA has initiated many innovative projects that have gained political acceptance and will be implemented. These projects appear bound to set new aesthetic, environmental, and sociocultural standards for the region. On the other hand, the positive picture may be overstated. Private sector interest in the project so far is closely linked to public support of private investment projects. Whether it is the project's socio-ecological focus (which is not widely accepted by the regional electorate) or the shift of investment interests to eastern Germany since unification, the fact is that independent private sector efforts are scarce. This in turn makes the whole initiative vulnerable and dependent upon political support "from above" for public funding. In fact, the experience so far with project selection processes points to top-down decision-making procedures and not to bottom-up ones as intended and announced.

The absence of IBA-EmscherPark funds for activities other than planning and communication means that the Agency only communicates, cooperates, and mediates rather than implements projects. The Agency's coordination efforts are thus constrained and there are few incentives for cooperating with it.

Implementation of the IBA-EmscherPark concept may fall victim to greater pressures for development investments from eastern Germany. Reunification and national policies for revenue sharing across the individual subnational states may draw resources away from the Ruhrgebiet and make it impossible for the innovative plans and proposals stimulated by the Agency to ever see the light of day. The prospects for any one development effort may lie less in its characteristics and value and more in the competition between that need and others for scarce public sector resources.

Mobilizing Private Funds for Regional Restructuring: The Role of the Initiativkreis Ruhrgebiet

Wir an der Ruhr, gemeinsam voran (We on the Ruhr, together ahead) is the label of the Initiativkreis Ruhrgebiet, a private effort launched in 1988 by the managing director of the Kommunalverband Ruhrgebiet and the Catholic bishop of the Essen diocese. The Initiativkreis Ruhrgebiet (IR) is a "club" of chief executive officers (CEOs) of major German corporations, banks, and enterprises that commits its influential members to promoting the Ruhrgebiet, to engage in its future economic and cultural revitalization, and to strive for success in restructuring the regional economy. Its thirty-five founding members agreed to pay an "entrance fee" of 1.5 million deutschmarks (payable in five annual installments of 300,000 DM each) into a project development fund and to invest in the future of the Ruhrgebiet. The membership rose to forty-eight by September 1989, providing annual revenues of almost 15 million deutschmarks. Its first prominent spokesman was the late Alfred Herrhausen, the general manager of the most powerful German bank, the Deutsche Bank.

The IR utilizes its endowments to increase the appeal of the region and to improve its image. Apart from eye-catching advertisements in regional and national newspapers, this is done along two independent strands:

1. Through sponsoring outstanding events in the region such as art exhibitions (e.g., in 1989, Max Pechstein; in 1990, van Gogh), music festivals (the annual Klavier Festival Ruhr), scientific congresses of national and international importance, and sports events (e.g., world championships, masters tournaments, world cups, and the like in tennis, athletics, and horse riding). This is primarily done to attract outside interest (and tourism) in the region and its comprehensive cultural infrastructure, but also to raise media coverage of the region and to reinforce regional pride and identity.

2. Through promoting innovative investment projects such as a chain of marinas along the regional industrial canal system, regional science and business parks, a world trade center park, and public golf courses, as well as more socially oriented projects such as the conservation of traditional workers' housing. Using the influence and power of its members, the

Initiativkreis removes real and perceived constraints and bottlenecks, which in the past have hindered the take-off of innovative projects in the region.

Members of the Initiativkreis Ruhrgebiet occasionally refer (wrongly!) to the public-private partnership concept in Pittsburgh as their model. Their intervention is more rooted in the civic and paternalistic traditions of the Ruhr, as exemplified by the late Alfred Krupp, the founder of the large Krupp Steel Corporation. The vested interests of the members are clear: the improvement of the region's image helps them to maintain their businesses and to retain their highly qualified labor force.

Discreet behind-the-scenes counseling, mediating, and promotion characterize the activities of the Initiativkreis Ruhrgebiet. There is little publicity on how projects are selected, and the decision-making process is opaque. A well-prepared press conference once a year reveals the new initiatives and projects to the regional and national public. This opacity appears to be counterproductive, raising suspicion rather than creating confidence.

Still, the IR must be credited with improving the external image of the Ruhrgebiet. It has also built an internal sense of identity while stimulating local and regional politicians to think in terms of the region's role in a world economic system. The events the IR has sponsored are net gains to the area, as they would not have occurred without its specific stimulus and subsidy. However, both the motivations and impacts of the Initiativkreis Ruhrgebiet have been questioned.

Institutionally and politically, this private initiative has been charged with simply trying to reestablish the dominance of the old large corporations in the region, bypassing more democratic decision-making processes through its "old boys' network," which generates public sector resource commitments to support private projects. Investments by member corporations credited to the initiative are said by many to be projects that would have been undertaken in any event. Finally, the IR's cultural and sports events appear to critics to service the local bourgeoisie or upper class, rather than functioning as tourism attractions or stimuli to greater non-local attention to the Ruhrgebiet.

On some level, this criticism seems plausible: the region simply cannot compete with Paris, Vienna, or Munich as a tourist or cultural mecca, regardless of its efforts. At the same time, the Initiativkreis Ruhrgebiet is an important watershed, as it constitutes a renewal of private sector commitment to the area. Large-scale, private-led new development projects of any sort have been rare in the region for decades, and the initiative does promise a new source of capital for revitalization and renewal.

CONCLUSION: PROSPECTS FOR THE NEXT DECADE

What are the main conclusions to be drawn from this regional case study and the three new approaches to regional restructuring? As we have shown, the context and the socioeconomic conditions of regional restructuring in the Ruhrgebiet differ considerably from that in comparable regions of the United States and Great Britain. Dortmund is neither Liverpool nor Pittsburgh. Comparative assessment must consider the varying contextual conditions.

The new approaches to regional restructuring in the Ruhrgebiet clearly depend heavily on public initiative and cooperation. Thus, they differ from the prevailing privatism strategies in the United States and Great Britain. All the initiatives take place in a traditional and value-conservative milieu of cooperation between the large corporate steel, coal, and energy corporations, politicians, and unions. These traditional coalitions and their resistance to change often hinder the implementation of innovative projects. However, many efforts have generated new coalitions of innovative actors and entrepreneurial investors in high-tech fields, especially near the new regional universities, albeit with heavy dependence on public support. The endogenous development strategies pursued by the state government have provoked many new projects and initiatives, but their stability and longevity remain questionable.

What the three strategies undoubtedly have brought about is an improved image of the region. In the eyes of outside observers and private investors, the Ruhrgebiet is no longer a loser, a place to avoid. Within a very short time period the region has become attractive for investors because of the human potential and an affordable quality of life, for others as an innovative laboratory of regional change. The new regional development efforts have contributed to this transformation.

However, the costs of reunification in Germany, the billions of deutschmarks needed to modernize the obsolete public infrastructure and to renew the outdated industrial base in the cities and regions of eastern Germany, will be considerable. Thus, redistribution will have to take place at the cost of the cities and regions in western Germany. Unconstrained transfers and state funds for innovation will no longer flow as readily to the Ruhrgebiet. The region, like other less well-off areas of western Germany, will have to rely on endogenous resources rather than the share of redistributed funds they used to get from the more affluent states and regions of the country.

All the initiatives launched in the Ruhrgebiet relied, to a greater or lesser degree, on this external source of public sector funds. Current implementation of these plans is impeded by the loss of funds, heightened interlocational competition for what resources (and new investment) remain in the poor regions of western Germany, and renewed lobbying for support of existing heavy industry in the region in the face of fears of greater job loss. The expectations for these efforts that were raised are now less likely to be met, not because of any flaw in the plans and programs themselves but because of external factors that could never have been anticipated in the development of the regenerational approaches, those associated with the demise of communism and the reunification of Germany.

ACKNOWLEDGMENTS

The authors are most grateful for comments they have received from Peter Meyer and Peter Roberts on an earlier version of this chapter. Their critical questions have caused the authors to add basic information on the institutional and political background of local economic development in Germany.

4

Employee Buyouts and Loans to Preserve Jobs: The South Bend Experience

Charles Craypo
Jerry Paar

South Bend, Indiana, is a typical midwestern factory town that lost half its manufacturing jobs after the mid-1950s. Total employment continued to grow, but mostly in the low-wage service sectors. From 1979 to 1990, jobs in old manufacturing industries (vehicles and machinery) fell by 8,100, while those in stable and expanding industries such as construction and plastic products rose by 5,400, and in services by 34,200. Because South Bend is a typical U.S. factory town in this regard, its experiences with government-financed attempts to save threatened manufacturing jobs and create new ones is relevant to the employment and income future of the United States.

This chapter examines the implementation and performance of an employee stock ownership plan (ESOP) buyout of the South Bend Lathe (SBL) Company of South Bend, Indiana, and of an industrial revolving fund (IRF) created in connection with the buyout to help the city retain and create manufacturing jobs. In 1975, the U.S. Commerce Department's Economic Development Agency (EDA), acting under the Employee Retirement Income Security Act of 1974, gave the City of South Bend a $5 million grant with which to finance the SBL buyout. The EDA also stipulated that as SBL repaid the buyout loan the city could use the money to make new loans to high-risk manufacturers under long-term, low-interest rates. The first section of this chapter describes the ESOP buyout and the post-buyout restructuring and operating performance of SBL. The second section describes the purpose and structure of the fund, loan experiences during 1978–1989, implementation problems, criticisms, and responses. Finally, the wider policy implications of the South Bend experience are analyzed.

THE SOUTH BEND LATHE ESOP

South Bend Lathe was organized in 1906; by the 1920s it was the world's leading manufacturer and exporter of small lathes. It remained a family enterprise until 1959 when it was acquired by Amsted Industries. Amsted initially profited from SBL and added product lines from other acquisitions (*South Bend Times* 1966), but it failed to make necessary capital investments and gradually fell behind industry products and technology. By 1974 SBL was for sale again, but the only buyer available wanted to liquidate the company. This prompted J. Richard Boulis, president of SBL under Amsted, to engineer an ESOP buyout.

Boulis drafted the proposed buyout in terms that led all concerned to believe that they had a choice between unqualified support for his plan or imminent plant shutdown. As a result of his misrepresentations, union workers voluntarily gave up their pensions and substituted ownership shares in the new company (Olson 1982:747–750).

The final buyout package totaled $10 million, $7.6 million of which went to Amsted for the sale of SBL and the remainder in a line of credit with local banks for the new company to finance capital development. The $7.6 million purchase price was financed by a $5 million EDA grant to the city — at 3 percent interest over twenty-five years — and a $2.6 million, five-year commercial loan at prime-plus interest rates. As SBL repaid the $5 million loan from the city, the latter deposited a corresponding number of ownership shares with the ESOP Trust, which in turn allocated them on the basis of an earnings and years-of-service formula among individual SBL employees with the restriction that only shareholders with three or more years of service could vote their shares. Since all other shares were voted by the ESOP Trust, the employee-owners did not acquire a majority of the votes until the late 1980s.

Boulis served simultaneously as SBL president, board chairman, and ESOP Trust director, giving him total control of what was nominally an employee-owned company.[1] At first he refused even to recognize the union and tried ousting it in two unsuccessful union decertification elections. A review of SBL's administrative authority structure concluded that the firm was controlled by its directors rather than by its worker-owners, with minimal internal corporate checks and balances on Boulis's decisions (Arnold and Porter 1981).

Differences naturally arose between labor and management over alternative operating strategies. Labor wanted to continue making SBL's traditional product lines using both traditional and advanced (micro-electronic) production processes. Management wanted to phase down certain lines and develop and build high-tech, computerized lathes in South Bend while importing small models from foreign producers for domestic distribution. A similar effort by Amsted had failed miserably, but Boulis spent his entire tenure at SBL trying unsuccessfully to develop a computerized numerically controlled (CNC) lathe.

With a work force of about 500 and $17 million in annual sales at the time of the buyout, SBL ranked among the nation's top twenty independent machine tool makers. Fifteen years later, while it had provided bonuses to employee-owners and retired its $2.6 million commercial loans, the firm was down to about 100 workers.

Boulis's response to foreign imports was to acquire other companies and transfer small lathe production overseas, actions consistent with his interest in preserving the company, regardless of what and where it produced. By contrast, the worker-owners wanted to save the company in South Bend as a high-wage and high-salary unionized enterprise. But the unionized worker-owners also wanted the company in South Bend to remain a union shop. These conflicting objectives and management's subsequent actions underscore the error the union and community made in accepting corporate bylaws that gave one person unchallenged control.

Boulis began importing parts from a Korean firm and expanding overseas production commitments. Then he made three corporate acquisitions, committing resources that could have been used to retrofit the South Bend plant and redesign established product lines to new business activities. It is impossible to say whether SBL would have survived under the union's strategies, but centralized managerial control ensured its eventual demise as a local manufacturer: machine tool lathes, historically SBL's key product line, fell from 32 to 11 percent of dollar shipments while parts and imports together rose from 52 to 79 percent and imports alone from less than one-fifth to more than one-half (Boulis 1985).

Employee-owners naturally resented Boulis's corporate acquisitions and the declining value of company shares on which they depended for retirement income. These shares could not be traded or redeemed except with the company and at a price determined jointly by SBL management and outside auditors. The per share value of SBL stock was put at $500 in 1975, but by 1989 it had fallen to $43 (Dodson 1989).

The employees as the risk-taking shareholders were the biggest losers from operating decisions that reduced production employment in South Bend and devalued SBL ownership shares. Unlike conventional shareholders, however, under the ESOP they had absolutely no power or control over management. After workers finally gained voting control, in December 1987 shareholders voted 2-to-1 against Boulis's reappointment to the board of directors. Despite this show of no confidence, the ESOP Committee, by a 3-to-2 vote — with Boulis chairing the meeting and casting the deciding vote — returned him to the board. Individual employees and the union then sued in federal court to have Boulis removed from all company and ESOP offices; Boulis voluntarily resigned his positions and retired from the firm in early 1988 (Dodson 1988a; 1988b).

In mid-1989 SBL defaulted on its ESOP loan payment and asked the South Bend Industrial Revolving Fund, which held the paper, to restructure SBL's existing debt and approve an additional capital loan, which the company needed to make plant and equipment improvements. The rejection by the IRF Loan Committee was tantamount to a public vote of "no confidence" in the company and its managers and an indication that after thirteen years of financial rescue missions for SBL the city no longer was prepared to chase good money after bad. Even the SBL local union — the only organized voice of SBL employee-owners — did not publicly support management's request or criticize the IRF action, which indicated that the production employees themselves had little faith in management. It also suggested that the situation was desperate and that by now the various parties were looking to minimize the damage to themselves in SBL's eventual collapse.

SBL management then demanded mid-term union contract concessions from production workers, which were rejected since the workers saw no future for the South Bend plant. Union officers remained convinced that management wanted to subcontract most of the work still being done and was in fact raising needed cash flow by cannibalizing existing SBL equipment and assets (Reynolds 1990). When the opportunity arose, the union supported a successful revolt inside management by local managers who feared the possible relocation of all production and distribution operations away from South Bend. Despite a new management commitment to South Bend, union-management relations deteriorated until some fifty-two production workers, having already extended the old contract eight months beyond its expiration date, refused to work any longer without an agreement and struck the plant for two weeks in May 1991 (Dodson 1991a; 1991c).

Thus, sixteen years after the ESOP buyout of South Bend Lathe, the experiment in employee ownership cannot be judged a success. A fraction of the original jobs remain, management has been in constant conflict with labor and itself, and the company has dim prospects as a machine producer. The administrative structure imposed at the time of the buyout clearly precluded meaningful and effective participation by employee-owners and contributed heavily to SBL's internal problems. It also made possible the diversion of financial resources and production away from the South Bend plant and greatly weakened the operating potential of the company as an employee-owned enterprise. These failures also diminished the performance of the industrial revolving fund created in South Bend at the time of the SBL buyout, which was to be capitalized by the ESOP's loan repayments.

THE INDUSTRIAL REVOLVING FUND

The South Bend Industrial Revolving Fund was established in 1975 under a "grant agreement" between the EDA and the City of South Bend covering the $5 million EDA grant to finance the SBL buyout. EDA intended that the IRF would be used (1) to finance similar employee buyouts in other threatened companies in South Bend, and (2) to assist the area generally in adjusting to economic dislocation caused by industrial restructuring (Economic Development Administration 1975). City officials named First Source Bank, the area's largest locally controlled commercial institution, to be the IRF "trustee" and, along with EDA, established a five-member administrative board.

This allocation of board positions gave administrative control of the Fund to local banks and private and public economic developers. Other groups having an interest in development projects, such as labor unions and neighborhood associations, were not included. Nonetheless, conflicting objectives became evident. Banks prefer low-interest, public loans that do not compete in the local lending market with high-interest, commercial paper; existing businesses prefer low-interest loans and government loan guarantees that go mainly to new and expanding businesses. Among government officials, those giving priority to private development objectives are inclined to promote expansion of any sort, while those favoring labor and neighborhood priorities are likely to insist that loan committees consider the quality of jobs being retained and created and the impact on community environment and neighborhood zoning. Finally, city authorities, regardless of competing development interests, wanted to coordinate development policies and programs rather than promote isolated efforts and, as it turned out, were prepared to assert administrative control over the IRF in order to ensure that loan criteria and allocations were consistent with the city's overall economic development strategy.

The original grant agreement acknowledged that the IRF would have to make risky loans if it was to preserve threatened manufacturing jobs; it also recognized that many loan recipients would not be able to provide collateral and in some instances would be unable to repay loans. Thus, the IRF charter instructed the board to "take more risk" than normal in approving unsecured loans (Industrial Revolving Fund 1975). Board members also agreed informally that because of numerous plant closings and phase-downs in South Bend, priority should be given to preventing additional closings, even when the policy necessitated loans that further increased risks (Gilcrest 1985).

The area's largest bank was made the principal administrator of the IRF although the Fund was designed to emphasize high-risk loans aimed at preserving existing manufacturing operations. This peculiar contraction was explained by a co-author of the IRF organizational plan:

> It was not deemed practical that such funds should be commingled with the municipal funds of the city of South Bend and it was deemed advisable that special arrangements should be conceived and developed to assure the use of such funds for the purpose intended. It was determined to place such funds for general administrative purposes with a trustee located in the South Bend area which had substantial experience and expertise in performing fiduciary functions. (McGill 1975; O-5)

Current IRF guidelines still commit the Fund to unorthodox loan criteria and non-competition with commercial lenders. Loans cannot be made to firms that need "continuous subsidies to remain viable business concerns," and only projects involving manufacturing and related transportation or warehousing activities and located in certain city-designated industrial areas are eligible for support. Among the criteria used in making loan decisions are the quality of the proposed project, the net impact on area employment, an anticipated ratio of one new job for every $15,000 in loan funds, and a maximum ratio of one dollar of IRF funds for every one dollar from other lending sources (Industrial Revolving Fund 1985). Although the SBL ESOP buyout took place in 1975, it took time for its loan repayments to fully capitalize the IRF, so lending started in 1978.

By 1983 another coordinated program was in place. A nonprofit development company called Business Development Corporation (BDC) was created to serve as a clearinghouse for and coordinate the activities of the Chamber of Commerce, Project Future (a Chamber subsidiary), and the South Bend Department of Economic Development. BDC was certified by the Small Business Administration (SBA) to administer its SBA Federal Loan Program. In 1984 it obtained an SBA loan for a new company called New Energy Corporation to construct a corn-based ethanol fuel plant in South Bend. As New Energy repaid the loan to BDC, the latter would make additional revolving loans to other businesses, much as the IRF does with SBL's EDA loan repayments. The major administrative issue involving the existing IRF then became whether it would operate inside or outside the BDC.

IRF Loan Performance. For this reason, it is necessary to distinguish between the periods 1978–1984 and 1985–1990. During the first period the IRF operated largely independently of BDC, and during the second period mainly in conjunction with BDC. As Table 4.1 shows, the 1978–1984 period involved fewer but larger loans to a smaller number of borrowers than the 1985–1990 period. The loan repayment and job performance experiences of the 1978–1984 borrowers were not encouraging. By the end of 1990, five of the eight loan recipients were still operating in South Bend, but only six of the sixteen loans they had received have been or were being repaid, the others having been refinanced or written off. Some one thousand retained and created jobs were attributed to these loans by the end of 1991, but a single borrower accounted for more than 80 percent of these jobs and South Bend Lathe for half of the remainder. Three borrowers had gone out of business or relocated, and on balance, the IRF board had to write off in excess of a half-million dollars in loans as a result of defaults.

Easily the largest borrower during this period was SBL. But its persistent operating problems forced the Fund to write off much of SBL's outstanding debt. This was critical to IRF performance, because at the time SBL accounted for two out of every three IRF loan dollars outstanding. In addition to the initial $5 million ESOP loan, SBL had obtained $780,000 in additional loans in four installments between 1979 and 1982. The funds were obtained on the grounds that SBL was experiencing operating difficulties and needed the cash for plant and equipment, without which it might go under financially and cause the IRF to lose most or all of its unrecovered investment in SBL — some $3.7 million. In 1983, SBL requested a moratorium on repayments due to the effect of the recession on company performance. Board members turned down that request, but it was renewed and rejected again in 1985, this time on the grounds that SBL was financially sound and that company management wanted to use the money elsewhere (Dodson 1985b). By the end of 1989, however, SBL was in default on its outstanding $3.7 million debt to the IRF.

Fund officers forced SBL into liquidation as a way of recovering part of its remaining investment in the company. So far the IRF has had to write off $1.5 million of the original $5 million loan and $552,000 of the additional $780,000. However, they also had to refinance $1.6 million on the original loan, under precarious terms: interest only payments until 1996, when the entire balance must be paid in a balloon payment, a questionable prospect in view of SBL's track record.

The second largest borrower, a molded plastic manufacturer that received support during the 1978–1984 period, was also the largest job provider and most successful of the loan recipients. The company obtained two loans totaling $500,000 to build a production complex in the city's newest industrial park. In 1990 it employed more than eight hundred workers making plastic auto components after it expanded its product line to the Great Lakes area during the 1980s. The company made three additional loan requests but the IRF turned down each of them, initially due to insufficient funds (because of supplemental loans the IRF made to SBL after 1975) and later because the board determined that an operationally successful firm did not need subsidized financing.

The reasons why only one out of seven borrowers during the period 1978–1984 was successful in subsequent loan repayment and job performance are as follows: (1) the IRF made several multiple loans to individual borrowers, especially South Bend Lathe, only one of which resulted in substantial job creation and continued loan repayments; (2) IRF loans usually financed the major portion of these projects, and as a result the Fund often had to make additional and precarious loans to borrowers that were in financial trouble; and (3) the IRF functioned independently of South Bend's overall economic development program, which precluded coordination in organizing, financing, and monitoring projects, so the IRF loan portfolio tended to have only isolated and high-risk borrowing prospects.

The net effect was to destabilize the Fund and diminish its contribution to manufacturing growth and employment in South Bend. In an internal memo to other board members concerning a loan reorganization request from one of the borrowers that later would default on its debt, South Bend's city controller noted that "serious problems" were created because IRF loan repayment often was "tentative and subordinate to most other debt incurred by any company receiving funding from us." He therefore questioned whether the board was exercising "sound judgement" in its loan policy. "I don't disagree that we are in a box with no other viable option," he wrote, but nevertheless he urged the board in the future to avoid "the continued position we seem to be in" (Vance 1985).

Also concerned about Fund implementation and performance was the EDA; its 1982 audit report criticized board procedure on six counts:

The South Bend Experience 63

1. Failure to specify and quantify IRF program and goals;
2. Failure to obtain EDA approval before making loans;
3. Failure to require financial reports from borrowers;
4. Failure to increase interest rates on loans above 3 percent;
5. Failure to complete formal documents before making loans;
6. Failure to gather and report to the EDA information on job retention and creation (Pross and Prosser 1982).

The IRF board responded to these charges — and to the implicit threat of EDA remedial action — with both formal and informal changes in procedure. Formally it assured EDA that it would tighten loan approval and monitoring practices, require financial statements and collect performance data from borrowers, and include the findings in annual reports to EDA (Gilcrest 1983). Informally, but more relevant to IRF performance, the board shifted priorities from job retention to job creation projects and began demanding loan collateral and first and second creditor claims on assets in the event of loan default. Most important, the board abandoned its practice of funding projects almost exclusively and operating largely independently of other economic development activities; instead, it allowed the IRF to become part of the city's overall job retention and creation efforts.

During the period 1985–1990, the IRF made more loans to more borrowers for a larger total loan portfolio than it had in the initial periods. As a result, average loan size was 23 percent smaller than in 1978–1984, and the average borrower received less than half the total amount of money as in the earlier period. The Fund also made *two* multiple loans to individual borrowers during 1985–1990 compared to *four* such loans to a *much smaller number of borrowers* during 1978–1984. Because the loans were more decentralized and diversified in the later period, in addition to being part of the city's overall development loan program, the job and loan payback performance was superior to that of the earlier period. As Table 4.1 shows, by the end of 1990 one of the 1985–1990 loans had been repaid in full and the other twenty-two were being repaid. Also at that time, some 620 retained and created jobs were attributed to these loans, a smaller but more evenly distributed number than for 1978–1984. All of the borrowers continued to operate in South Bend.

Finally, most loans were for new jobs in start-up firms rather than job retention in threatened ones and covered a broader range of industries than

Table 4.1
South Bend Industrial Revolving Fund, 1978–1990

A. Loans and Borrowers

Period	Total Loans	Total Borrowers	Total Loan Amount*	Average per Loan*	Average per Borrower*
1978–84	16	8	2,487	155	311
1985–90	23	21	2,749	119	131
1978–90	39	29	5,236	134	181

B. Status of Loans, December 1990

	Paid		Active		Refinanced		Written-off	
	Loans	Dollars*	Loans	Dollars*	Loans	Dollars*	Loans	Dollars*
1978–84	2	400	4	750	4	780	6	557
1985–90	1	150	22	2,599	—	—	—	—

*Amounts represent thousands of dollars.

in the past. Once the board shifted its priority from job retention to job creation and in practice retreated from its initial high-risk loans, it followed that start-up and expansion projects in conjunction with other development agencies would receive the bulk of IRF funding.

The Fund's more balanced and stable loan policy during this time also reflects the emergence of the city's Department of Economic Development as principal coordinator of all public and private financial assistance to new and expanding firms and the Fund's integration into this wider funding network and range of projects. It is important that the city assume the role of coordinator and central source of information and direction because it can be the most impartial — though not impeccable — representative of the diverse and opposing interests within the community. In addition, funding opportunities and procedures are complex; the rules surrounding them vary among government agencies and private organizations, so it is advisable to have a recognized facilitator who can determine which funding "pot" can support which development project.[2]

PUBLIC POLICY IN THE SBL BUYOUT AND IRF LOAN PROGRAM

Two policy guidelines emerged from the experiences of the South Bend Lathe ESOP and the IRF Fund. First, attempts to save failing manufacturing operations through publicly subsidized reorganization schemes are not likely to succeed in the absence of (1) financial support that extends beyond the reorganization itself to include needed capitalization and product research and development, and (2) sustained monitoring by the appropriate public development authorities of the borrower's repayment and job performance. Second, local industrial revolving funds should be integrated into the wider area's larger economic development program rather than being administered as independent agencies by private lending institutions and development organizations with narrower interests.

The South Bend experience shows the futility of using limited public funds to try to rescue traditional manufacturing operations that have become uncompetitive through age, neglect, and industrial change. Due to (1) years of mismanagement and conglomerate failure to invest, and (2) lagging product quality and design, it was not possible for the SBL ESOP to become a competitive producer with the limited resources available to it under the terms of the 1975 buyout and in the years that followed. Thus, most of the jobs at SBL were lost. This is not unusual, however, because small, undercapitalized tool-making firms have been in decline across the country as a result of rapid changes in product design and production technology (Holland 1989). The IRF and local money market institutions simply could not provide SBL the capital it needed to rebuild itself into a global competitor.

But it is also clear that SBL managers neither initiated nor tolerated efforts to implement the kind of cooperation and participation among interested parties that advocates of more local commitment and employee ownership say are necessary if such firms are to achieve satisfactory levels of production, job retention, and tax revenues (Bradley and Gelb 1983; Woodward, Meek, and Whyte 1985; Simmons and Mares 1982; Whyte et al. 1983). Management of SBL simply showed *no* commitment to South Bend — and none was demanded as a condition of the loans.

The second policy implication from these experiences involves several "lessons." The first is that industrial revolving funds *should* stress local commitments because they are components of overall community development programs. The second is that such funds can only rarely serve as primary lenders and that they rarely can afford to commit major proportions of their resources to "non-bankable" loans. Finally, administrators of loan funds committed to local economies must make explicit choices between retention of existing industrial jobs and creation of jobs in expanding economic sectors, which may not employ current workers without sizable targeted retraining efforts and resources.

The South Bend IRF experienced two distinct stages in this regard. During 1978–1984, implementation policy was to consider and fund only capital projects that commercial banks considered too risky. As a result of this approach, the Fund found itself making subordinated loans to South Bend's declining durable goods sector and precarious firms in expanding industries. Single loans to weak borrowers soon became multiple, unsecured debts, and the Fund found itself dependent on repayments from a small number of troubled recipients.

After 1984 the board revised its policies and procedures under pressure from the EDA. The changes redefined and redirected the Fund from a principal to a supplemental lender, improved administrative policy and procedure, integrated activities into the city's overall capital financing program in conjunction with the Business Development Corporation and the Small Business Administration, and shifted loan criteria from job retention in traditional manufacturing to job creation in expanding areas. Improved implementation policy and procedure resulted in improved "performance" in a financial sense. However, since the latter shift in emphasis was not accompanied by sufficient resource commitments to retraining for displaced workers, the IRF goals of creating jobs for South Bend's workers were never attained.

CONCLUSION

The reasons why the SBL buyout failed are similar to the reasons why nine other ESOP buyouts of troubled manufacturing firms also failed: rundown plant and equipment and uncompetitive product and distribution methods due to neglect and mismanagement by previous owners, management refusal to implement genuine employee participation and involvement, lack of sufficient capital and other operating resources to make the firm a viable competitor (Whyte and Craypo 1988). Hindsight clearly shows that government-supported ESOP buyouts were a well-intentioned but tactically flawed public policy. The idea was objectively sound but insufficient in nature and financial scope to overcome the enormous impact of U.S. industrial decline at the level of the individual firm and operating plant. The EDA apparently has discontinued such buyouts.

The South Bend IRF experience reflects U.S. industrial development policy generally, which is deliberately to have no policy at the national level. The result is that each state, region, and community embarks on its own industrial policy with no rational coordination and purpose. Each competes with the other, although each can make the convincing case that it does so out of necessity and for protective as much as aggressive reasons. The effect of bidding wars for jobs is to forego tax revenues and endanger public services at the same time that business leaders criticize governments for inadequate educational systems and crumbling infrastructures. Until recently, South Bend boasted a thriving machine tool industry associated with the region's auto and steel sectors. But with deindustrialization the number of machine shops has declined considerably and today it is difficult for experienced machinists to find desirable jobs in South Bend (Reynolds 1990). This is ironic in view of the structural resurgence of both auto and steel production in the Great Lakes region.

Such is the economic development system that has evolved in the United States; although it may be a fallacy of composition for competing regions to behave as if what is good for one area is good for all areas, the competition presents a national dilemma that cannot be resolved by the actions of a single community. Thus, Indiana and South Bend will continue to lure certain types of jobs from Michigan and Illinois, and South Carolina and Tennessee will do the same to them. A survey of plant closings and phase-downs in South Bend during the period 1961–1988 revealed thirty-five closings involving 37,000 workers at recent peak employment levels. The competitive failures of South Bend are indicated by the fact that twenty-five of the closings occurred in order to relocate production to low-wage (often newly constructed) plants in the U.S. South (Craypo 1988).

A more farsighted policy would be to target scarce development resources (1) in the areas in which individual regions and communities have recognized strengths and comparative advantages, and (2) on existing firms or firms that have a natural interest in locating in that area without the lure of subsidies and abatements. EPA grant money and the IRF Fund might have been better used to target the local machine tool industry for revitalization along the lines of the industrial districts that have attracted considerable interest, first in northern Italy and now in various other European regions. These are locally integrated productive systems of highly specialized small and medium-sized firms engaged in various stages and aspects of production in a particular product line, such as machine tools. What distinguishes economic growth in these regions from that in South Bend and other traditional U.S. factory towns is that instead of being fragmented and randomly market-determined, it is conceived and carried out as an interrelated social, political, and economic activity involving the entire community (Pyke, Beattine, and Sengenberger 1990).

NOTES

1. In the opinions of Boulis and other top managers, salaried and production workers were entitled to view certain financial and operating reports, but like all other share-

holders, they had no right to participate directly or indirectly in the day-to-day management of the company. On the other hand, as employee-shareholders they were obliged to conduct themselves on the job in the best interests of the company. "The only real difference at South Bend Lathe now," Boulis said a few days after the buyout, "is that each employee has a bigger personal stake in our company's ultimate success" (*South Bend Times* 1975). The union had no formal role in managerial decision making and only token representation on the board of directors.

2. For example, it is prohibited to use federal grant monies to relocate jobs from one labor market to another. Therefore, when a large pharmaceutical manufacturer decided to relocate a recently acquired production unit to South Bend, at a declared cost of $3.8 million, the Department coordinated a $300,000 assistance grant and loan that avoided any improper use of federal funding to relocated jobs: it involved a $150,000 grant directly from the Business Development Corporation and a matching loan made by the city but funded by the Indiana Department of Commerce. By contrast, Total Composites, a start-up company, received a $936,000 capital financing package arranged by the Department with the federal Small Business Administration, various private sources, and the IRF (Business Development Corporation 1989:5).

5

Policy Instruments in West Central Scotland and Their Local Authority Context

William F. Lever

Of all the local and nationally driven responses to the deterioration in the British economy in the late 1970s and early 1980s, the most extensive range of different policies may have been implemented in the west central Scotland conurbation based around the city of Glasgow. Initially, local authorities were empowered to develop their own economic development policies. As it became apparent that many were either unwilling or unable to generate effective policies, a wide range of other actors — development agencies, the private sector, and the voluntary-community sector — have come to play a growing role in local economic development policy. Increasing concerns over cost effectiveness, measured in terms of cost per net new job and in terms of targeting on the most disadvantaged groups in the labor force, has led to some "churning" of alternative implementations.

In this chapter, I review the economic decline of the Glasgow conurbation and then examine the broad policy approaches adopted and the local politics of economic development program implementation. Within this context, I then discuss seven major dimensions of local policy and how the political context has shaped implementation of each approach.

INDUSTRIAL DEVELOPMENT AND DECLINE

As one of the first European centers to industrialize, it was perhaps inevitable that west central Scotland would epitomize the problems associated with deindustrialization. The region, centered in Glasgow and based on the estuary of the river Clyde, first developed in the seventeenth and eighteenth centuries as an industrial processing center for raw materials from the trans-Atlantic trade. The conurbation's most rapid period of development, however, was in the latter part of the nineteenth century, driven by its shipbuilding, which dominated the world market. (It has been estimated that in 1900 almost one-half of the world's seagoing shipping had been built on the Clyde.) This industrial base was supported by strong local steel-producing and heavy engineering sectors. World War I trade disruption and the Depression of the early 1930s began the process of Clydeside's industrial demise. After a short boom in replacement demand immediately after World War II, the economy of the west central Scotland conurbation continued its decline.

Whatever the causes of this decline (and in Rowthorn's 1986 trichotomy, the main failure seems to have been competitive, rather than maturation or excessive trade specialization), the effects have been devastating. Employment fell 27 percent from a postwar peak of 844,000 in 1952 to 615,000 in 1987. Manufacturing, however, lost a full two-thirds of all its jobs, falling from 424,000 to 142,000 workers.

Service employment clearly did not absorb the slack created by the decline of manufacturing. In fact, during the period 1980–1986, service employment actually fell annually. Even if the service sector had grown, the sectoral shift would not have allayed a major restructuring in the composition of the employed labor force. Most of the manufacturing sector layoffs were of male manual workers, who were not likely to be hired by the new and growing employers, because the service sector tended to prefer females and school dropouts for its lower skill positions.

Over the past twenty years, the conurbation as a whole has virtually never shown male unemployment rates below 10 percent; the rate peaked in 1984 at 20.9 percent. The uneven spatial distribution of employment across the conurbation has heightened the severity of impact. The core city, Glasgow, has always had the highest rates of unemployment, and within the city, lack of work has been further concentrated in depressed public housing estates. The peripheral housing estates built on the edge of the city after World War II became the hardest hit after the decade of the 1970s. They remain so in part because they are relatively inaccessible to the locations in which new business development has occurred. By contrast, the dormitory suburbs and the two New Towns built after World War II have had as little as one-third the unemployment rate of the city itself.

Housing and land use planning policies throughout the postwar period clearly had the effect of socially polarizing the population of the conurbation. The virtual exclusion of private housing construction from the central city has had the effect of driving the middle classes to the suburbs and at the same time restricting the poorer households to public sector housing in the core city and the older industrial towns. Although the New Towns were creations of the public sector, they have been quite selective in their housing allocation policies and have excluded the unemployed and "problem" households; thus, they more closely resemble the middle-class suburbs than the core city of Glasgow. Similarly, the combination of closure of nationalized heavy industries and failure to sell or dispose of industrial sites has led to construction of new employment poles at locations far distant from workers in need of jobs.

THE POLITICS OF POLICY FOR THE LOCAL ECONOMY

Historically, the British approach to areas with a consistent or recurrent pattern of high unemployment relative to the national average has been to designate those areas as development districts or areas and to provide assistance, usually in the form of central government grants toward capital investment within the range of 12 percent to 40 percent of the cost. Over time, the areas given such assistance have increased and the value of aid has fallen, at least until 1984 when both the defined areas and the levels of assistance were reduced (Townsend 1987). The size of the local areas defined was often so large that companies could locate in relatively unproblematic areas well away from problem labor markets and still receive substantial levels of assistance. Both of the major grants systems in operation in Clydeside in the period 1979–1983 channeled most of the assistance to the areas least in need (Lever 1986). Although the highest rates of unemployment were to be found in the inner city, the outer ring gained £68.6M in Regional Development Grant and £26.1M in Selective Assistance, while the totals for the inner city were £30.8M and £7.4M, respectively — although the inner city contains 55 percent of the manufacturing employment.

The failure of the central government schemes to accurately target the areas of greatest need was one of the major reasons for the downgrading of regional policy and the introduction and expansion of more locally based urban policy operated by local government after 1978. Legislation in the late 1970s conferred upon local government powers to intervene in the local economy for the first time. Powers initially were conferred by a national Labour government to metropolitan and urban local authorities who for the most part were in Labour Party control. The powers were gradually pulled back after the 1979 election of a national Conservative government.

The local consequences of these national patterns have been shaped by the peculiar characteristics of local government politics in west central Scotland. The social polarization in the conurbation is reflected in the political composition of the electorate and of political control, especially in the district (lower tier) authorities. The working-class base of the west of Scotland has throughout the postwar period virtually guaranteed Labour control. After local government reorganization in the mid-1970s, the Labour Party has steadily consolidated its control of the region (conurbation, rural exurbs, and freestanding towns).

Labour has consistently drawn on its strength not only in the core city of Glasgow but in the surrounding industrial and mining areas as well. Since 1974, the Conservatives have lost votes as local authority voting seems to reflect national election trends in which the growing North-South divide within Britain has entrenched Labour in the North and the Conservatives in the South. Notwithstanding a spike in the popularity of the Scottish Nationalist Party in 1978 and a revival of the centralist Liberal/Democratic Alliance in the mid-1980s, political power within the conurbation remains under the Labour Party's overwhelming control. Only in the more affluent suburbs did the Conservatives or Liberal/Democratic Alliance gain any power; the nationalists have tended to concentrate, interestingly, in the New Towns.

The political complexion of local government has two implications for the formulation and implementation of policies to combat the problems associated with high levels of unemployment. First, the prevailing political ethic of the ruling party in local government will influence how they try to reduce unemployment. Conservative local authorities are more likely to produce programs designed to help the private sector reduce costs, raise profits, and expand employment. This has been termed a "supply-side" approach to local economic regeneration. Labour local authorities are more likely (1) to expand demand for goods and services through public sector expenditure — and hence create employment, and (2) to protect employment through planning agreements and local authority contracts. Second, where local authority control lies in the hands of one party and national government in the hands of the other major party (as in the case of Glasgow), it may be difficult for local authority executors to implement nationally derived programs.

This conflict characterized Glasgow throughout the 1980s. Historically, the city and the west of Scotland have relied upon very high levels of public sector economic participation. Approximately 60 percent of housing in the conurbation is publicly owned, and in some towns the proportion may be as high as 80 percent. Throughout the postwar period the area has always qualified for the highest level of regional assistance grants to industry. The nationalized industries such as coal, steel, railway locomotive manufacture, and some shipbuilding were overrepresented in the region's industrial structure. Thus, many of the private sector businesses were heavily dependent upon public sector purchases, notably the region's heavy engineering and machine tool sectors.

Consequently there is a public sector dependency culture and a belief that where urban environmental or economic problems arise, it is the responsibility of government, local or national, to solve them. Urban problems in the west of Scotland therefore have been seen as soluble by a major public sector clearance and rebuilding program, often with little regard to its real economic effects (Donnison and Middleton 1987). The disruption caused by such comprehensive renewal programs may itself be one explanation of the movement of industry and business from the core city to the more predictable environments of the suburbs.

The historical primacy of *public* action may explain why, when Labour-controlled councils were given powers to intervene in local economies in the late 1970s, many had difficulty in cooperating with private sector enterprises. Although local councils were able to raise local property taxes and use the revenue for economic regeneration, the use to which such monies were put was quite limited and in some cases substantial underspending resulted. C. Moore and S. Booth (1986) reviewed the extent to which the eleven local district authorities that make up the conurbation engaged in local economic development. Efforts involved three elements: hardware, such as the provision of sites and buildings; software, such as the provision of business advice; and rational planning of local economic assistance. (Education is a regional authority function.) All authorities showed a marked preference for the first of these three elements: it was clear that local authorities preferred to use the money available in the creation of permanent assets such as prepared sites and advance factories and workshops, which would survive even if they never were rented or if the businesses occupying them closed. Money sunk in the form of business advice, grants, or soft loans would be lost with the closure of assisted companies. Consequently, few of the local authorities created business advice schemes, and only one local authority, Glasgow District Council, created an economic development plan that took into account the needs of the assisted companies. While much of this bias was attributable to the reluctance of Labour councils to assist profitable enterprises, some local authorities felt that they lacked the expertise or knowledge to offer advice to business or to enter into dialogue with business in the preparation of economic development plans.

However, the regional upper tier authority, Strathclyde Region, had much greater resources and expertise, so it was able to mount significant programs of assistance. Given that the two major functions of regional authorities — education and social work — are person-oriented, the most successful region-level programs have dealt with labor supply through training and work experience. But such efforts could not be coordinated with spatial impact wrought by district authority physical development efforts.

Given this need for coordination and its commitment to urban regeneration and economic development, the Scottish Development Agency (SDA) founded several jointly focused area programs collaboratively with the regional and selected district councils. The SDA, however, has a commitment to the development of economic potential, while local authorities may prioritize assistance to their most deprived communities. There is thus considerable room for conflict between the Agency and the local authority. In its most extreme form, this conflict may lead to the demise of the area-based initiative. Nonetheless, five area programs were launched in the conurbation. In contrast to the effects of regional policy, the balance of the Scottish Development Agency's expenditure is in favor of the inner city projects (£71M to 1987) compared with the outer conurbation (£70M to 1987), although private sector investment is higher in the outer conurbation (£133.5M) than in the inner city (£105.5M). Thus, although the SDA initiatives have not suffered from the emphasis on the expanding periphery in the way that central government's regional policy has, the equally important political question concerns selection of the area-based programs. A program designed to promote cooperation and coordination has resulted in the emergence of new points of implementation conflict.

The apparently unavoidable conflicts between central and local government intervention in local economies in the west of Scotland have been mediated by both sides bringing other parties into the equation.

1. The Scottish Development Agency was set up in the mid-1970s by the then Labour Government and was charged, among other things, with revitalizing the Scottish economy. Its objectives over time have focused more and more on economic matters. The Agency is funded by central government; it is not electorally accountable and is subject to changes as London's policy emphases shift.

2. The mobilization of the private sector reflects the recognition by many local authorities that they lack business expertise. Partnerships have been established in the form of Enterprise Trusts in which local authorities supply premises and some fi-

nance and private companies supply expertise and seconded labor (that is, company employees on temporary assignment to the trusts). These trusts were promoted by a network of large U.K. firms.

3. The voluntary-community sector has become involved as a result of local recognition that the for-profit sector was unlikely to be able to absorb the unemployed, while the local public sector was restrained from action by restrictions on spending imposed by central government. Thus, community businesses and similar enterprises have been developed "not only to create employment and work experience opportunities" but to supply socially desirable goods and services that the for-profit sector seemed unable to supply profitably. The roles of these actors have become more prominent as policies have been pursued "on the ground" in west central Scotland.

LOCAL ECONOMIC DEVELOPMENT

We can identify seven major policy approaches to the revitalization of local economies within the west central Scotland conurbation. These are (1) work experience and training, (2) financial assistance to small firms, (3) the provision of workshops and small industrial premises, (4) support for worker cooperatives, (5) enterprise zones with tax and planning concessions, (6) employment and training subsidies, and (7) equity participation in larger industrial ventures. Ranked in this order, these seven types of programs extend from the highly targeted and worker-specific schemes, through area-based projects, to more widely available assistance with much less accurate targeting and greater risk of deadweight (Turok and Wannop 1990).

The seven types of programs exhibit different implementation geographies, due in part to the nature of the agency delivering the program and in part to the scale at which economic regeneration is deemed to operate. On the one hand, there are schemes of assistance focused on individuals, usually identified by personal characteristics such as skills, unemployment record, or age. Although such schemes are ostensibly placeless, they tend to be concentrated wherever the largest collections of such individuals occur. At the other extreme are area-based programs, which may have one of two geographic rationales: some may represent spatially focused attempts to regenerate areas that have suffered a major economic loss, such as the closure of a steelworks or coal mine; others may be focused on "growth poles," or areas of potential growth within a regionwide economy, such as New Towns.

Moreover, since implementation occurs at three public sector levels — district, region, and Scottish Development Agency (Scotlandwide) — there is considerable room for conflict over the spatial focus of priorities. Proposals for new infrastructure, for example, have been the objects of conflict between an industrial town (which wants to boost its economy), the regional authority (which proposes to choose a site of greatest benefit to the whole conurbation), and the SDA (which often recommends developments midway between Glasgow and Edinburgh that lie outside the Strathclyde region). Coordinated location decision making has thus proven to be elusive.

Work Experience and Training

The region has two quite successful schemes aimed at providing work experience, Heatwise and Workwise. *Heatwise* is a voluntary sector project funded from various public sources, founded in 1984 to provide work experience and training for the long-term unemployed by engaging them in insulating and weatherproofing public sector housing. There were over 1,000 participants in 1984–1987, mostly single males from areas of high deprivation. Most were long-term (more than one year) unemployed, and 60 percent had no educational qualifications. About 45 percent of the participants gained subsequent employment or went on to other training schemes, possibly because Heatwise itself provided only limited training. This low placement rate gives the scheme a high cost per job created/filled of £22,000 per job. However, there were additional benefits in the form of upgrading the public sector housing stock. Since this housing is concentrated in the peripheral estates of Glasgow, the program is vulnerable to attack from other local authorities that do not benefit directly from the program's output.

Workwise is a Youth Training Scheme initiated and supported by the private sector that also started in 1984. It offers training in retail and commercial skills for school leavers (high school dropouts), placing trainees in known vacancies, most of them in the city center. On average, 64 percent of trainees obtain jobs after training. Workwise draws its funds largely from the National Training Agency, with private sector support taking the form of seconded staff and the local authorities supplying premises and equipment. The cost of each placement is about £5,000 (Hayton 1990). Although it is ostensibly people-oriented, the focus of this program on the city center has a distinct regional connotation. The SDA has stressed the development of Glasgow's central business district for corporate offices, for business services, and for tourism as part of a regional strategy to help the city compete with other non-capital cities in Western Europe. The benefits of such development are then assumed to spread throughout the region. Again, however, the rest of the region is neglected by the geographic focus, in this case on "showcase" locations.

Financial Assistance to Small Businesses

Two distinct forms of aid are available: one is aimed particularly at the young unemployed, the other is more general assistance to small businesses either at start-up or subsequently. *Enterprise Funds for Youth* (EFY) is run by Glasgow Opportunity, the local Enterprise Trust, on behalf of the Scottish Development Agency. It was created in 1984 out of concern for rising youth unemployment, and it aims to promote the establishment of new viable businesses by persons 16 to 25 years of age by offering unsecured loans of up to £3,000. Some 75 new businesses were assisted in 1984–1987, of which 37 percent were business services, 30 percent were personal services, 25 percent were retailing, and 8 percent were manufacturing. Seventy percent of EFY recipients were unemployed, though few were long-term unemployed. There was a high degree of deadweight, as many of the businesses would have been founded without EFY assistance; the failure rate was comparatively high. The cost per job created was in the range of £3,800 to £6,700. A more modest scheme is *The Prince's Business Youth Trust*, funded by the Department of Employment to provide small loans (up to £1,000) to young people setting up in business. About 240 awards were made in 1984–1987, but there are no estimates of deadweight and survival, so costs per job cannot be estimated. These forms of assistance are person-oriented, but surveys of applications suggest that the businesses created tend to be dependent on local customers; thus, they achieve more success in relatively buoyant local economies than in the most deprived areas. Even though they do not involve local funds, these efforts are thus perceived as not serving areas of acute need.

The more wide-ranging system of financial assistance to small businesses is operated by the Small Business Division of the SDA. Assistance usually takes the form of loans, up to £50,000, both for new start-ups and for business expansion. After allowing for both deadweight and displacement, it was estimated that help to small businesses provides or sustains about 2,000 jobs in the west central Scotland area at an average cost of £1,700 per job, although related public expenditure probably doubles this cost per job (Coopers 1986). The program's implementation is *not* targeted; it responds to the geographic pattern of loan requests. A more specific example of assistance to small business is to be found in the Clydebank Venture Capital Fund, financed by the SDA and the Bank of Scotland. Recipients of such loan finance must be located in Clydebank, one of the most depressed industrial economies in the area. The Fund supported about 65 businesses in the town in the period 1982–1987, providing some 120 extra jobs (after deadweight) at an estimated cost of £4,250 per job (Coopers 1988). The Small Business program fits well with other area-based programs and has a full regional focus. It serves areas of potential such as designated growth points and provides emergency programs for areas such as Clydebank, a town that recently lost three-quarters of its manufacturing employment. Integration with other efforts is, however, limited by the program's dependence on the initiative of individual companies.

Managed Premises (Incubators) for Small Firms

Clyde Workshops is operated and financed by British Steel (Industry) Limited, having been set up following the closure of the Clyde Ironworks in 1979. Making use of the vacated premises and offering management services, the Workshop contains about 75 companies employing about 280 people. The majority of tenants had been unemployed, but in the absence of targeting other than by location, the disadvantaged groups (such as long-term unemployed or youth) had not been particularly attracted to the scheme. Given that the premises were already available and that the scheme is intended to be self-financing with rents covering management costs, the cost per job figures are extremely low. The role of British Steel Limited is markedly regional in character. Its programs are intended to help former steel-producing areas revitalize after a plant closure, so it is not a locationally flexible tool of redevelopment.

The Regional Council funded five *New Enterprise Workshops* (NEW) in 1985 in partnership with other bodies. The purpose of NEW is to provide workspaces and facilities to new enterprises, which, once established, will move on to larger premises. About 10 to 12 projects per year employing about 30 workers move on to this second stage. However, it is difficult to estimate how many jobs are attributable solely to NEW support, as the intention is that assisted enterprises continue to expand once they move on from NEW. The region also funds a Start-Up Units program, intended in part to house growing enterprises leaving NEW. Units are provided in accessible locations at low cost. Although they are not deliberately targeted at disadvantaged groups, their geographic location and characteristics influence the type of people and firms interested in leasing them, which leads to a focus on the neediest areas. Currently about 120 workers are employed in these Start-Up premises at an average cost of £3,900 per job.

Comprehensive Small Business Assistance

The conurbation contains two schemes combining finance, premises, and business services to small businesses: Strathclyde Community Business, and Practical Training for Business.

Strathclyde Community Business is a regional agency set up in 1984 by the Regional Council to promote and service the training, development, and financial requirements of community-owned enterprises. Funding of about £500,000 per annum comes from the SDA, the National Urban Program, local authorities, and the European Social Fund (ESF). Community businesses are designed to create jobs, provide local services, and retain incomes in areas of high unemployment and deprivation such as the public sector housing estates. By 1987 there were 18 Community Businesses in Glasgow providing about 800 jobs. They are highly targeted on the local unemployed, but their economic and social objectives often come into conflict. Their social objectives are to provide employment and to offer services that the market is unable to provide. Their economic viability, however, often depends upon a professional manager whose objectives may not coincide with those of the community. An ongoing concern for the supply of services to deprived communities has required continuing subsidies for many community businesses. Costs per job have thus been about £1,000, although the scheme was originally intended to be self-financing (Turok and Wannop 1990).

Practical Training for Business is run by Strathclyde Regional Council and is funded jointly by the region and central government. The program was founded in 1978 to create permanent jobs for the long-term unemployed by providing comprehensive support to potential entrepreneurs with good business ideas. Due to difficulties in providing effective support and identifying viable business ideas, the scheme has suffered a high level of business failure, resulting in a high cost per job of between £5,000 and £12,000.

Worker Cooperatives

The *Scottish Cooperative Development Committee* was founded in 1976 to expand the cooperative sector and create jobs by helping to establish viable employee-owned enterprises with funds from local authorities, the SDA, and the ESF. It provides a wide range of advice, training, finance, and general support to new and existing cooperatives. Substantial technical assistance is typically provided on the grounds that individual cooperators are inexperienced and lack technical, financial, and managerial skills and that sizeable businesses are usually being created that require extensive planning. There are thirty-eight cooperative enterprises in Glasgow with about 250 jobs. Most of the workers were previously unemployed, and recruitment tends to be extremely localized. After allowing for deadweight effects, the estimated costs per job are £4,100 to £5,000.

Enterprise Zones

Central government belief that industry was being constrained by local planning and other regulations led to the creation of *Enterprise Zones* (EZ) in 1981. One of these is located in Clydebank within the west central Scotland conurbation. Initially the major attraction to companies was the relief from local property taxation for a period of up to ten years. This factor led to significant numbers of existing businesses making moves within the conurbation to get into the EZ. The Clydebank EZ had the advantage that much of the site had already been managed by the Scottish Development Agency, which had already begun to create factories and workshops before the EZ incentives became available. Intraregional competition for businesses and local employment has been accentuated by the creation of the EZ. By 1986, the Clydebank EZ contained 250 firms employing about 5,400 workers, but estimates of additionality suggest that only 31 percent of these jobs are directly and solely attributable to the EZ incentives (PA Cambridge Economic Consultants 1987). After allowance is made for job losses off the zone through short-distance movement of firms, the cost per job constitutes £23,000. Enterprise Zones are managed by the SDA and give the impression of having been imposed externally. The non-local imposition heightens the conflict engendered by the inequality of the EZ itself.

Employment and Training Subsidies

Strathclyde Region has developed an extensive range of employment and training subsidies. The *Employment Grants Scheme* was set up in 1982 and is funded jointly with the ESF. The wage subsidy varies between 40 percent and 60 percent of a recruit's gross wage for a six-month period (the highest levels apply to the long-term unemployed and the disabled). Some 14,500 grants were made between 1982 and 1987, with most of the recipient firms being small. All recruits are unemployed and most are young and semi- or unskilled. The estimated cost per job is £18,500, which is quite high but is justified on the basis of its very effective targeting on the most disadvantaged groups.

The *Training and Employment Grants Scheme* is run by SDA with joint funding from the ESF. It was started in 1982 to help residents of disadvantaged areas secure jobs and employer-based training by subsidizing 66 percent of a trainee's wage for up to six months and up to 100 percent of any off-the-job training costs. Unemployed youth and long-term unemployed are eligible. Between 1982 and 1987 the scheme attracted 4,000 recruits; 90 percent were aged 25 years or less. However, the estimated cost per placement of £14,600 is quite high.

A related scheme is the *Youth Employment and Training Initiative* funded by Strathclyde Region and the ESF. Started in 1985, the Initiative provides a 100 percent subsidy for off-the-job training costs and 30 percent of wages during on-the-job training for up to two years. The scheme provides about 150 places, of which 70 percent are taken by 17- and 18-year-olds. The cost per job of £5,800 is significantly lower than that for other subsidy programs because of the much closer scrutiny required to avoid subsidizing jobs that do not require assistance. All these programs are non-place specific within the conurbation and the region.

Equity Participation in For-Profit Companies

The SDA's *Scottish Development Finance* is a fund set up to assist larger companies that require financial assistance. The fund refinances companies by acquiring ordinary or preferred shares while assisting with National Loan Fund loans and other forms of assistance. After both displacement and supplier effects are taken into account, investments under this program created around 2,000 jobs in the west of Scotland at a cost to the agency of £2,900 per job. However, if all other public assistance to the companies concerned is added in, the cost per job figure rises to

£6,300. Once the SDA's shares are sold, then these costs may fall significantly and in the longer term the fund may become close to self-financing. The fund has prioritized assisting major companies that dominate their local labor market, thus favoring large plants in relatively small towns over the larger urban centers.

CONCLUSION

The growing switch from regional policy to local urban economic policy in the west central Scotland conurbation increased the implementation burden on local authorities. District Councils, however, proved to be either unwilling or unable to devise policies to assist private companies. Given that many of the councils were Labour-controlled, there was considerable conflict between their objectives of helping the most deprived groups within the community and central government's objectives of freeing the private sector to make increasing profits. As a result, nongovernmental agencies came into being to engage in urban economic regeneration. However, the conflict over objectives remains, with bodies such as the Scottish Development Agency still being oriented toward private profitability and bodies such as community-voluntary organizations and local authorities still stressing the need to target job creation for the most deprived groups and areas within the conurbation.

The multi-tiered structure of the agencies now delivering programs has accentuated these conflicts. The uppermost (Scottish) tier is managed by the Scottish Development Agency, whose concern to expand the Scottish economy means that it is wedded to a growth pole philosophy that leads it to prioritize new business attraction. Only through its environmental arm has the SDA become involved in programs oriented toward the inner city. Area-based programs such as Glasgow Eastern Area Renewal (GEAR) in the east inner area of Glasgow, Clydebank, and Motherwell have been developed to improve the quality of the environment, but a part of the approach is the use of vacant land for new small-scale industry. There remains considerable debate whether such employment creation benefits the local deprived population or whether the benefit leaks out to the larger community.

The two tiers of local government clearly have different geographies of development, and in a conurbation such as west central Scotland the potential conflict between a city center authority (such as Glasgow) with acute economic problems and little space and the peripheral authorities (such as New Towns) with ample space and a confident business environment is manifest. The Region, which is responsible for the whole conurbation in a strategic planning sense and which has more resources than the districts, has responded with the integrated planning approach introduced by the West Central Scotland Plan. This plan, directly or indirectly, has had the effect of stimulating new employment — perhaps as many as 50,000 jobs in the central business district of Glasgow. It has also helped to create an attenuated ring of growth around and beyond the periphery of the conurbation while leaving a zone of economic deprivation in between (the peripheral public housing estates and old single-industry towns). In a dynamic sense, one can identify waves of growth passing outward, having originated in or close to the city center and moving outward in search of cheaper land, easier planning regimes, and more pliant labor. The nineteenth-century manufacturing wave now seems to be fifteen to twenty miles from the city center, while the new tertiary wave has yet to move more than two to three miles from the heart of Glasgow.

6

Regenerating Urban Neighborhoods: Local People as Implementers of Economic Development Policies

Alan McGregor
Andrew A. McArthur

Despite a lengthy tradition of policy intervention by the national, state, and local governments in the United Kingdom, urban economic and social problems persist. In a number of British cities substantial progress in revitalizing the older, inner urban areas has been counterbalanced by the deteriorating position of peripheral, public sector housing estates (McGregor and Mather 1986). More recently, attempts have been made to promote the private sector as a leading agent in the process (Barnekov, Boyle, and Rich 1989).

In the 1980s, a new force in neighborhood regeneration emerged from communities located in some of the most disadvantaged areas of urban Britain. Although it would be an exaggeration to call this a movement, a range of community-based economic initiatives has developed, sharing similar objectives and philosophies. These initiatives rely on local people coming together to actively tackle the problems of local unemployment and poor service provision.

These efforts are varied. Among the primary concerns are

1. creating employment opportunities that can be steered toward local people;
2. taking control over the local housing stock and running this service collectively; and

3. provision of a local banking and credit facility to local residents.

These activities represent a new wave of economically oriented community initiatives operating at the neighborhood level.

The efforts directly involve local residents in the running of income-generating activities and aim to be economically freestanding in the marketplace. In this important sense they differ from the long-established tradition of community activity as a campaigning force or in running projects that depend ultimately for their survival on a continuing flow of program grant assistance from public agencies. There are also some parallels here with the experience of the United States in the 1980s when community economic development became a major concern of neighborhood organizations (Teitz 1989).

Policy makers and practitioners are now trying to get communities, themselves the target of regeneration policies, to become more actively involved in the process. In many cases neighborhood groups are seen as potentially valuable partners. Until recently, policy efforts have been dominated by professional and centralized agencies operating at arm's length from the communities they serve. The introduction of an active neighborhood component potentially enriches the scope for local economic development by mobilizing new resources and ideas from within local communities that outside agencies can link up with and draw on in the process of policy implementation.

The main purpose of this chapter is to consider the nature of these community development efforts in the U.K. context, and their importance as implementation tools. We begin by looking at some of the broader influences that lie behind the new wave of economic activity by neighborhood organizations. Next, we consider some of the key features that characterize community enterprise activity and the different forms this activity has taken. Here we present some of the main models and examples of community enterprise that exist and map out the main ways in which they have been supported and encouraged by outside agencies anxious to see local communities become more actively involved in the process of policy implementation. We then assess some impacts of community enterprise to date, examining the job creation efforts of community businesses and the value of local services provided by community credit unions. We conclude with some final thoughts about the possible future role for community economic initiatives in economic development program implementation.

ECONOMY, SOCIETY, AND THE GROWTH OF COMMUNITY ECONOMIC ACTIVITY

Although various forms of community-based economic activity predate the 1980s, this decade witnessed a dramatic upsurge in the number of such organizations in the United Kingdom. The economic events of the period are the context in which these initiatives flourished, and in which their impacts on low-income neighborhoods were felt. At a more analytical level, review of the broader trends of the decade permits an assessment of the extent to which neighborhood development efforts are the creatures of a particular set of economic, political, and social circumstances. If they are, then their "success" may be as short-lived as the climate that allowed them to emerge in the first place.

Between 1979 and 1983 Britain suffered a severe economic recession that led to reduced employment, particularly in traditional manufacturing sectors. A net loss of 2 million jobs was experienced, roughly 1 in 11 of the United Kingdom's jobs. Over 1 in 5 of the economy's manufacturing jobs were lost over the same period. The massive shifts, however, were felt on a differential scale in the regions making up the British economy.

In the North 1 in 8 jobs were lost compared to 1 in 15 in the more affluent South. In some of Britain's northern cities this gave rise to rates of unemployment unprecedented since the 1930s: Glasgow and Birmingham had unemployment over 16 percent in 1983. Within these cities, individual neighborhoods experienced substantially higher rates of unemployment, particularly for men. A number of areas of Glasgow's east end had male unemployment rates in excess of 50 percent as late as 1985. In short, the early years of the 1980s witnessed the consignment of many urban neighborhoods, some previously stable blue collar communities, to the economic dustbin.

As the economy began to recover, the gains have gone disproportionately to the more prosperous regions (MacInnes 1988). New jobs tended to be in the service sector, which expanded in the higher income, densely populated regions like the southeast conurbation with London as its core. Between 1983 and 1987 employment grew 6 percent in the southern regions while it stagnated in the traditional manufacturing regions of the North.

This increasing inequality can also be seen in the United Kingdom's income distribution: poorer households experienced below average increases in real incomes as the economy began its recovery from the nadir of the early 1980s (Department of Social Security 1990).

While the private sector restructuring proceeded, the Conservative central government began to withdraw "the state" from many areas of activity that impacted directly on Britain's lower income urban neighborhoods:

1. regional policies for economic development weakened;
2. the system of financial supports for the lagging regions was progressively eroded, and funding for local authorities' maintenance of their public sector housing stock fell;
3. the quantity and quality of services available to low-income neighborhoods declined as cost-effectiveness, not service provision, became the public priority.

These trends increased the demands in low-income neighborhoods for some form of action. Community-based organizations stepped in to assist (or substitute for) local and governmental agencies. On balance they have provided services on a relatively cost-effective basis.

The 1980s were also marked by a common perception of the failure of top-down urban initiatives and investment programs to have a real impact. Many of the poor inner city areas were the focus of major investment programs. These efforts served to change the face of many older urban neighborhoods and attracted existing firms into the areas. However, they have been less successful in opening up opportunities for local people to start new businesses or for the unemployed to secure the jobs that are available (McArthur 1987).

The emergence of community economic action over the 1980s can be seen as a response to national economic trends and weaknesses in the effectiveness of mainstream urban policies. The implementation of community business initiatives, however, was also shaped by the adoption of the strategy by the state. Central government claims an important role for local community organizations in the process of urban regeneration (Scottish Office 1989). This claim reflects past funding and institutional support for such local initiatives.

Local governments also exhibited widespread involvement in promoting the community-based initiatives. The approach provides an alternative to reliance on conventional small firm policies in areas with very limited traditions of entrepreneurial behavior. A number of local authorities have set up specialist agencies to provide development assistance to, and funding and training for, community enterprise initiatives.

SHARED CHARACTERISTICS OF COMMUNITY ENTERPRISE

Despite the diversity in the structures and activities of community enterprise, most have a number of common features:

1. they are revenue-generating enterprises;
2. while many have enjoyed considerable financial support from public agencies, they aim in the long run to be economically freestanding;
3. the enterprises are "owned" by individual members of the communities within which they are located; and
4. a concern with the social problems of the neighborhood is typically an integral element of the organization's objectives.

Control in most community enterprise initiatives rests with the residents of the neighborhood, individually or in groups. The members or shareholders select a board of directors or a committee of managers. This body takes principal responsibility for the running of the enterprise and is accountable to the membership or shareholders through annual general meetings at which all or part of the board or committee is elected.

It is possible for a community enterprise to extend eligibility for membership to different types of groups. Eligible categories can include residents of an area, people working but not living in that area, or individuals or representatives from outside bodies who may not be part of the community but who have a positive contribution to make to the work of the business. The integrity of local control can be protected by ensuring that individuals from outside the enterprise's community cannot exceed 49 percent of its membership or its controlling body.

Overall, community enterprises appear to be part of the "ethical sector" in the attitude they adopt to the conduct of their business. Although they have employees just like a conventional business, they tend to stand for fair wages, good employment conditions, and trade union rights, and they try to hire residents of their neighborhoods (Buchanan 1986). Similar considerations could apply to the price and quality of their goods and services — especially if sold to members of the community they are set up to serve. Thus, there is a potential conflict between the pursuit of ethical and commercial objectives for the community enterprises. To the extent that they compete with other firms in their areas, they may be forced to trim their ethical commitments if these add significantly to their operating costs.

VARIATIONS IN COMMUNITY ECONOMIC ACTION: SOME EXAMPLES

The involvement of communities in their local economies has taken a variety of forms. Typical activities for community businesses include environmental and construction-related work, neighborhood security patrols, the provision of small industrial units for rent in complexes of managed workspaces, community transport, and a range of recycling and local shopping services, including retailing. Some examples illustrate this diversity.

Ferguslie Park Community Holdings is situated in a high unemployment housing estate in a town close to Glasgow and is run by a board of directors largely elected by the "members" drawn from the local community. With full-time managerial employees and a workforce that has reached 100 people, the business engages in environmental and construction work and provides security services. In existence for about ten years, it no longer receives public subsidies. It has been successful in bidding for contracts from public agencies involved in the regeneration of the housing estate and is by far the largest employer in the local neighborhood.

Govan Workspace, Limited, was launched in the late 1970s to set up and run managed workspaces for small businesses to help stimulate local employment in an area hard hit by the decline of shipbuilding. It now owns its own properties, formerly derelict industrial and school buildings, which have been renovated to provide 100,000 square feet of workspace. Five hundred people are employed by the small firms occupying the premises.

Community cooperatives are a form of community business often focused on the provision of local retail and service facilities. These organizations involve more pooling of local capital, as residents purchase shares in the enterprises. Community cooperatives are thus less dependent on state support to get started than many other community economic initiatives.

The Galliagh Community Co-operative Society, located in a housing estate in Derry in Northern Ireland, runs a supermarket and post office — important local services in an area with only limited retail outlets. Regular share contributions for a period of over a year from about 2,000 local residents enabled the community to raise sufficient capital to borrow additional funds and build the supermarket. The enterprise has 30 employees, 1,500 current local shareholders, and an annual turnover of £1 million.

Community credit unions, another type of community business, offer the basic elements of a banking system and a source of low-interest credit in neighborhoods where the problems of multiple debt and illegal money lending can be rife. They are probably the fastest growing example of community-based organizations; of the 164 credit unions founded in the 1980s, the vast majority were community-based, rather than workplace-based.

Cranhill Credit Union, set up in the late 1970s, was one of the first community credit unions in Britain. It operates from premises owned by the local authority and serves 1,000 members in one of Glasgow's massive peripheral public sector housing estates that has no bank. This development owes less to public policy than most other forms of community enterprise initiatives. The origins of many of the new credit unions can be traced to encouragement and support from U.S. and Irish credit union movements and the national trade organization, the Association of British Credit Unions. Thus, credit unions reflect a different external influence on impoverished neighborhoods, that of the nonprofit sector.

Community-based housing associations and housing cooperatives provide low-cost rental housing by taking over and modernizing stock previously administered by public housing departments or owned by private landlords. Queens Cross Housing Association has taken over blocks of nineteenth-century tenemental properties, renovated them, and rented them at affordable prices to people in an inner city area of Glasgow. More recently, the association has created workspaces for start-ups and businesses dislocated by housing renewal projects. This expansion of activity is indicative of a trend toward such housing associations becoming involved in wider local economic initiatives.

Collectively, these examples of community enterprise represent a new tier of activity at the neighborhood level that is now providing jobs and services in run-down areas and building self-confidence and managerial capacity among the individuals from those communities who are involved in the development and management of community-based enterprises. Public sector support for these efforts remains fragmented, compartmentalized, and specific to particular forms of community economic action. It is possible that this neglect reflects some weakness in the political commitment toward genuinely empowering local neighborhoods. But it could also result from an imperfect appreciation of the nature and extent of the contribution of community enterprise to neighborhood regeneration, from evidence that such organizations have minimal impacts, or from data demonstrating the inefficiency of community-based initiatives.

We thus turn to assess the impacts of two specific forms of community economic action: community business and community credit unions. These models illustrate the two main areas covered by the emerging tradition of community enterprise activity — that is, the creation of jobs through commercial activity of different kinds and the provision of services needed within the neighborhood. Once we have data on experienced impacts, we can draw conclusions about the reasons for minimal organized public sector support for such initiatives.

THE IMPACT OF COMMUNITY ECONOMIC ACTION ON NEIGHBORHOOD REGENERATION

Job Creation through Community Business

The search for new ways to generate economic activity and jobs in deprived urban environments and to direct a larger proportion of any jobs created toward the more disadvantaged groups in the local labor market, such as the long-term unemployed, is high on the British urban policy agenda. Creating jobs that will benefit the local community is the principal objective of most community businesses. Indeed, it is this local job-targeting objective that has excited much of the interest among policy makers in Britain.

The following discussion presents findings from a survey of 57 of the 66 existing Scottish community businesses carried out during 1987 (McGregor, McArthur, and Noone 1988). These businesses directly employed 360 people at the time of the survey. Over 1,000 additional workers were employed by a small number of community businesses acting as agents for national temporary work programs. Other jobs were generated by some of the community businesses that rented workspaces to other small enterprises.

Taking these employment figures at face value, this does not appear to be a significant contribution to employment. Setting the 360 jobs existing within community businesses against the 340,000 unemployed in Scotland in 1987 vividly illustrates the limited overall contribution of community enterprise. However, the appropriate yardstick against which to judge community enterprise is its contribution to the employment needs of specific local areas, not those of the nation as a whole. For example, Ferguslie Park Community Holdings, with its 100 employees, is located in a severely depressed housing estate that had around 850 unemployed residents. Nearly 20 percent of them had been out of work for at least five years. The 100 jobs created by the community business may have helped place 12 percent of the jobless, if the jobs created went to local people. The issue of who gets the jobs in community businesses is thus central to claims of their efficacy.

Table 6.1 describes the employment status of individuals recruited by conventional and community-owned small enterprises. It shows that community enterprises score on two counts over conventional small businesses aided by urban policies, namely:

1. they are much less likely to recruit people already in employment (13 percent as opposed to 31 percent);
2. they are much more likely to hire the *long-term* unemployed (46 percent versus 7 percent).

Other things being equal, an urban program based on conventional small businesses will need to create roughly twice as many jobs as a program built on community enterprise if it is to achieve the same short-run impact on hiring the *local* unemployed. This is a telling criticism, given the difficulties involved in creating any kind of employment opportunities in the hostile common environments of low-income neighborhoods.

Table 6.1
Status and Residence of Employees Prior to Recruitment

Employment Status	Community Enterprise	Conventional Small Business
Employed	13%	31%
Unemployed (under a year)	29%	62%
Unemployed (over a year)	46%	7%
Other	12%	1%
Area of Residence		
Local area	83%	42%
Elsewhere	17%	57%

Note: Percentages do not all add to 100 due to rounding error.

In 1987, three community-based organizations in Glasgow managed 108 occupied workspace units employing a total of 629 workers. This in itself was a substantial job creation effort, given that none of the workspaces had been in existence before the early 1980s. Interviews with the tenants of the workspaces revealed that:

1. two-thirds were genuine gains to the locality, representing either transfers from outside the area or new business start-ups;

2. fewer than 1 in 5 (17 percent) of the owners/managers lived within the locality;

3. 31 percent of the owners/managers had been unemployed prior to the start-up of the business;

4. for 75 percent of the owners/managers, this was their first experience of self-employment or running a business.

It is difficult to assess the contribution of these community-based workspaces in the absence of comparable figures for other workspace provision efforts. The number of start-ups is below the average of the schemes included in the Department of Environment's review of managed workspaces (1987). This suggests that community efforts may complement *existing* entrepreneurial efforts rather than stimulating new businesses, which is a more daunting — and expensive — task.

The picture is less promising when we examine the workforce of the firms renting the workspaces (Table 6.2). Most employees were either employed or short-term unemployed prior to recruitment; moreover, only 33 percent were recruited from the local area. These figures compare very unfavorably with the recruitment behavior of community enterprises summarized earlier in Table 6.1.

The statistics suggest that when the community enterprise is an indirect facilitator of employment creation, the link to jobs for local residents and the long-term unemployed becomes tenuous. However, many of the jobs were provided by small firms transferring into the depressed areas with their existing labor force, which explains the poor figures on local recruitment. With turnover and expansion it is likely that more local people will find jobs with these firms.

Table 6.2
Status and Residence of Employees of Workspace Firms Prior to Recruitment

Previous Status		*Area of Residence*	
Employed	41%	Local area	33%
Unemployed (under a year)	39%	Elsewhere	67%
Unemployed (over a year)	8%		
Other	13%		

Note: Percentages do not all add to 100 due to rounding error.

Taking account of various traditional factors (additionality, displacement, and local multipliers), costs per job created by community businesses came out at roughly £5,000 in 1987 prices. This compares with a figure of £4,300 for a one-year place in the United Kingdom's national job creation scheme — the Community Program. Thus, if the jobs created by community businesses lasted longer than fourteen months, their creation was more cost-efficient than the Community Program. This comparison raises the question of the viability and longevity of community enterprises.

Insufficient empirical evidence on viability exists to arrive at a firm prediction. However, out of fifteen community businesses we studied in depth in 1987 that were then relatively mature, 33 percent closed their doors by 1990. This figure, while somewhat discouraging, compares favorably to the experience of the small firm sector as a whole: P. Ganguly (1985) found that 40 percent of start-up firms in the United Kingdom fail by the end of their third trading year. Nevertheless, by the end of the 1980s, supporters of community businesses, particularly in Scotland where substantial public resources had been committed, were becoming noticeably nervous regarding the long-term future of these enterprises.

Provision of Local Services: Community Credit Unions

As we noted earlier, rapid growth has been taking place since the late 1980s in the area of community credit unions. Much of this expansion occurred in communities poorly served by banks in which the problems of multiple debt and extortionate money lending by loan sharks were intensifying.

Tackling these problems is a tall order for any local organization. Nevertheless, recent work we have carried out at Glasgow University on credit unions (including interviews with over 500 individual members) points to some very positive economic and social contributions. In the first instance, credit unions are able to reach relatively large numbers of local residents with the service they provide. Even a small credit union will normally cater to several hundred members. The largest community credit union in Britain (Dalmuir) has over 2,000 members. In Northern Ireland, where credit unions have a longer history than in Britain, large unions have over 7,000 members.

We found that people joined credit unions because they needed credit, because there was nowhere else locally they could save, or because they felt more comfortable with the service provided by the credit union than the more formal atmosphere of a bank. The relatively small amounts that many people were able to save (half our respondents deposited £2 or less on each visit) made visits to banks potentially embarrassing. Moreover, such sums precluded spending on transportation to non-local branch banks.

Most members interviewed (88 percent) had an outstanding loan from the credit union. Of the borrowers, 60 percent reported that they would not have been able to make needed purchases without the credit union loan. This group felt they were either unable to obtain credit elsewhere or were reluctant to take on the financial burden that an alternative credit source would have involved. The benefits to members also extended beyond the economic circumstances of the individual to embrace the social life of the neighborhood. Many credit unions are lively community facilities, places where people come and meet their neighbors, share some gossip, and find out about other things that are happening in the neighborhood. They serve as a community facility in areas in which such institutions tend to be lacking or are externally imposed by local authorities.

In our survey of credit union members, we asked about people they had met through the credit union. We found that credit unions exert an important influence on the development of social relationships. Seventy-three percent of respondents reported making new acquaintances — people they would feel happy to stop and talk to in the street. More significantly, a full 40 percent reported making new friends — people they would invite to their house — through their membership in the credit union.

The experience of community credit unions and other locally provided commercial services opens up some exciting possibilities in relation to the regeneration of deprived communities. They can, of course, increase local purchasing power, but they also serve as focal poles for community organizations. This aspect of the institutions is particularly important when communities have been devastated by economic decline and social ties have been disrupted by urban renewal programs. Credit unions and other retail providers appear to be very effective in terms of bringing relatively large numbers of local people together as volunteers. It is common to find between twenty and thirty local residents actively involved in running individual credit unions. The skills of local people and the capacity of the neighborhood are consequently enhanced and strengthened.

CONCLUSION

The emergence of neighborhood organizations as new actors in neighborhood regeneration reflects the growing plurality of the economic development effort in British urban policy. Although many of the developments discussed in this chapter remain small in scale and in many ways marginal to the economic life of their communities, they have a potentially distinctive role to play. Being locally based and sensitive to neighborhood conditions, they are in a good position to articulate and pursue solutions for local problems without the distractions and competing responsibilities with which other development agents must deal. The ability of community economic initiatives to direct jobs toward the unemployed in their service areas and provide widely used and valued local services is a major reason for the current interest being shown among local authorities and other development agencies in this sector of activity.

Community enterprises offer some prospect of reconciling the tension between policies that are "place" and "people" oriented. On one hand, policies targeted toward geographic areas often have very limited impacts on disadvantaged local groups. On the other hand, policies seeking to improve the employment prospects of certain groups of people may succeed but do little to enhance conditions in an area if people leave to pursue opportunities elsewhere. What community enterprise may offer is a policy device that manages to do both. These are enterprises that are rooted in disadvantaged communities. They are unlikely to pack up and leave. They are also enterprises that offer a way of directing the benefits of economic activity toward some of the poorer groups in an area. As such they have a unique niche in the array of policy implementation alternatives.

However, despite recent successes in job targeting and local service provision, such neighborhood economic initiatives often struggle for viability. Their long-term survival is still very much in doubt. The ability of community initiatives to be sustained well into the future will partly depend on the continued involvement of local people coming forward and playing an active voluntary role. More often than not, the excitement and challenge associated with community action comes at the early stage when people are struggling for resources to launch new projects. Faced with everyday tasks of running community initiatives, the battle may appear to have been won. Indeed, there are examples in which the dynamic quality has diminished or disappeared from community economic initiatives once they are up and running. For example, S. McCrystal (1990) found that the Galliagh supermarket is no longer seen as a special *community* institution, and as a result, it has proved more difficult to find new local volunteers to serve on the store's management committee.

Maintaining the positive contribution that community economic action potentially offers may therefore partly depend on looking for new challenges and opportunities. Here, outside agencies are in a position to help maintain momentum. Assisting community economic initiatives is not merely a question of providing financial resources for locally inspired projects. An ongoing community development effort to build skills and confidence within the neighborhood is required along with a commitment to empower local organizations' capacities for policy development and implementation. This is not always an easy task for professionalized agencies more familiar with "doing things to" rather than "working in partnership with" neighborhoods where renewal programs are being applied. However, past policies have been found wanting, and the possibilities associated with community economic action offer a new and hopeful route for implementation of innovative local economic development policies.

ACKNOWLEDGMENTS

The research reported in this chapter enjoyed the generous financial support of the Economic and Social Research Council, the Joseph Rowntree Trust, the Scottish Development Agency, and the Scottish Development Department.

Part III

Spillovers and Community Response: Local Forces Shaping Economic Development Program Implementation

Local development efforts are often focused on narrow geographic areas. Concentration of resources and programmatic effort can maximize the impact of programs, but such a focus increases the danger that unanticipated spillovers may damage the broader local economy. This problem is nowhere more evident than in programs addressing urban waterfronts. Such efforts may pay more attention to the land-water boundary than the relationship between the land area addressed and adjacent neighborhoods.

The transformation of urban waterfronts embodies the shift of the post-modern city from an industrial base in which ports, providing transportation access, bulk commodity shipments, low skill employment, and dumping grounds for waste, have declined in importance. Today, development pressures on waterfronts have transformed them from sites of industry and shipping to locations for marina slips, tourist attractions, new office facilities, and high-income condominiums.

This shift in waterfront orientations embodies the trajectory of the post-modern city whose economy runs on tourism, services, and high-income residential districts, and whose land-use patterns and infrastructure require substantial public intervention. The three cases discussed in the following chapters exemplify the conflicts engendered by urban redevelopment and economic structural change. However, they illustrate another facet of public policy conflict: the narrow, and sometimes inconsistent, geographic focus of development efforts.

Robert Giloth's discussion of southeast Baltimore demonstrates the negative consequences of an excessively narrow vision. Impacts on older, stable working-class residential neighborhoods were ignored in efforts to redevelop derelict waterfront areas. The resultant conflict arose because residents of the affected areas protested the negative effects on their neighborhoods and were able to challenge the dominant urban development coalitions in the city.

Describing similar problems in south Cardiff, Wales, Huw Thomas and Rob Imrie show that the spillover effects ignored by the waterfront development organization adversely affected small industrial firms, rather than residential areas. In contrast to the ability of the Baltimore residents to coalesce, the Cardiff businessmen, perhaps because of their individualist orientation toward running their own firms, were unable to mount a coherent and politically powerful response to the threat to their continued operation in their traditional locations.

Finally, Alma Young and Robert Whelan's discussion of conflicts over the facilities of the Port of New Orleans demonstrates that spillovers are not just intentionally overlooked by powerful development organizations. Neither the Port nor the City can be characterized as inherently weaker than the other. Conflict emerged from differences in perspectives and understandings of the role that waterfront development can play; the relatively equal power of the two protagonists resulted in recurrent failures to take advantage of opportunities that might have benefited both parties. Better recognition of the spillover effects of each other's efforts by both the Port and the City might well have avoided the stalemate and inaction that are described.

7

From Cannery Row to Gold Coast in Baltimore: Is This Development?

Robert P. Giloth

The story of southeast Baltimore during the past three decades illustrates the difficulties that neighborhoods face when they contest waterfront transformation. Local efforts tend to emphasize the preservation of working-class neighborhoods, affordable housing, and industrial districts along urban waterfronts (Louv 1983; Giloth and Betancur 1988; Giloth and Mier 1989). Neighborhoods' priorities are their own preservation rather than the maximization of exchange values from new economic development (Logan and Molotch 1987; Clavel 1986).

Southeast Baltimore neighborhoods have blended working-class protectionism with the planning language of historic preservationists as they have contested the development of the southeast waterfront, stopping a highway in the 1970s and downscaling new high-income, Gold Coast development in the 1980s. Over time, while not halting development or its negative impacts, they have contributed to a better process of planning, pace of development, and integration of new development with the existing city. Along the way, they have attained a degree of political power through persistent community organizing and grassroots electoral politics.

This chapter portrays the community conflict about the emerging city using Baltimore as a case that illustrates a more general pattern of urban development implementation politics. After acknowledging the challenges of economic development implementation and sketching the recent history of southeast Baltimore, I discuss the housing price impacts of waterfront development on neighborhood affordability in southeast Baltimore and three community responses to those impacts. I conclude by reflecting on the opportunities and limits of public and community planning to remedy the recurring shortcomings evident as contemporary urban development strategies are implemented.

ECONOMIC DEVELOPMENT CHALLENGES

Local economic development frequently stumbles in implementation as the result of four unresolved dilemmas. First, the private sector largely shapes the direction and modes of implementation of local economic development; but the public sector must provide infrastructure, zoning changes, incentives, and planning legitimacy (Barnekov and Rich 1989). The result is that public planning often follows development. Second, local officials justify economic development by promising public and private benefits; yet there is widespread skepticism about what benefits are produced, in part because inadequate resources are committed to evaluation of urban development projects (Giloth 1992). Third, the public sector is supposed to manage social conflict, but it has neither the commitment nor the resources to resolve conflicts about who pays and who benefits from local economic development. Fourth, economic development is evolutionary — opportunities and impacts only emerge over time; yet the urban development process is underplanned and anxiety-driven in the present (Pressman and Wildavsky 1973).

Baltimore's waterfront renaissance illustrates these problems. The city's inner harbor is being redeveloped for residential, commercial, recreational, and office uses. This planned development is exemplified in its ten-year-old HarborPlace Festival Market, developed by James Rouse at a cost of $22 million in the late 1970s (Levine 1987; Giloth 1990; Stoker 1987; Hula 1990). The twelve-mile stretch of waterfront extending southeast from HarborPlace, including the historic Fells Point and Canton neighborhoods, has been dubbed Baltimore's "Gold Coast." That strip of waterfront formerly housed numerous port-related industries — at one time being called Cannery Row — and thousands of jobs, but it now contains high-income residential and commercial projects valued at $1 billion. More projects are expected to be built as the real estate market revives in future years. What is not widely acknowledged or recognized is that much of Baltimore's recent waterfront development has failed (Jacobson 1990a; 1990b).

Southeast residents and organizations have objected to this development on historic preservation and neighborhood affordability grounds. They have opposed the high density development of the Gold Coast because it blocks public view corridors and access to the waterfront, expands truck and automobile traffic, and escalates housing prices and speculative buying in adjacent neighborhoods, thus raising property taxes. They have challenged specific waterfront projects, proposed alternative waterfront design plans, introduced urban renewal amendments, won state legislation to expand property tax exemptions for older homeowners, sponsored "linkage" legislation that would require developers to help preserve affordable housing, and run their own city council candidates. Taken together, community outcry has slowed development along the Gold Coast and probably has scared off developers in some cases.

These efforts of southeast Baltimore citizens may reduce the density of waterfront projects by one-half, but they have not stemmed the development tide. There are several reasons for this. First, the civic consensus promoting development in Baltimore is quite strong because of a precarious local economy, municipal fiscal shortfalls, the minimal supply of developable land, and the lack of independence of City Council and government officials from the real estate industry (Stoker 1987; Giloth 1990). Second, citywide opposition to southeast waterfront development has been lacking because both middle-income and poor neighborhoods (and their representatives) frequently deem increased economic development as good and opposition to development as particularistic and perhaps self-serving. Finally, community opposition to urban land-use changes confronts global processes of economic restructuring and financial speculation that are reordering the external and internal spatial order of cities, constraining government discretion, and making anti-growth claims appear unpatriotic (Fainstein and Fainstein 1987).

History and Evolution of Southeast Baltimore

Southeast Baltimore is a collection of ethnic neighborhoods typifying the kinds of neighborhoods that urbanologists rediscovered in the 1960s (Kuttner 1976; Cassidy 1980; Rich, Netherwood, and Cahn 1981). The Fells Point and Canton neighborhoods in particular illustrate the historical forces that shaped southeast Baltimore and the challenges that now confront its neighborhoods as economic change has transformed a working waterfront to a Gold Coast during the past twenty years. These neighborhoods also typify waterfront districts found in most cities. Fells Point was one of the original three towns that joined together to form Baltimore City in 1773, and it became a center of shipbuilding; maritime trade of coffee, flour, and tobacco; a port-of-entry for newly arriving immigrants in Baltimore — many Eastern Europeans settled in nearby neighborhoods —

and a raucous sailor's enclave of saloons, dancehalls, and flophouses (Keith 1982; Reps 1972; Shopes 1991; Zeidman and Hallengren 1991).

Canton, immediately east of Fells Point, was developed in the nineteenth century by Captain John O'Donnell, a trader who settled in Baltimore in 1785. His son consolidated the family properties into the Canton Company and developed them for industry and residences. Eventually, Canton became the port-terminus for the Pennsylvania Railroad, which bought the Canton Company in the 1920s. Even today the landmark that signals entry into Canton's waterfront is the now-closed American Can complex, once the largest can-making plant in the world and at the center of Cannery Row (Keith 1982; Olsen 1980).

At the close of World War II, Fells Point and Canton remained working neighborhoods. Twenty years later, Fells Point and Canton witnessed plant closings and relocations along the waterfront, the shrinking of port shipping from containerization and competition from ports such as Norfolk, the suburbanization of the children of southeast families, and the decline of neighborhood commerce (Reutter 1988). Changes in southeast Baltimore mirrored transformations taking place in Baltimore as a whole and in other industrial cities. Industry relocated, citizens suburbanized, and downtowns staggered. Baltimore lost 200,000 residents between 1950 and 1980, one-quarter of its population.

Favored public policy responses to these changing urban realities were highway building, urban renewal, and downtown revitalization (Mollenkopf 1981; Frieden and Sagalyn 1989). Baltimore pursued all three. Since the 1940s, Baltimore's roadbuilders had plotted alternative highway routes to link Baltimore via interstates and beltways to the north, south, and west; all the plans included routes that cut through East Baltimore. The development logic guiding these plans emphasized increasing the suburban, regional, and national accessibility of Baltimore so that it could be more competitive as a port, downtown, and business location. In particular, downtown advocates, such as the corporate-dominated Greater Baltimore Committee, viewed the expressway system as key to the regional success of its Charles Center office district and the inner harbor revitalization (Olsen 1980).

Hundreds of homes were demolished in Canton for the highway right-of-way and many rowhouses stood empty in Fells Point awaiting the bulldozer as the neighborhood destabilized. A coalition of neighborhood activists and historic preservationists called SCAR — Southeast Council Against the Road — ultimately defeated the planned highway by using the federal funding requirement for an environmental impact statement to argue that the elevated highway structure would irreparably damage the historic buildings of Fells Point and Canton. They were part of a citywide anti-highway coalition called MAD — Movement Against Destruction (Bailey 1969). Fells Point residents succeeded in having a large portion of their neighborhood designated as a historic district on the National Register of Historic Places in 1969; Canton became a historic district in 1978. The national Advisory Council on Historic Preservation agreed with SCAR that highways and historic districts did not mix, one of the few times it disagreed with Baltimore development officials (Truelove 1977).

The initial results of the environmental impact statement confirmed the community's point of view: highway planners were sent back to the drawing boards, now as an interdisciplinary group called the Urban Design Concept Team (Owings 1973; Allison 1969; Campbell 1967; Bailey 1969). Ultimately, eight new highway options proved no more workable and revealed the inherent weaknesses of the highway logic: the inner harbor and Rosemont sections of the plan were dropped in 1969; the highway plan for Fells Point and Canton was finally scrapped in 1977 (Truelove 1977; Brambilla and Longo 1979; Carlson 1987).

The defeat of the Road set the stage for southeast Baltimore history from 1970 to 1990. The South East Community Organization (SECO), the successor to SCAR, grew in membership and stature, taking on a range of neighborhood issues (Truelove 1977; Crenson 1983; Baroni 1983). Stopping the highway also set the stage for the high-income development boom; indeed, preservationists and community developers unwittingly laid the foundations for the Gold Coast along the southeast waterfront in the 1980s.

By 1977, when the Road was defeated, the economic value of Baltimore's waterfront had already begun to skyrocket. At this point, two sets of private forces came into play: private developers as part of the urban real estate boom of the 1980s, and the back-to-the-city movement that combined young people migrating to cities, new higher-income residential growth related to service economy expansion, and neighborhood revitalization by existing residents (Berry 1985). Private commitments were augmented by public resources, including possible gifts of city-owned property (often acquired for the right-of-way for the highway that was not built), which permitted urban homesteading.

Between 1980 and 1990, twenty-five waterfront projects were built or approved in Fells Point and Canton, approximately 2,000 residential units and 500,000 square feet of commercial space together representing approximately $1 billion of private and public investment. Fifteen hundred marina slips were also planned or built. When completed, this middle- to high-income housing will increase the population of Fells Point and

Canton by 5,000 people, 25 percent of the 1980 base (Jacobson 1990a; 1990b; Waterfront Coalition 1990).

Gold Coast developers were mostly Baltimore-based and had close ties to the Baltimore growth coalition and former mayor William Donald Schaefer, the acknowledged leader of the Baltimore Renaissance (Giloth 1990). Many of the Gold Coast projects received public subsidies such as Urban Development Action Grants (UDAGs), promising to create jobs and expand Baltimore's tax base. Gold Coast developers also took advantage of land swaps and write-downs and massive infrastructure improvements funded by unused interstate highway monies and federally funded $1 million blocks of cobblestone streets in Fells Point.

The City of Baltimore benefited from this southeast waterfront development in several ways. The yearly property tax revenues from all First Councilmanic District properties — including those in the Gold Coast and part of downtown Baltimore — increased 300 percent from 1976 to 1990, producing approximately 29 percent of Baltimore's total property tax revenues (Department of Finance 1991). The city also obtained commitments from developers to rebuild waterfront infrastructure and to contribute toward the building of a promenade along the water's edge.

Gold Coast Impacts on Fells Point, Upper Fells Point, and Canton Neighborhoods

The southeast Baltimore Gold Coast has not demolished hundreds of homes, as the planned interstate highway would have done. It has, however, imposed costs on the residents of adjacent areas and threatens the future affordability of nearby neighborhoods. These indirect impacts raise two questions for southeast waterfront activists and for economic development practitioners in general: Who should bear the costs of new waterfront development? Do residents have the right to remain in and improve their neighborhoods?

Community research has documented the transformation of the land value gradient in southeast Baltimore. Since the mid-1970s, properties near the waterfront have dramatically increased in value as Gold Coast planning and development started (Giloth 1989). Property value increases and decreases in Fells Point/Upper Fells Point between 1985 and 1988 were influenced by their distance from the southeast waterfront. An analogous pattern is emerging in Canton as well.[1]

What is the overall impact of waterfront development on southeast Baltimore neighborhoods? There are approximately 8,000 housing units located between one and six blocks from the waterfront in Canton, Fells

Point, and Upper Fells Point. Of these, 60 to 70 percent are owner-occupied. Prices in Fells Point/Upper Fells Point increased $9,000 between 500 feet and 2,000 feet from the waterfront between 1985 and 1988. Assuming no further price escalation, each of these 8,000 housing units has increased or will increase an average of $4,500 in housing price because of its waterfront proximity, a feature to which residents attached no special value.

Southeast Community Responses to the Waterfront Transformation

Ten years of waterfront planning and project development passed before southeast Baltimore neighborhoods banded together to say "too much!" As with neighborhoods in many cities, southeast residents did not initially perceive a problem with the transformation of its tattered waterfront to a Gold Coast. And when they began to have doubts, they did not feel empowered to challenge the wisdom of city government.

Three southeast Baltimore coalitions eventually emerged in the late 1980s that confronted the transformation of the southeast waterfront to a Gold Coast. These coalitions overlapped in membership, including old and new residents, although each emphasized a different set of concerns about waterfront development impacts. The Waterfront Coalition battled the physical development plans of the City of Baltimore and specific developers; the Joint Tax Committee of Canton and Upper Fells Point initiated statewide legislation to reduce the impacts of increasing property taxes on elderly homeowners; and the Southeast Linkage Group advocated that waterfront developers fund the preservation of affordable housing.

Waterfront Coalition. In fall 1987, southeast Baltimore organized anew to confront the adverse impacts of development. The precipitating reasons were a City Council bill to rezone the southeast waterfront to allow more high-rise development and a mega-development proposal for redevelopment of the soon-to-be-closed American Can factory on Boston Street. Neighborhood residents and organizations formed the Waterfront Coalition. In November 1987, they rallied at St. Casimir's Church in Canton to protest the proposed rezoning and its likely impact on neighborhood property taxes (Field 1988).

The political vacuum created by the departure of long-time mayor William Donald Schaefer for Maryland's governorship in 1986–1987, the weakness of the acting mayor, and his losing mayoral election campaign with Kurt L. Schmoke provided the opportunity for neighborhood-sensitive city planners to act. They developed a guide plan for the southeast waterfront and educated southeast neighborhood organizations and leaders about upcoming waterfront projects (Department of Planning 1987). These municipal planners introduced a critical language of urban design (e.g., view corridors, density, height and bulk regulations) that enabled the Waterfront Coalition to translate its visceral opposition to waterfront development into formal and properly phrased planning recommendations.

From 1987 to 1990, the Waterfront Coalition conducted a feisty campaign that questioned the wisdom of high-density waterfront development, building high-income housing on piers, blocking view corridors, and disrupting working-class and historic neighborhoods. Their outcry forced newly elected Mayor Kurt L. Schmoke to commission another southeast waterfront plan in spring 1988 simply to buy political time. Despite constant public testifying, community outreach, the development of an alternative waterfront plan that won an American Institute of Architects award, project scrutiny, and the drafting of alternative urban renewal amendments, however, the Baltimore City Council passed Canton and Fells Point Urban Renewal Amendments in the fall of 1989 that largely ignored its own commissioned waterfront plan and the Waterfront Coalition's recommendations.

The Coalition had better luck opposing and reshaping implementation of specific projects. The struggle over one such project including 15 buildings on a 9.3-acre site illustrates the Waterfront Coalition's tenacity and the global dimensions of the southeast waterfront transformation (Merrifield 1991). By 1988, when the American Can complex was permanently closed as a result of the company's regional consolidation, there was not much left of Cannery Row in Baltimore. In 1988, Triangle Industries, a junk bond–financing holding company, brought in a Drexel Lambert real estate associate to redevelop the southeast Baltimore site for housing and retail (Kelly 1988a; 1988b; Plaza Land Associates 1988; Bruck 1988).

American National Plaza was first conceived as four and then two twenty-story, residential towers containing 450 high-income apartments and a mixed-use commercial development costing $150 million. Market uncertainty and community opposition forced a redesign to a 200,000 square foot strip shopping center with a supermarket, multiplex theaters, and neighborhood retail; a second phase anticipated residential and office uses. The federal Department of Housing and Urban Development (HUD) awarded the City of Baltimore and American Plaza Associates an $8.5 million Urban Development Action Grant in 1988 to subsidize this $52 million development; other financing included $9 million from American

National Can, $1 million from the now defunct Washington National Bank, and the remainder from CitiCorp. If American National Plaza proved financially successful, the City of Baltimore would ultimately receive a 15 percent return on its $8.5 million UDAG investment.

Community opposition focused on how the project overwhelmed the adjacent rowhouse streets and how it required the demolition of four historically significant buildings (Macsherry 1988). In the fall of 1988, the Waterfront Coalition launched a "Recycle the Can" petition drive that gathered 3,000 signatures requesting that the American Can buildings be saved. Because of the federal monies involved, an environmental and historic review was necessary for the development. The Advisory Council on Historic Preservation, after a site visit and public hearing, for only the second time in twenty years (the first being its opposition to the planned interstate through Fells Point and Canton) ruled against the City of Baltimore and recommended that serious attention be given to preserving the American Can buildings (Kelly 1988b; Gunts 1988).

The developer and the City of Baltimore revised their plans to save one building on the western edge of the site, but the entire development proposal was withdrawn in March 1989 after two mysterious toxic chemical spills occurred in the American Can buildings. There are numerous explanations about why Triangle Industries scuttled the American National Plaza plan: (1) community opposition; (2) withdrawal of financing; or (3) more profitable deals elsewhere (Samuel 1989; 1990). Whatever the precise explanation may be, the City of Baltimore lost its $8.5 million UDAG and the development efforts stalled.

In the spring of 1990 the Waterfront Coalition established an American Can Committee to envision options for the reuse of the American Can complex. They invited Southeast Development, Inc. — the nonprofit development affiliate of SECO — and the Neighborhood Design Center to participate, and they contacted the American National Can Company to request its cooperation. The committee established three criteria for developing reuse options: (1) preservation of historic buildings; (2) provision of retail businesses to meet the shopping needs of southeast Baltimore residents; and (3) development that is compatible with the urban rowhouse neighborhoods surrounding American Can.

The committee decided that its role was to assemble market and site information and urban design concepts that would help private developers generate community-sensitive proposals. This was a departure from its previous advocacy efforts and suggested a new type of community-inspired public-private partnership. The Waterfront Coalition convened Recycle the Can 2 in November 1990, at which time residents responded favorably to reuse plans for a full-service supermarket, elderly housing, office space, and neighborhood retail (Gunts 1990; Kelly 1990). Planning continued with the participation of forty public, private, and community representatives, and Southeast Development, Inc. submitted a proposal to the federal government for $500,000 toward the development of a supermarket on the eastern portion of the American Can site in August 1991.

Despite this neighborhood initiative and the participation of a broad implementation coalition, the American National Can Company has refused to cooperate or to allow the American Can Committee into its buildings. Those close to American National Can say that tearing down all the buildings remains their favored option.

Joint Tax Committee of Canton and Upper Fells Point. The development pressures of the southeast waterfront transformation eventually translated into higher home prices and higher property taxes. Yet those who must pay the taxes are often on low or fixed incomes: elderly homeowners may have to sacrifice building repairs or other life necessities to remain in their homes.

The Joint Tax Committee of Canton and Upper Fells Point had two points of origin. The first was the work of the Upper Fells Point Neighborhood Association and the Julie Community Center — a low-income, advocacy center — to fight the designation of their neighborhood as a historic district, a case in which the coalition of preservationists and existing residents broke down over the issue of housing affordability. Community residents feared that historic district status would encourage housing speculation and their eventual displacement. The historic district passed, but in November 1986 activists decided to continue the fight by advocating property tax relief for residents of historic districts.

The second emerged from a Canton church-sponsored SECO informational meeting on State of Maryland property tax relief for senior homeowners in early 1987. At that meeting residents agreed that escalating property taxes constituted a serious problem; they formed an ad hoc committee to examine options for property tax relief.

Eventually these initiatives joined forces. They turned first to Baltimore City Council for tax relief but received little support; they then approached the Maryland General Assembly. State legislation introduced in 1988 failed to pass, but efforts in 1989 were more successful.

Members of the Joint Tax Committee lobbied effectively for their state bills, enlisting support from the Baltimore Taxpayer's Coalition, city and state officials, and southeast residents. They surveyed 420 homeowners in Canton and Upper Fells Point and found that 48 percent of the senior citizen homeowners had experienced an increase in property taxes of more than 45 percent between 1985 and 1988. Citizen support and media coverage were mobilized at local rallies, and a busload of southeast residents went to the state capitol in February 1989 to testify. The Maryland General Assembly passed legislation in March 1989 that increased the maximum property tax credit available to senior homeowners to $2,000 (English 1989).

Southeast Linkage Group. In early 1989, SECO convened neighborhood leaders to discuss the potential for using linkage techniques to solve waterfront development impacts. Linkage policies require developers of market-rate development to provide resources to solve housing and employment impacts caused by that development (Keating 1986; Casale 1989; Andrew and Merriam 1988). Using innovative neighborhood research and taking advantage of political schisms in southeast Baltimore and citywide, the Southeast Linkage Group (SLG) advocated inclusion of a linkage requirement in the urban renewal amendments that were to have public hearings and City Council action in the fall of 1989. The SLG SECO staff developed and recommended a fee of $2.25 per square foot to be paid over five years into a housing trust fund by developers of new waterfront projects that contained more than 100,000 square feet of space.[2] The fund, in turn, would oversee the use of the linkage fees and would incorporate community input and plans in its expenditure decision. Together with private financing, the linkage fund could finance the construction of 60 new homes, rehabilitate 75–125 homes, or construct 50–75 affordable rental units.

The SLG presented its research and trust fund proposal at the Planning Commission and City Council hearings at the same time that the Canton and Fells Point urban renewal amendments were being heard (Ruby 1989). Their research and the recommended $2.25 fee received widespread media coverage but little support. City officials, nervous that the explosive waterfront issue would never end, asked that the proposal be considered separately from these amendments. The Linkage Group agreed, acknowledging its latecomer status and reassured by the promise that the southeast district councilman would introduce separate linkage legislation in City Council.

Given more time to develop its ideas, the SLG refined its linkage proposal into a citywide enabling ordinance so that neighborhoods anywhere in Baltimore could better confront the negative impacts of new development. The bill awkwardly combined two concepts: a targeted linkage program for development "hot spots" in Baltimore, and reform of citizen review of major development projects. The bill called for designation of Impact Zones, within which development applications had to document the negative impacts of the proposed construction, recommend specific remedies (fees or inclusionary components such as housing), and propose administrative mechanisms to ensure the appropriate use of resources. As became apparent, implementing the Impact Zone bill would still depend upon neighborhood vigilance and advocacy.

The Impact Zone bill was introduced in April 1990 and public hearings took place in November 1990 (Adler 1990; Atwood 1990; Kotschenreuther 1990). The Linkage Group brought together allies from other harbor neighborhoods and neighborhood planning advocates; the hearings also attracted growth coalition boosters and real estate lobbyists. City planning officials steadfastly denied that anything was wrong with their planning process; in contrast, waterfront developers admitted that there were serious problems with the development process but argued that Impact Zones were not the answer.

Although the bill did not pass, political pressures led the president of Baltimore City Council to convene a task force in March 1991 of community, city, and developer representatives to devise alternatives to the Impact Zone bill. Three months later, the task force reported back to the City Council and the mayor. Its recommendations included (1) changes in development review procedures; (2) the commitment of income generated from public incentive loans in southeast Baltimore to a Southeast Trust Fund; and (3) the development of a southeast neighborhood plan that could be used to bargain with developers and to articulate the community's sense of the future.

CONCLUSION

The efforts of southeast Baltimore citizens to influence changes on the city's waterfront have attempted to insure that planning take account of housing affordability, neighborhood stability, public access, and appropriately scaled development. Their struggle has asserted the importance of the use values of community building, challenging the narrow criteria of profit and property tax maximization. Some public accommodation to these concerns has been achieved. However, the planning process remains essentially unchanged. Many of the participants in the waterfront struggle concluded that southeast residents must elect more responsive City Council members; two participants in these community struggles launched successful electoral campaigns in the spring of 1991.[3] Their election changed the balance of power on the waterfront issue and holds hope for reshaping the dynamics of the development process so that neighborhoods are better represented.

The transformation of southeast Baltimore from Cannery Row to Gold Coast illustrates the limitations of municipal planning in balancing neighborhood preservation and city economic development. Cities like

Baltimore, on the edge of social, economic, and financial disaster, feel compelled to promote large-scale development at all costs. Yet this uncritical boosterism can be destructive, and the national real estate recession and banking crisis have shown how economically precarious and neighborhood-destructive unconstrained real estate promotion can be.

Is a different type of urban development possible? Can there be a more rational, neighborhood-sensitive approach to designing, reviewing, and implementing large development projects? Or is future urban development to be characterized by still more community conflict, the boom and bust of real estate cycles, and anxiety-fueled planning and growth promotion? The southeast Baltimore case holds a number of lessons for other cities and neighborhoods:

1. The dramatic restructuring of urban space in the post-modern city reasserts the importance of public planning: it is both a locus of social conflict and a set of substantive ideas, standards, and processes that can be used by neighborhood advocates to develop counter-plans. Increasingly, neighborhood organizations are taking responsibility for this planning.

2. More is at stake in contemporary urban development than who bears its costs and benefits: new urban development creates isolated, protected downtowns and high-income enclaves. Too often, urban neighborhoods containing displaced workers, retirees, or the underclass are viewed as irrelevant and potentially dangerous and are subject to removal.

3. Neighborhood and city advocates must build bridges among diverse populations. The southeast Baltimore case shows how middle-income preservationists and working-class, white ethnics forged alliances to preserve their neighborhoods. However, it also shows the difficulties of building citywide coalitions around issues of economic development and redistributive urban policies.

4. The passage of time frequently demonstrates the wisdom of neighborhood advocacy: southeast Baltimore activists saved their waterfront from a highway so that it could become a Gold Coast; their recent struggle has balanced the new and old city. Ironically, the marketplace has confirmed the economic rationality of neighborhood preservation and a slower pace of development.

5. These four lessons imply a critical final finding: the rush to action and absence of deliberation in many crisis-led implementation efforts may doom them to inefficiency in long-run economic terms. "Irrationality" and "emotional" argument by neighborhood and community groups may merely reflect differences in priorities and goals (the economists' "objective functions"). The differences in objectives are not recognized, nor is their appropriateness considered, in the pressure to act, not debate. Critical local insights that can contribute to the economic efficacy of plans are thus lost.

Unfortunately, the combination of urban fiscal stress, regional fragmentation and competition, and the anti-city bias of the federal government during the Reagan and Bush administrations have made substantial reform of the urban development process in the United States improbable. Consequently, balanced urban development will continue to be advocated (and sometimes achieved solely through community conflict) until new political coalitions gain power and articulate alternative urban development visions and a more autonomous, evaluative, and inclusive planning process (Giloth and Mier 1989).

ACKNOWLEDGMENTS

The author would like to thank Chris Ryer, Bobbie English, Peter Meyer, Steve Janes, Curt McKnight, and Anne Shlay for their ideas, information, and helpful advice.

NOTES

1. Research examined 419 properties in Canton, Fells Point, and Upper Fells Point; the properties represent approximately 9 percent of owner-occupied dwellings and 5 percent of all housing units. The primary data were property tax assessment records for each of the sampled properties for the years 1985 and 1988. Other data controlled for factors that influence changes in property values such as housing sales, zoning, building permits, and distance from the waterfront. A multivariate statistical model was used to establish the effects of waterfront proximity on housing price changes taking into account other market and institutional factors.

2. The fee was derived by discounting the total economic impact of waterfront development by factors such as housing turnover, percentage of below-median income families, and percentage of renter population. An adjusted waterfront impact of $4.5

million divided by 2 million square feet of potentially developable space along the waterfront resulted in the $2.25 fee.

3. In the September 1991 primary, the First District machine was soundly defeated — a stunning turnaround given its victory in 1987. There are many partial explanations for the defeat: low voter turnout; redistricting; new in-moving residents; and collapse of political machines. Neighborhood and voter dissatisfaction also were important factors — regarding waterfront development, in particular, and the future of southeast neighborhoods. In a sense, the winners were those who stood up — in contrasting ways — to the impacts of waterfront development; the losers were those who acquiesced or who actively and uncritically supported the developers.

8

Industrial Change and Conflict in Urban Redevelopment: The Case of South Cardiff, Wales

Huw Thomas
Rob F. Imrie

Patsy Healey and her colleagues (1988:219–243) have described decision making about land use and development in Britain as consisting of a number of policy processes, each characterized by different rules governing access, style, and procedures of debate, legitimation, and evaluation. They have illustrated how planning projects may involve one or more policy processes, and they point out that some social and economic groups have privileged access to the processes involved.

This chapter explores the policy processes involved in the implementation of major urban renewal projects in south Cardiff from the perspective of small businesses that have been affected by them and wish to influence them. It is based on over forty interviews with small businesses impacted by two waves of redevelopment proposals from the mid-80s onward, on interviews with technical officers of the local councils and other agencies involved in urban renewal, and on a long-term project examining the policy innovations represented by urban renewal in south Cardiff (Thomas and Imrie 1989; Imrie and Thomas 1992). We find that small firms have been generally unsuccessful in influencing urban renewal decision making despite the adverse effects of the proposals for many of them, and we examine why this pattern has prevailed.

Implementation of urban renewal projects in south Cardiff have involved a mix of four policy processes. In Healey and colleagues' (1988) terminology, they can be distinguished as follows:

1. Techno-rational policy processes, in which "professional experts" limit entry to discussions, define the terms of discourse, and dictate criteria for evaluation.

2. Semi-judicial policy processes, in which formal hearings with statutory functions are used to conduct an open but formal debate in accordance with prevailing norms of justice and fairness (typically used in challenges to compulsory takings).

3. Consultative processes, allowing regulated access and discussion to those deemed by the state to have an interest of some kind in the project. They may, at one extreme, allow for "public participation" (often merely information provisions); at the other, some kind of corporatist bargaining (such as meetings between property developers and local politicians and officers to hammer out acceptable renewal packages).

4. Politico-rational processes — the area involving elected politicians, characterized by discussions and debates in a wide range of public, semi-public, and private forums.

Efforts to dispossess small businesses of their premises in order to create large sites for redevelopment have involved all four policy processes. Two have been of particular significance. First is the politico-rational process, since the area's prospects have depended upon continuing central government support and a compliant local state that provides coordination "on the ground." Second is semi-judicial processes, taking the form of legal intervention rights, which have represented a fallback option for businesses unable to influence implementation policy in any other way. Particular attention will be paid to the relationship of small businesses to these processes in subsequent sections.

THE BACKGROUND TO ECONOMIC CHANGE AND DEVELOPMENT IN SOUTH CARDIFF

In March 1987, Cardiff Bay Development Corporation (CBDC) was formally set up by Britain's central government, charged with the responsibility of redeveloping a large portion of the Cardiff docklands. With a mission in common with other Urban Development Corporations (UDCs), CBDC was launched "to transform utterly an area of dereliction, wasteland, and low order uses . . . generating new forms and levels of development in economic, housing, cultural, leisure, and tourism terms"

(CBDC 1988:2). CBDC is an example of the well-established British political phenomenon, the quasi-autonomous non-governmental organization, or "quango." It is a creation of central government, which appoints all the members of the board that governs it; however, it has considerable day-to-day autonomy in pursuing its tasks, along with freedom from much local government interference.

As one of the second wave of urban development corporations (Lawless 1988; Stoker 1988), CBDC's ten-year mission is to stimulate private sector regeneration of Cardiff's docklands by providing necessary infrastructure, consolidating land holdings, and creating an overall regeneration strategy — a vision of the future. Its central government grant (at 1987 prices) will be £250 million over the ten years, but it can supplement this by, for example, trading in land. It has powers of compulsory purchase (eminent domain). CBDC is now responsible for a docklands area of 2,700 acres, which is far from abandoned: there are 6,000 residents and 1,000 companies employing over 15,000 people in the area (Alden et al. 1988).

Cardiff's docks achieved international significance at the end of the nineteenth century. They have, however, contracted consistently since the end of World War I and are now only marginal to the city's economy (Thomas 1989). However, the dockland itself continued to be the main industrial area in the city. Contrary to its popular image, Cardiff was never a manufacturing center: even in the 1950s, the sector accounted for no more than one-third of Cardiff's workforce, and this proportion has now stabilized at around 15 percent. Thus, the manufacturers within the Cardiff Bay Development Area provide a substantial proportion of their sector's total employment of the city and its immediate hinterland. Not only are they an important element of employment diversification, but their proximity to residential areas characterized by poverty and lack of mobility means they may serve as a source of economic opportunity (Alden et al. 1988).

The industrial firms of the docklands area are by no means homogeneous. The largest industrial employer is the locally based Allied Steel and Wire. A manufacturer of steel products ranging from rods to rails, it has two large and related complexes and employed some 2,000 people in 1991. However, the small firms clustered along Collingdon Road are more typical of the area.

Collingdon Road is, in effect, a ribbon development of a kilometer in length, squeezed in between a railway and the first of Cardiff's modern docks, the Bute West Dock. In 1988, there were 77 businesses along the road employing 706 people (Alden et al. 1988:77). The majority of businesses are small manufacturers and machinist shops, but depots and small assorted warehouses are also prevalent. The road exhibits a kind of patchwork quilt of landownership and tenancies, with buildings of varying ages, styles, and states of repair — a familiar picture in dockland areas.

Until the 1970s, the road itself was privately owned and maintained and was in a poor condition. However, it was upgraded and adopted by the local South Glamorgan County Council in the late 1970s and was included in the City Council's North Docklands Industrial Improvement Area initiative from 1979 to 1986. Under the initiative, £314,583 was given in grant aid for the refurbishment and improvement of old industrial buildings in the area.

From 1986 to 1988, a separate City Council initiative focused exclusively on supporting buildings in Collingdon Road. During that time four grants totaling £18,520 were provided, which generated a total investment of at least £97,000. Other forms of assistance for small firms were also set up that benefited companies on the road. Until the advent of the CBDC, local authority economic policies were aimed at sustaining and building upon the small-firm industrial economy of areas such as Collingdon Road.

However, the nearby Atlantic Wharf development, which was begun in 1983 by the South Glamorgan *County* Council with firm financial support from central government, involved the legally unchallengeable "compulsory purchase" of the premises of thirty-two small firms akin to those on Collingdon Road (Thomas and Imrie 1989). The ambivalence of the *City* Council toward Atlantic Wharf can be explained by this displacement of local enterprises, which their policies had been designed to assist (Thomas 1992).

Thomas (1992) argues on the basis of documentary and interview evidence that by the mid-1980s, senior officers and politicians in the County Council were convinced that the economic future of south Cardiff no longer lay with small-scale manufacturing. Small indigenous industrial firms could see little place for themselves in the new-look dockland that was being proposed by the County Council. Not surprisingly, they resented it. The CBDC approach has reinforced their fears.

In its first year, CBDC commissioned a firm of private planning consultants, Llewellyn-Davies Planning, to draw up a strategy for its area. This was never intended to be a master plan, but rather to provide an overall direction and to point out development opportunities. The tone of the regeneration strategy reflects CBDC's overall aims. It envisages a substantial change in the nature of the area, a central dimension of which will be the replacement of low-value, low-density uses and vacant land by high-value, high-density, prestigious uses. In this respect it is an orthodox urban renewal document (Weiss 1986). A taste of CBDC's strategy is provided by its role for Collingdon Road. It proposes a grand, almost ceremonial, mall along its length to connect Cardiff city centre with the waterfront of the Bay. This major route would be flanked by a mixture of high-value, prestige uses, especially up-market residences and office complexes.

Clearly, the existing industrial uses are incompatible with such a prestigious feature, and indeed, Collingdon Road falls within an area in which CBDC has indicated it will use compulsory purchase powers to acquire property if necessary. Compulsory purchase orders have not been served because CBDC cannot yet confirm that a central plank of its strategy, a proposal to enclose Cardiff Bay and turn it into a freshwater lake, will go ahead. Pending a decision on this project, there will be no attempt to redevelop Collingdon Road. This has created a climate of uncertainty, although CBDC has acknowledged the very natural concerns of existing industrial operators in the Bay, including those in Collingdon Road:

> The existing industries in the Bay need to be protected and nurtured as the economy changes. . . . [S]ites and premises should be made available in association with the industrial development strategy to allow local firms to expand and move as necessary. This will be particularly important in relocating those industries that need to move for reasons of site assembly, environmental impact, or infrastructure development. A process of close liaison with the industrial and commercial communities, and the handling of each move individually is necessary to maintain the enterprises and jobs and avoid misunderstanding, blight or loss of confidence. (CBDC 1988:21)

CBDC has taken steps to put these intentions into practice. The Development Corporation commissioned a local enterprise agency to act as intermediary between it and firms in the area. Furthermore, CBDC has prepared six sites to provide facilities for relocation of businesses from Collingdon Road. Our analysis indicates that these facilities are far from satisfactory in enabling relocations to take place, which reflects the corporation's failure to understand the firms' real needs.

THE IMPACT OF URBAN RENEWAL ON SMALL FIRMS IN SOUTH CARDIFF

The impact of recent large-scale urban renewal proposals in south Cardiff on small businesses in the area has been in line with the experiences of small businesses affected by earlier urban renewal projects in the United Kingdom and the United States (Falk 1980; Frieden and Sagalyn 1989). Of the twenty-two small firms affected by the Atlantic Wharf redevelopment that could be traced and interviewed five years later, four claimed that the loss of their premises had led directly to loss of employment in the business, and three had gone out of business rather than relocate (Thomas and Imrie 1989). The majority of firms regarded their location (as opposed to the premises themselves) as an important element in the successful operation of their business (McIntosh and Keddie 1979).

More recently, a survey of Collingdon Road businesses identified a number of firms that were losing orders, and were certainly shelving plans for expansion, because of the implications of the CBDC regeneration strategy for the area (Imrie and Thomas 1992). The experiences of two quite different industrial concerns in Collingdon Road are indicative of the problems caused by renewal plans. One company is a small metalworking and machining shop (employing seven people). Its customers demand assurances of both quality and security of supply. The latter requirement has resulted in serious constraints on sales, as a spokesman has noted. "We're tendering at the moment, but the customer would want us to do a four-month job and is worried about whether we'll be around. . . . We certainly can't take on longer-term projects and we wouldn't be given them in the present climate."

The second company is larger (over forty employees, and looking to expand), and represents the field of specialized industrial services (cleaning and decontamination). Its proposed extension to its premises at Collingdon Road has been refused planning permission because it is inconsistent with CBDC's plans. As a result, important training and decontamination facilities cannot be built. An internal company memo concludes that "both existing and potential customers now have cause for concern in the areas of backup for our asbestos removal facilities."

Not all small businesses in the docks suffered or are suffering in this way, but it appears as if the majority are. This is not entirely surprising, because the evidence points to the perceived importance of the dockland location and/or the relatively cheap premises found there for the competitiveness and development of businesses.

The reality that the physically dismal docklands area continues to represent an excellent low-cost business location ensured a degree of opposition to plans for urban renewal. Businesses that owned freeholds of their sites and considered their land as investments as well as bases for current trading have additional reasons to resist displacement. Natural antipathy toward plans that disrupt their business has been reinforced by a perception that the agencies displacing them have had no real interest in understanding how the companies function and what they need to survive and flourish. As one company representative in Collingdon Road put it, "CBDC are really poor at looking at the company from the company's point of view. . . . [T]hey'll make the area look better but it's having a terrible effect on my business. . . . [H]ow many people will they put out of work for a few flowers?" (quoted in Imrie and Thomas 1992).

The approach of the two quangos that have had the task of assembling redevelopment sites in south Cardiff has hardly served to endear them to the companies whose activities they have been disrupting. Both the Land Authority for Wales (LAW) at Atlantic Wharf and CBDC in south Cardiff have taken narrow legalistic approaches. The LAW appears to have been under pressure to assemble the Atlantic Wharf site as quickly as possible, and it did the minimum it was legally obliged to do to assist the businesses that its acquisitions displaced.

CBDC appears to have learned lessons from the LAW experience and has employed a local enterprise agency to act as its eyes and ears, talking through problems of disruption and relocation with businesses affected by its renewal strategy. Grants are available to cover the difference between the compensation paid to firms forced to vacate old premises and the costs of acquiring new facilities. However, by 1991 early optimism that most firms would in fact benefit from the jolt caused by imminent relocation (Williams 1989) has been dimmed. A widely leaked report by the enterprise agency found that most of the firms that relocated had done so without any assistance from CBDC (and as a response to uncertainty about the future of the dockland area). The remaining firms were reportedly uncertain about the future and exhibited a sense of stagnation. Informed opinion in the area now holds that the activity of the CBDC has been wholly unhelpful to local businesses to date, and that its grant aid and attempts to provide alternative sites have been undermined. Blame has been placed on CBDC's reluctance to compromise in negotiations over the compensation levels to be paid to businesses forced to relocate.

In interviews, almost all the businesses from Collingdon Road alleged that CBDC deliberately prevaricates in negotiations, being aware that continuing uncertainty will weaken small businesses far more than it will affect a government-sponsored renewal agency. Clearly, such an allegation is difficult to evaluate, particularly when businesses are involved in complex and often conflict-fraught discussions. However, our interview data were collected some four years after CBDC adopted the main elements of its strategy. It is significant that not one of the businesses interviewed had finalized details of terms of purchase and/or compensation with CBDC, though all recognized the need to negotiate and three were committed to specific new locations. One major Collingdon Road landowner claimed not to have been approached at all by CBDC, while others have had intensive discussions. This pattern suggests that a very selective strategy of acquisition is being pursued, one that smacks of an adversarial approach rather than constructive discussion.

It is against such a background that small businesses have had to devise responses to the prospect and reality of urban renewal. As might be expected, few firms accept without question the initial offer made for their premises. However, such a rejection is only the first step in formulating a constructive response and resistance. Rejection alone is not effective.

STRATEGIES OF RESISTANCE

In principle, businesses affected by urban renewal proposals have a number of avenues open to them to try to influence events:

1. political lobbying in an attempt to influence the state at one or more levels (entering the politico-rational process);
2. lobbying the technical/professional personnel (entering the techno-rational process);
3. exercising their legal rights to object to compulsory acquisition of property, to applications for planning permission, or to local plan proposals (use of consultative and semi-judicial processes).

Allied Steel and Wire (ASW), which has 2,000 employees, has access to politicians and technical officers at the highest level through the position of its chief executive as a member of the board of CBDC. Even before the creation of CBDC, the power and influence of ASW were evident in the care that was taken to ensure that the Atlantic Wharf proposals did not endanger its functioning. It has been kept fully informed of the implementation of the project, and vital water supplies have been protected from disruption.

Small businesses, on the other hand, have no direct access of this kind. Interviews with close to forty small businesses affected by redevelopment proposals in south Cardiff indicate that they did not lobby either officers or politicians. Instead, they relied on either or both of two strategies for improving the outcome for their business: (1) attempts at hard bargaining; (2) exercising their legal rights of objection. In general, it has to be said that neither strategy has been successful in affecting the details of the urban renewal proposals, but some businesses have been more successful than others in securing good sites on which to relocate.

The general reluctance to lobby has had three bases. First, a number of companies found the general principles of urban renewal in the docklands wholly acceptable and were concerned only with assuring a reasonable deal for themselves. This seems to have been particularly true of the more limited Atlantic Wharf redevelopment, in which case the six businesses that pursued their objections to compulsory purchase at a public inquiry still did not question the need for large-scale redevelopment in the area. They only attempted to show how this goal was compatible with retaining their own premises.

Second, given the overwhelming support for renewal from local authorities, central government, and the media, it has been very difficult for any small business to seriously question the overall proposals. Local newspaper coverage of the early years of the Atlantic Wharf redevelopment was entirely supportive of the principles of renewal, paying no attention to the costs imposed on local small firms (Thomas 1992). Media accounts have generally stressed the political and institutional unanimity in support of renewal, creating a forbidding impression of the inevitability of large-scale dockland change. Not one of the companies interviewed doubted that urban renewal would take place, whatever their views of it.

The final explanation for the lack of lobbying activity is, simply, a lack of political and organizational sophistication — particularly with respect to the quangos, which have non-local lines of authority. Only a few of the small businesses in south Cardiff showed any inclination to explore the political and institutional complexities of the proposals.

One dimension of organizational failure was the inability of firms to get together to form a coalition to oppose urban renewal schemes. In Atlantic Wharf, in particular, each company was aware of exactly which other companies were affected and even, as time went on, which companies were especially hostile to the compulsory purchase orders. Yet no attempt was made to pool ideas or resources. Indeed, each of the six companies that pursued its opposition to a public inquiry arranged to be represented separately. In Collingdon Road, one or two tentative attempts appear to have been made to form a common front. The initiative collapsed quickly in the face of CBDC's refusal to negotiate on anything other than an individual basis. The ethos of small firm entrepreneurialism and the individualizing tendency of legal and planning processes appear to have combined to undermine any efforts at coalition-building.

Moreover, the companies affected by these urban renewal proposals were (and are) very different (Thomas and Imrie 1989). They are all relatively small, but some are industrial, others are in wholesaling, others provide services to consumers. Some are static in terms of turnover and employment; others are growing and have high aspirations. Some owners are looking toward retirement; others are younger and seeking a brighter future. Some rent their property and would be just as happy renting elsewhere; others own their premises and are as interested in returns from property value increases as they are from trading. In short, the material significance of urban renewal to these firms varies greatly from one to another, and this in itself creates difficulties for collective action.

As individuals, however, small businesses in south Cardiff have made little impression on changing the face of urban renewal. Those that have done best in negotiations with the renewal agencies are the ones that have an appreciation of the political will behind urban renewal and the imbalance of strength between them and their opponents. They have used legal procedures (such as registering objections to compulsory purchase orders) as irritants in the urban renewal process, seeking thereby to increase the price they can demand (in the form of compensation) for cooperation in the future. One or two firms have achieved good deals in this way. Others have misjudged matters and have pursued their objections too far, finding themselves enmeshed in legal processes that have drained their companies of time and money. No objection to a compulsory purchase order has yet been upheld, and it is unlikely that this will happen in the immediate future. Central government has the final say, and its commitment to urban renewal in south Cardiff is total, for the present.

CONCLUSION

Small businesses in south Cardiff have found themselves shut out of, or minor players in, policy processes that have been significant in promoting urban renewal in the area. Lacking political and technical skills, and sharing an individualistic ethos and suspicion of government, they have been unwilling and unable to lobby either officers or politicians engaged in policy making. Collective action has eluded them, and they have found the semi-judicial processes fair in a technical sense but all too ready to produce results that mirror the balance of political power in the region.

Thus, the renewal efforts have created an increasingly embittered and disillusioned small business stratum in the renewal area that sees an uncertain future for itself and its workforce. No technical solutions are available to overcome or defuse such bitterness. In the south Cardiff case, this impact appears to have been irrelevant; it seems an accurate reflection of the objectives and priorities of the agencies responsible for promoting urban renewal.

9

Strategic Planning for the Port of New Orleans

Alma H. Young
Robert K. Whelan

Strategic planning is "a disciplined effort to produce fundamental decisions and actions that shape and guide what an organization is, what it does, and why it does it" (Bryson and Einsweiler 1988:1). While the roots of strategic planning are primarily in the private sector, there is some history of public sector strategic planning, especially in military organizations.

Bryson (1988:48) identifies an eight-step strategic planning process for organizations. This process includes the following: (1) initiating and agreeing on a strategic planning process; (2) identifying organizational mandates; (3) clarifying organizational mission and values; (4) assessing the external environment for opportunities and threats; (5) assessing the internal environment for strengths and weaknesses; (6) identifying the strategic issues facing an organization; (7) formulating strategies to manage the issues; (8) establishing an effective organizational vision for the future.

A number of state governments, and some cities, have used a strategic planning process for economic development. This process has varied from "strictly in-house, professional bureaucratic participation to an elaborate, consensus building 'corporationist' effort among labor leaders, business people, and government bureaucrats and elected officials" (Eisinger 1989:27). In 1986, P. Eisinger identified seventeen states that had written a strategic plan for economic development. Cities such as San Francisco, Pasadena, and San Antonio have prepared strategic plans for economic development. Other localities, including Oak Ridge, Tennessee, and

Hennepin County, Minnesota, have substantial economic development components to their strategic plans.

This chapter focuses on the implementation of the strategic plans of the Port of New Orleans, a public sector organization. We introduce the subject first, with a discussion of the historical and environmental context. Then we discuss the strategic planning process. Finally, we address two areas of special concern to the Port: the capital improvements program and the sale of riverfront properties.

HISTORY AND ENVIRONMENTAL CHANGES

The Board of Commissioners for the Port of New Orleans (known locally as the Dock Board) is the state agency charged with governing the port. The Dock Board has jurisdiction over a tri-parish area (Orleans, Jefferson, and St. Bernard). The Dock Board has seven members appointed by the governor: four representatives from Orleans Parish (i.e., the city of New Orleans), two members from Jefferson Parish (a large suburban parish west of New Orleans), and one member from St. Bernard Parish (a smaller suburban parish south of New Orleans).

The facilities of the Port of New Orleans are located in two main areas. General cargo facilities are located along a nine-mile stretch of the Mississippi River. This stretch of the river abuts eleven historic neighborhoods, including the French Quarter, as well as the Central Business District (CBD). Container and dry bulk facilities are located along the Mississippi River Gulf Outlet (MRGO) and the Inner Harbor Navigation Canal (IHNC), which connects the river and the MRGO.

In the mid-1980s, the Port of New Orleans faced a crisis situation because of a changing global external environment. Worldwide problems were compounded by serious difficulties at the local level. Changes in the external environment included the following:

1. The growth in foreign trade in the Pacific Rim reduced the Gulf of Mexico ports' share of foreign trade from 30 percent in 1960 to 18 percent in 1985.

2. Reductions in oil and agricultural prices in the 1980s hurt both the New Orleans local market and its main service area in the Midwest.

3. Transportation changes, such as "mini-bridging," made it cheaper to transfer cargo to railroads and send goods east-west than to send cargo through the Panama Canal. Containerization

hurt ports like New Orleans, which had not built new physical facilities able to accommodate these changes.

4. Deregulation and the construction of new projects (such as the Tennessee-Tombigbee Waterway) stimulated competition from other ports. New Orleans competes with large ports such as Houston and Tampa, but in some instances it competes with smaller ports such as Mobile, Alabama, and Biloxi, Mississippi (*Strategic Plan* 1986).

New Orleans, like other ports, had two main problems in the internal environment. First was the value of the land: riverfront property became valuable for condominiums, retail shops, and museums. After the 1984 World's Fair, traditional dock usage was jeopardized by development for "higher and better" uses as commercial usage expanded. The second problem involved developments in labor demand and supply: longshore jobs were lost as the industry became less labor intensive. New Orleans handles three times more cargo today than it did in 1965, with only 22 percent of the dockside labor. New jobs are emerging in shipping-associated administrative functions and information processing. These jobs demand higher labor-force skills than displaced dockworkers can supply.

By 1985, the Port of New Orleans faced a crisis situation as a result of these shifts. General cargo trade had declined dramatically (down a third by 1984 from a peak of 8 million tons in 1974). As a result, the Port expected a deficit in fiscal year 1987 of $12.8 million and a negative cash flow of $5.1 million, associated in part with decisions taken by the Board in 1986 to reduce port pricing. Due to operating losses, spending on capital facilities had been drastically reduced at the same time as demands for new dockside infrastructure were growing (*Strategic Plan* 1986).

STRATEGIC PLAN PROCESS AND RECOMMENDATIONS

Faced with these significant challenges, the Dock Board in 1985 commissioned a strategic planning study. In assessing the Port's situation, the Board's consultants, operating with a sixty-member advisory committee, noted the problems just cited and a number of strengths, primarily the Port's location and general facilities. The consultants set out a number of options that would enable the Port to enhance its role as a major economic generator for the New Orleans tri-parish region and the state. They recommended a shift in orientation from a traditional "landlord" role to that of a customer-oriented, service-providing port organization. The Port then redefined its objective as becoming a "service organization whose primary purpose is to maximize the flow of foreign and domestic waterborne trade and commerce with relevant markets by providing, directly or through third parties, highly productive facilities, equipment, and support services to meet the specialized needs of shippers and ship operators" (*Strategic Plan* 1986:34). To serve this end, the Port adopted three general goals:

(1) To increase cargo volume and surpass within the next decade the Port's general cargo tonnage . . . by competing effectively with other U.S. ports;

(2) To restore financial health by generating revenue and cutting costs; and

(3) To contribute to state and regional development by promoting trade and developing Port property. (*Strategic Plan* 1986:34–35)

Our discussion will stress the economic development aspects of the strategic plan by emphasizing the third goal, highlighting how the Port has sought to develop its property. In 1986 there were three types of property owned or controlled by the Port. First was the land and wharf area along the downtown riverfront, which is highly prized for commercial and other development. Second was the Rivergate, a downtown convention and exhibition facility owned and operated by the Port since 1968 but long since superseded by other facilities. Third were the industrial properties in the MRGO and upriver areas, where there is potential for developing additional maritime facilities.

The consultants offered a number of strategies for developing Port property. First, they recommended that the port negotiate a comprehensive approach with the City, the Exhibition Authority (which operates the Convention Center) and other interested parties for use of the Central Business District waterfront, including the Rivergate, for commercial purposes. A comprehensive approach would enable the Port to exploit most efficiently the revenue potential from commercial development of key downtown properties while eliminating the financial drain of Rivergate operations and debt service. In implementing its strategy, the plan says that the Port "should assume the role of catalyst and guide and allow other private and public entities to assume the role of developer" (*Strategic Plan* 1986:39). The plan had a March 1987 deadline for completing an agreement with the City and other governmental agencies on the Rivergate, as well as the preparation of a development plan for the CBD riverfront by April 1987.

Second, in the area of capital improvements to maritime properties, the consultants recommended that the Port pursue relatively low-risk, flexible capital improvement projects in the near term, given financial constraints, while actively planning more substantial developments over the long term. In the short term the plan proposed that the container service along the MRGO at France Road and the wharves along the uptown riverfront be enhanced by rudimentary infrastructure improvements, including new container cranes. In the long term, the plan proposed beginning a planning process to determine where to locate additional container-handling capacity, the need for which is likely to become apparent beginning in the mid-1990s. A detailed five-year capital spending plan was to be completed by April 1987, with infrastructure improvements at France and Jourdan Roads to be completed by December 1988 and improvements on the MRGO to be completed by June 1989.

The plan assumed that the Port will take "a proactive role in commercial and industrial development, provided such development is not in conflict with its maritime interests" (*Strategic Plan* 1986:39). The latter proviso is critical, given the Port's central place in the New Orleans local economy: it has generated some $1.3 billion annually for the New Orleans area economy and has been responsible for 54,000 jobs (Ryan 1992). The fragmentation of the city's economic development effort also gave the Port a tremendous opportunity to exercise a leadership and coordinating role in its efforts to improve maritime-oriented capital facilities and develop downtown riverfront properties.

In June 1986 the Board hired J. Ron Brinson, an energetic, young entrepreneurial bureaucrat, as its new executive director. As the former head of the American Association of Port Authorities (AAPA), he had the experience needed to implement the strategic plan. Through his cost-cutting efforts, the Port succeeded in generating $41 million in cash reserves by 1990. Brinson restructured the organization and made it more entrepreneurial, bringing in new talent and more qualified staff after getting civil service exemption for twenty-one key positions. He also negotiated a new statement of relative Board and management roles and responsibilities, with the Board clearly limited to setting the policy orientation. Finally, Brinson made the Port a more visible player on the local economic development scene.

IMPLEMENTATION ACTIONS AND RESULTS

Capital Facilities

Unlike many other ports, the Port of New Orleans lacked a dedicated source of revenue or tax base to finance capital improvements. Through 1989, the Port had only been able to undertake improvements on a piecemeal basis as self-generated, excess operational revenues became available.

Shortly after Brinson assumed his new duties, the Dock Board began to search for sources of financial support for meeting the major capital needs of the port. At the same time, the newly elected governor, Buddy Roemer, was pushing for additional funding sources to remedy the state's infrastructural deficiencies in order to enable it to meet its economic development potential. Thus, in 1988 the Port leadership, along with other public officials, launched a campaign to gain voter approval of a statewide referendum to increase the gasoline tax by one cent per gallon in order to fund infrastructure improvements throughout the state.

The passage of the Louisiana Transportation Trust Fund amendment on October 7, 1989, afforded the Port an opportunity to rectify infrastructure problems and to construct "market-driven, state-of-the-art facilities needed to effectively compete with other well-financed ports" (Board of Commissioners of the Port of New Orleans 1989). The $100 million provided to the Port through the Fund will be combined with an additional $87 million of the Port's own monies to finance a five-year (fiscal year 1990–1995) Port Improvement Program (PIP) implementing major elements of the strategic plan. The projects along the Upper Mississippi River in uptown New Orleans illustrate the processes of interaction between a special purpose authority (i.e., the Port) and the city in which it operates. We focus on these efforts next.

The master plan for Upper Mississippi River facilities was accepted by the Board on September 11, 1989. This stretch of wharves along the Mississippi River is the busiest in the Port and one of the busiest areas in the country for break-bulk cargo. This area is also seen by the Port as the most viable for growth in the foreseeable future. Current improvement projects (totaling $103 million) are designed to create state-of-the-art wharves with enough berthing capacity to suffice until the year 2010. However, no riverfront development can stand alone. Land access and roads are critical adjuncts. Access to the uptown wharves will be provided through the Tchoupitoulas Corridor.

Thus, the Tchoupitoulas Corridor Project was critical to the Port's efforts. Funds for reconfiguring and widening the existing Tchoupitoulas

Street (a city-owned and city-managed street) to four lanes of traffic were approved with the passage of the Transportation Trust Fund in 1989. The construction of the Tchoupitoulas Corridor project is to be managed by the City and will provide the primary link for trucks carrying cargo between the river wharves and the interstate highway system. The Port has sought to work closely with the City to ensure the upgrading of this artery; the project is also of political importance to the City, since Tchoupitoulas Street is currently inadequate for today's traffic demands, much less for the future increased truck traffic that it will see because of the Port renovations as well as the scheduled closing of the present four major truck routes servicing the port that run through residential neighborhoods. The expansion of the street will take port-related traffic away from residential streets while facilitating easier access for trucks to the uptown wharves and other port-related facilities.

Coordination of the Port and City efforts, however, was difficult. By the fall of 1990, the Port was ready to begin construction work on its biggest project, the consolidation of two uptown wharves into one multipurpose terminal, which will be an unbroken wharf two miles long, one of the longest in the world. At the time, the Port still lacked an agreement from city officials that they would proceed expeditiously on the Tchoupitoulas Corridor project. The Port reasoned that spending millions on upriver capital improvements would be a wasted effort if sufficient access to the new facilities was not forthcoming. Therefore, it was imperative that the two projects — Tchoupitoulas Corridor and Upriver Facilities — be started and completed in tandem. After much negotiation with the City, the Port had in hand by January 1991 signed copies of a tripartite agreement committing the Board, the State, and the City to a confirmed and integrated planning and construction schedule for the Tchoupitoulas Corridor project (Hughlett 1991).

Why was the City so slow in starting the work on the Tchoupitoulas Corridor? In brief, Mayor Barthelemy's office delayed the process. The delay reflected the mayor's anger over Donald Mintz's decision to run against him in the 1990 mayoral race and Mintz's use of his position as chair of the Dock Board as a launching point and a part of his media campaign. The fragmented nature of the bureaucracy within City Hall makes it difficult to implement large projects. Thus, without someone in the mayor's office pushing the project, it was likely to languish. Ultimately, it took pressure from Governor Buddy Roemer and members of the state legislative delegation to get the Tchoupitoulas Corridor project moving. Only after the state threatened to have Tchoupitoulas Street declared a state highway and have it run by the Department of Transportation and

Development did the mayor take a more active role in having a timetable for construction developed.

These events were not atypical. Relations between the Dock Board, an independent state agency, and city government were often conflictual. During the statewide financial crisis of the 1980s, the city-state relationship was highly acrimonious. In the years from 1987 to 1991, Governor Roemer and Mayor Barthelemy frequently disagreed over how much financial assistance the state should provide New Orleans; the Dock Board was often caught in the middle.

This situation is rooted in the port's legal independence from, but economic integration within, the city. The fact that the City has little control over the Dock Board's activities has galled a succession of mayors. The governor appoints Dock Board members from lists of nominees provided by a number of civic organizations; the city government is not a part of the nominating process. Among city officials, the Dock Board is thus viewed as an agent of the state, and this upsets them because the port has such a major impact on the city and its economy. The styles of the two organizations also differ greatly. The Dock Board seems to be a progressive, action-oriented organization, while the city administration is perceived as patronage-ridden and inept. Comparisons between the two are often made, which puts the city at a disadvantage in some quarters, including the administration of Governor Roemer, which had promoted a reform-oriented agenda (see *Times-Picayune* 1990; Warner 1990).

The current city administration shows little appreciation for the maritime industry and the economic role it plays in the city. Indeed, the Barthelemy administration has made tourism the keynote of its economic development strategy. The City Council shares the administration's concern that the City lacks control over the Dock Board. Whether or not the focus on tourism is a valid *economic* decision, politics dictates that City economic development efforts be addressed to sectors it is capable of influencing. In the current structure, the maritime industry is not within its control.

During earlier city administrations, the Dock Board, composed largely of maritime interests, was less visible to the public. Now there is a different composition to the Board and it perceives a need to go to the public more frequently, consistent with Port Director Brinson's management style and personality. The Board is also caught up in issues that are more publicly oriented including the use of public funds for capital projects and disposition of riverfront properties for non-maritime purposes. It is ironic, but perhaps inevitable, that at a time when the Port has come to accept more of its responsibilities relative to the local community and broader economy, relations between the City and the Dock Board have become more strained. Instead of development agendas becoming fused, political imperatives and differing personalities and styles keep them apart. These differences between the Dock Board and the City were nowhere more apparent than in the controversy surrounding the disposition of the Rivergate and other riverfront properties.

RIVERGATE AND RIVERFRONT PROPERTIES

Riverfront Properties

The riverfront in downtown New Orleans has been a blend of maritime and port activities, tourism, and residential development, all in close proximity. Thus, efforts by the Port to develop its properties have unavoidably run into conflict with the City's priorities for adjacent lands.

Many non-maritime interests in the community have argued that the Port should relinquish control of its properties in the downtown riverfront so that these properties can be available for "higher and better uses," namely, upscale commercial and recreational activities. On the other hand, maritime interests have argued that the wharves should be retained permanently for maritime uses in fear that once the property was turned over for alternate activities, it could not be reclaimed. This debate has raged at least since 1969 when the Centroport Study called for the relocation of the port "away from the congested city riverfront" (Bechtel Corporation 1970). More recently, however, there is a growing awareness among some in the maritime community that as expansion of upriver facilities provides opportunity for relocation of cargo activity, certain wharves along the CBD riverfront can be made available for alternate uses. Given the Port's financial dependence on its own revenues, the fact that new uses of its central city properties could be used as "cash cows" to finance additional maritime facilities and operations has not gone unnoticed.

The Port's 1989 master plan for its Mississippi River facilities emphasizes the eventual consolidation of marine terminal operations in a small number of state-of-the-art upriver complexes. This shift will permit the long-term redevelopment of the downtown riverfront, an area covering 4.6 miles. Approximately 1.1 miles is already occupied by the Audubon Institute's Aquarium of the Americas/Woldenberg Park and by two festival marketplaces on either side of the aquarium (Rouse/Riverwalk on the uptown side, and the renovated Jax Brewery Marketplace downriver). The remaining 3.5 miles of riverfront properties will eventually become available for alternative uses, including non-maritime uses. While nearly all of these remaining wharves are presently fully utilized for ship and cargo functions, the Port understands the substantial economic development opportunities attending an eventual transformation of the riverfront.

Attempts at transforming the downtown riverfront have spanned almost a half-century and have pitted major civic and political interests against each other (Katz 1990:40). Throughout this period, the Dock Board has been a major actor, although until recently a rather "invisible" one. The first riverfront battle centered around plans to construct an elevated expressway along the French Quarter banks of the Mississippi River connected to a new Mississippi River bridge on Napoleon Avenue, a major uptown street (see Baumbach and Borah 1980). The pro-growth interests, including the Dock Board, were opposed by preservationists who argued that the riverfront expressway would harm the historic fabric of the French Quarter and forestall any future non-maritime uses of the riverfront. The preservationists won the battle by gaining national support, and the riverfront expressway and the uptown bridge ideas died.

In the place of those ideas came plans to redevelop the riverfront for commercial uses (see Brooks, Baumbach, and Drake 1985). The first major project to involve the Dock Board and the use of downtown wharves was the construction of the Hilton Hotel in 1979 by the International Rivercenter Corporation (IRC) on twenty-three acres adjacent to the Poydras Street Wharf. In return for use of the air rights over the wharf, the Dock Board required a maritime use at the wharf. The IRC partners agreed to the development of an international cruise ship passenger terminal at the Poydras Street Wharf. This pattern of requiring developers to include maritime uses for the wharves adjacent to the land being redeveloped became the standard criterion for the Dock Board in approving the use of its riverfront property through the mid-1980s. These developments included the Rouse Riverwalk, a residual of the 1984 World's Fair, and the Jax Brewery Marketplace.

By the time the Dock Board was faced with a request for one of its wharves for use as the site of the Aquarium of the Americas/Woldenberg Park, the composition of the Board was changing and so was its major concern. No longer dominated by maritime interests, and in need of cash to stem a rising deficit, the Dock Board was willing to negotiate a deal with the City and the Audubon Institute (the nonprofit organization that runs the zoo and the aquarium) for use of the Bienville Street Wharf in return for adequate compensation. After much negotiation, an agreement was ratified by the Board in July 1986 that gave the Audubon Park Commission the right to use of the Bienville Street Wharf for fifty years in return for 9 percent of the gross receipts of aquarium sales, up to a maximum of $25 million.

Strategic Planning for the Port of New Orleans 141

The Dock Board's success in negotiating compensation for use of the Bienville Wharf intensified its acrimonious relationship with the City. City officials felt that the Dock Board should not have requested as much compensation as it did for use of the wharf, given its historical pattern of requiring minimal compensation. The Board was seen as being less than cooperative in the City's efforts to enhance tourist developments along the riverfront. Moreover, city officials were upset that the City had gotten so little in direct revenue from the deal, while the Port was seen as having gained so much. In future negotiations with the Dock Board over riverfront properties, city officials would start with the position that the Dock Board was out to gouge the City and therefore could not be trusted.

Relations between the Dock Board and the City reached such a low level that toward the final weeks of the 1990 mayoral campaign, Mayor Barthelemy and Governor Roemer publicly announced major new riverfront plans without first informing or consulting the Dock Board (*Times Picayune* 1990; Warner 1990). "Riverfront 2000" proposed the use of a number of active downtown wharves for projects ranging from an expanded aquarium to a wildlife museum. The Dock Board responded with indignation that public and private groups (mainly the Audubon Institute) would announce the development of riverfront projects without first consulting the Board, and that the needs of the tourism industry would take precedence over the needs of the maritime industry (which was still using many of the wharves in question).

The Dock Board then called for the development of a master plan to define public interests and public policy standards for redevelopment in the downtown riverfront area, and it indicated its willingness to work cooperatively with the City of New Orleans planning initiatives. However, concerned that projects were being approved on the riverfront in a piecemeal, uncoordinated fashion, the Port held a series of public meetings in the spring of 1990 to receive comments from individuals and interest groups on their vision of future uses of the riverfront. The Port was, in effect, *independently* beginning the public dialogue on what form master planning for riverfront redevelopment should take.

As a result of these meetings the Dock Board in August 1990 adopted a set of standards and values that are to guide planning and redevelopment of the riverfront. It asserted that

> The Board will reserve in perpetuity the waterside of all its riverfront servitude for appropriate ongoing maritime uses. . . . The Board will respond to proposals for alternate landside use of its riverfront wharves that address public objectives identified through credible, highly disciplined planning processes guided by

the broadest possible community participation. Adequate funding for redevelopment projects must be in place prior to Board authorization for reuse. The Board will seek fair and reasonable compensation for the value of maritime facilities which may be adapted for alternative uses. (Board of Commissioners of the Port of New Orleans 1990:26)

The Board will relinquish control of cargo-handling facilities only when replacement capacity is available elsewhere.

The Dock Board did not adopt a pro-active role for itself in the development of a master plan for the riverfront. It felt that such a plan should be developed by the City Planning Commission, but the Board pledged its support to the master planning process. However, the Board stressed that a plan for riverfront redevelopment needed to be in place before downtown wharves would be relinquished for alternate uses. In effect, the Board demanded coordinated citywide development planning by the City. However, the Dock Board did not adhere to its own demand when it sold the Rivergate to the Audubon Park Commission, on behalf of the City, in 1992.

Rivergate

The Rivergate opened in 1968 as the city's first convention center. The Dock Board owned the facility and 20 percent of the land under the Rivergate. The City owned the remaining 80 percent of the land, which was leased to the Dock Board for ninety-nine years with the stipulation that the Board continue to use the facility as a convention center. This restriction made sense when the center was first developed, but it became an onerous burden thereafter.

Due to the construction of other convention facilities and the Louisiana Superdome, the Rivergate became a financial drain on the Dock Board for over twenty years. Like almost all convention centers, it ran large annual deficits in its early years, even when used regularly. Later, when inflation could have raised revenues to levels that would cover operating costs and the $700,000-a-year debt service required for original construction bonds, the inland competition from other convention facilities limited its use. City-imposed restrictions on the use of the property ceased to be appropriate.

In conformance with its strategic plan, the Dock Board pressed for modification of its agreements with the city, so that its land could become a revenue-producing asset providing funds that could be utilized for much-needed maritime facilities. As Director Brinson argued, "if the hospitality industry is unable or unwilling to fulfill this role [of making Rivergate a revenue-generating asset], then the Board's strategic plan requires that it seek the highest and best use of this property in a manner consistent with the City's planning standards" (Brinson 1990).

In November 1987 the Dock Board signed a lease contract with the New Orleans Exhibition Hall Authority (the board responsible for the New Orleans Convention Center) for management and operation of the Rivergate for a three-year period: January 1, 1988, to December 31, 1990. The terms of the lease provided sufficient funds to cover the Dock Board's bonded indebtedness for the Rivergate, and thus the Rivergate ceased to be a financial burden to the Dock Board. The lease was extended for an additional year (through December 31, 1991) because the Exhibition Hall Authority wanted to be able to use the Rivergate for overflow crowds during the time that a 300,000-square-foot extension to the Convention Center was under construction.

The often strained relations between the City and the Port made resolution of the Rivergate problem very difficult and time-consuming. The depth of the strain was at no time more apparent than during negotiations for the use of one wharf, owned in fee simple by the Port, for further extension of the Convention Center. The Port offered to sell the wharf to the City for $1.00 and a change in the Rivergate lease, deleting the requirement that the building be used as a convention-type facility. Concerned that the Port might redevelop the site in such a way as to exclude it from receiving its "fair share" of the proceeds, the City chose instead to leave the Rivergate lease as it was and pay the Port $4.5 million for the wharf. The Port used the sale revenues to buy an additional (used) crane for its docks.

By early 1991 it was obvious to the major actors that a resolution to the problem had to be found, and it came as a result of discussions between the two entrepreneurial leaders of the Dock Board and the Audubon Institute. The Dock Board was under renewed pressure because the Exhibition Hall Authority had served notice that it would be ending its contract with the Dock Board for the use of the Rivergate at the end of 1991. Thus, the Dock Board would again be responsible for the day-to-day management of the Rivergate, and for generating sufficient funds to pay the remaining debt service on the facility. The Audubon Institute was finding payment to the Dock Board for use of the Aquarium site to be onerous, especially since the two differed on how revenue should be calculated. The Institute was also interested in acquiring additional downtown wharves in order to be able to carry out its "Riverfront 2000" plans.

The Audubon Institute served as intermediary with the City, and it convinced Mayor Barthelemy of the need to work with the Dock Board in order to move forward with riverfront redevelopment and to acquire the Rivergate, which was seen as a perfect site for a land-based casino. At that time the legislature was about to pass a bill legalizing a casino for New Orleans, a measure that Barthelemy had long advocated as an economic development tool for the city.

By April 1992, the Riverfront Economic Development Agreement had been signed by the Dock Board, the Audubon Park Commission, and the City Council. Among its major elements, the agreement gives the city full title to the Rivergate and the chance to redevelop it, most likely as a casino; ends the Dock Board's obligation to run the money-losing Rivergate (although it is still responsible for paying off the remaining debt on the facility) and gives it $13 million from the Audubon Commission; and gives the Audubon Park Commission the right to redevelop three additional downtown wharves and end its obligation to pay the Dock Board for the use of the Aquarium site. According to the city's chief negotiator, the Dock Board's desire to cancel the Rivergate lease has been "the fuel that drives this engine" (Eggler 1992).

Because of politics, personality differences, and conflicting management styles and priorities, resolving the Rivergate problem took almost six years. It was only after the leaders of the Dock Board and the Audubon Institute worked out a deal that made sense to their two organizations that they were willing to bring the City into the discussion. Because of the close working relationship between the mayor and the head of the Audubon Institute, the Dock Board was able to get what it wanted — to rid itself of the Rivergate.

CONCLUSION

In assessing the implementation of strategic planning efforts in the Port of New Orleans over the past six years, it seems clear that the Port has done well in achieving goals *internal* to the organization. It has done less well in achieving goals that involve the *external* environment. Without better coordination of efforts with the City as a whole, the Dock Board has simply been unable to efficiently and expeditiously attain its strategic planning objectives.

Two major factors have proved to be problematic in the implementation of these development plans. First and foremost are the different perceptions of the importance of the port in the city's economic development. The port was New Orleans' raison d'être. Historically, it was a

Strategic Planning for the Port of New Orleans 145

major employer and a key economic component. There are those who believe that a revitalized port is central to New Orleans' economic future. Others believe that the city must emphasize a tourism-based strategy in which non-maritime uses take priority over maritime uses on the riverfront. These value differences are reflected in the actions of various political and bureaucratic actors in the implementation process. Second, like many other cities, New Orleans exhibits a high degree of fragmentation in its business and political leadership. The inability to coalesce around common objectives is compounded by an exceptionally high degree of bureaucratic proliferation. The absence of a common set of objectives on the part of local elites has made coordinated efforts by political and business leaders extremely difficult to achieve. At the same time, no independent power bases in neighborhoods or other groups have been able to impose an alternative political agenda.

The result has been inefficiency and delay. Without a common set of objectives shared by all the major power brokers and actors in a city, strategic planning simply cannot succeed. The best-laid plans do not, in and of themselves, lead to full-scale or efficient implementation. In many instances the Dock Board's strategic planning process was more advanced than the City's comprehensive planning process and its economic development strategy. However, fragmentation of goals and power outside of the organization has impeded attainment of its objectives.

Part IV

Comparitive Analysis:
A Case and Some Lessons

10

A Tale of Two Cities: Revitalizing Corby, Northamptonshire, and Youngstown, Ohio

Terry F. Buss

Many public officials try to promote economic development by offering private firms subsidies and incentives to create jobs. Tax abatements, low interest loans, land at below market rates, low rents, grants for employee training, and subsidized wages are the principal tools in this strategy.

Most economists argue that subsidies, although widely used, are either unnecessary or even detrimental to economic development (Rhoads 1985; Sowell 1980; Vaughan, Pollard, and Dyer 1984). Most firms locate or start up in communities because they enjoy competitive advantages: lower production costs, availability and lower cost of materials, and proximity to markets. Subsidies are often too small and short-term to affect this basic calculation. Most firms would have located in the community even without such inducements. Subsidies, therefore, are often simply government giveaways. Subsidies are detrimental to local economies because needed capital or resources are transferred away from potentially viable firms into others that are less competitive and more likely to fail. In any case, the probability of attracting new firms is low: "virtually none of the employment change in an area is due to firms moving" (Birch 1981:5).

Even though subsidies for development make little economic sense, there is much to recommend them politically (Wolman 1988). Public officials argue that if they do not offer subsidies, other communities that do will end up with the jobs. Subsidies are a highly visible means for public officials to demonstrate that they are working for community revitalization. Public officials can reward or punish political interests by offering or withholding incentives. On the other hand, public officials suffer political pressures to distribute subsidies to satisfy influential political interests (e.g., the Chrysler Corporation bailout). Subsidies are preferable because they are expended off-budget, that is, out of public view with little or no public accountability (Redburn and Clarke 1983). Subsidies can make it look like other people are paying for redevelopment — with federal and state, rather than local, monies. But most public officials continue to subsidize simply because they do not understand development finance (Rhoads 1985).

Regardless of economic arguments to the contrary, communities will continue to use subsidies as a development tool.[1] This is especially true in communities experiencing economic crises when political leaders are compelled to take action. The question for many public officials, then, is not whether to use subsidies but how to make the best use of them.

This chapter analyzes economic development strategies of two cities — Corby, England, and Youngstown, Ohio — that heavily employ subsidies. Corby has used subsidies effectively to turn around its distressed economy, but Youngstown, also using subsidies, has continued to decline. Why did one community succeed and the other fail? The sections that follow describe economic crises and recovery in Corby and Youngstown. I next discuss the revitalization strategies of each city. The chapter concludes with some of the lessons learned about implementing effective economic development policy. Methodologically, the findings are based on a combination of participant observation and extensive interviewing.[2]

BACKGROUND

Steel Mill Closings

Both Corby and Youngstown were major steel producers until the late 1970s when demand for steel plunged into permanent decline and world competition, much of it subsidized, eliminated obsolete or unproductive facilities. Corby ceased basic steel production in 1979 when British Steel Corporation laid off about 5,000 workers initially, followed later by another 3,000. The tube works, employing 3,000, remains open. Unemployment in the community of 50,000 rose to 30 percent, second highest in the nation (Brooke Associates 1989).

From 1977 to 1980, Youngstown witnessed the closing of Youngstown Sheet and Tube Company, U.S. Steel Corporation, Jones and Laughlin, and Republic Steel Corporation, a process that idled 7 percent of the total labor force (Buss and Redburn 1983). By 1980 unemployment reached 22 percent — the highest in the nation.

Initial Responses

In the face of mass unemployment, both communities initially responded in the same way — pressuring their respective national governments to reopen the mills. In Corby, the mills were already nationalized under the British Steel Corporation, so closures were perceived as political. In Youngstown, the closures were seen as an opportunity to pressure government into creating a worker-owned, publicly subsidized steel facility (Redburn and Buss 1984).

It soon became clear that Corby could not pressure British Steel Corporation into reopening its mills. British Steel had been forced to close many facilities throughout England, Scotland, and Wales. No community had the political power to reverse these decisions in the face of high taxes and economic decline. Rather than continue to press for a reopening, public officials sought other mechanisms by which to turn around their economy.

Unlike Corby, Youngstown continued to lobby for different schemes to reopen its mills long after it became clear that basic steel production was no longer viable (Redburn and Buss 1984). In 1977, a group of prominent church leaders formed the Ecumenical Coalition of different faiths to raise capital from local citizens and state and federal government to create a steel-working facility that would be worker/community owned. Others were attempting to reopen the mills as a subsidized research center to study steel-making. Later, in 1980, remnants of the Ecumenical Coalition unsuccessfully sued U.S. Steel Corporation to prevent it from closing and hoped to revive the worker/community ownership scheme. Eventually, private entrepreneurs began, with modest success, to reopen portions of the closed facilities.[3]

Corby began its revitalization strategy early after the mill closings. Youngstown delayed for nearly three years, while pursuing what proved to be futile schemes to reopen the mills.

Achievements over a Decade

In the decade following the mill closings, Corby attracted more than 500 new firms to the district and added 13,000 new jobs. Most new jobs are in diversified light manufacturing. Unemployment is now at the national average — around 6 percent. The population is beginning to grow and is projected to nearly double by the year 2000. Some 250 new houses are being added each year, with about £22 million spent on houses so far.

Corby has leveraged more public capital and spent it in more innovative ways than has any other community in Europe or the United States. Youngstown over the decade has attracted many new firms but has failed to retain those firms already in place (Buss and Gemmel 1990; Ledebur 1986). Employment has lagged from 203,983 workers in 1979 to 181,151 workers in 1986, down 11.2 percent. The unemployment rate has dropped to about the national average, but this may be attributable to loss of population and workforce dropouts (Buss and Redburn 1988). The population in the city declined by 9.4 percent from 1980 to 1986, a loss of 11,000 people. During the decade only three new houses were constructed in Youngstown, and thousands of vandalized homes have been demolished.

Youngstown has obtained fewer grants from state and federal government than Ohio's twelve other urban areas. Using the same subsidies and incentives, both cities implemented diametrically opposite strategies.[4]

CORBY'S STRATEGY

Corby's strategy had three components: (1) developing a political structure that could effectively pursue revitalization; (2) marketing the land, buildings, and most of all, the workforce of Corby; and (3) raising unprecedented amounts of public capital so that other British and European taxpayers would pay for revitalizing Corby.

The Politics of Revitalization

Once it became clear that the steel mills would not reopen, Corby's political structure temporarily fell into disarray (Brooke Associates 1989). Local political leaders (23 of 27 were Labour Party members) were faced with the prospect of seeking aid from the newly elected Conservative government of Margaret Thatcher. Many leaders saw no hope for recovery and lacked technical skills and knowledge about economic development. In order to avoid blame for what they perceived would be failure, they allowed two small groups of community leaders a free hand in developing and implementing a revitalization strategy.

The parent group — Joint Industrial Development Committee (JIDC), comprised of representatives from the Corby District Council party leadership and officers, the Northamptonshire County Council, the regional Commission for New Towns, and British Steel Corporation (Industry) — developed the strategy and worked on its implementation.[5] The other group emerged out of the Corby District Council. It implemented the strategy.

The JIDC was critical. It channeled the funds it controlled into Corby and provided valuable contacts to secure funds from others. Most of all, it represented an emerging consensus among community leaders about how to approach revitalization.

But to succeed, Corby had to reform its political structure so that it could take charge of its own destiny. Corby District Council reorganized by eliminating four of its seven executive positions, leaving only the Chief Executive Officer (CEO), the Director of Finance, and the Director of Technical Services. Twenty percent of the Council staff positions were eliminated even though the jobs could have been funded. This was a bold act in a country where more government rather than less is valued by many. An initial action of the streamlined Council was to promote Duncan Hall, a young attorney serving as assistant district chief executive officer, to chief executive officer with primary responsibility for revitalizing the community. The CEO had the support of the party leadership to do whatever was needed to succeed. Revitalization would not have been possible without political power being exerted at the right place and right time without faltering.

One of the first official acts of the CEO was to reassign or retire the local government planners who usually would have been responsible for economic development. The CEO and other officers assumed these duties themselves. The CEO, finance and technical services officers, and party leaders in the District Council formed a select group who would mastermind recovery. Later they created the post of Director of Industry to manage all facets of industrial development in what they called their Industrial Development Centre.

As a first step, the select group and JIDC prepared a blueprint, *A Strategy for Corby: A Community Plan*, that specified what they wanted to achieve as economic goals for the community, how much money or resources would be required, and who was going to pay for the implementation. The blueprint would lead to the leverage of hundreds of millions in pounds sterling. The plan was only about twenty pages long and was completed in a few days without the assistance of expensive outside consultants.

As implementation of the plan progressed, the group, backed by the District Council, learned to waive, ignore, or circumvent the cumbersome planning and development regulations that have stultified the British economy. When a new road was needed at an industrial site, they simply went ahead and built it. When a factory was unable to comply with some building codes, these were waived. The new authorities asked only: "What does industry need to locate here?" Then they supplied it. Even though they were willing to suspend almost any regulation, the group was not willing to support polluters or other undesirable firms simply for the sake of jobs.

As more and more firms were attracted by the ease with which new businesses could be started, and as jobs were offered to laid-off workers, the group accelerated its efforts. The group was authorized to pursue almost any deal on behalf of the community and to offer every imaginable incentive. Several anecdotes illustrate the extent of this activity. An American industrialist was negotiating with the CEO to locate in the community. The deal hinged on the industrialist's request for the antique Jaguar that at the time was the city's official car. In most cities handing over the car, no matter how many jobs were to be created, would be seen as illegal at best. Corby's CEO without a moment's hesitation handed the industrialist the car keys. In another case, an industrialist wanted a street named after his company — Curver, a major multinational producer of plastics — and wanted the grand opening of the company to be presided over by a member of the royal family. Corby District Council immediately named the street, built an asphalt heliport pad, and arranged to fly in a member of the royal family to welcome the new company. Another industrialist needed to break ground immediately in order to insure financial backing for his venture. At the time, the Corby public works crews were busy at another site. The CEO moved the crew in order to land the new firm even though he did not have time to consult the District Council or the unions. Complaints were answered with the question, "What's more important, jobs or regulations?" Few complained after that!

Ultimately, members of the group marshaled enough authority to travel around the world in search of companies, often at considerable expense. Tolerance is the prevailing attitude in the community: if they bring in jobs, then let them wander.

Marketing Corby

Marketing was the cornerstone of Corby's strategy. The group, upon observing other communities, understood that simply advertising a community's image is ineffective and expensive. They realized that any advantages or amenities available in Corby were also available elsewhere. Nearly every community has available land, vacant buildings, infrastructure, locational advantages, and a trained labor force. The group took a different approach. They convinced Oxford University Press to locate its distribution center in Corby. Then they began marketing by boldly stating that the oldest business in the entire country had the confidence to locate in Corby. To maintain their steel-making tradition, they came up with the slogan "Corby Works," a word play on the closed steel facility known as the Corby Works and the fact that its laid-off steelworkers were ready, willing, and able to work. They spent hundreds of thousands of pounds advertising Corby in prestigious publications such as *The Economist*. Their unique marketing approach was wildly successful. At one point, officials were receiving so many inquiries and so many firms were moving to the community that the group took out ads telling prospects not to apply for help in locating in Corby. This stimulated even more inquiries.

In the early years, the group was criticized by the local media, rival politicians, and academicians for being undemocratic and for not creating enough jobs at wages comparable to those in the steel industry (Boulding, Hudson, and Sadler 1988). Adding fuel to the fire, the CEO had written an article for the Association of District Councils' *Review* suggesting that the democratic processes of the council form of government precluded the effective use of economic initiatives and that only a small core of senior officials with broad powers could successfully undertake development activities. The group responded by publishing its own newspaper, *The Ecorbyist*, named after *The Economist*, to which they owed so much of their marketing success. *The Ecorbyist* presented facts and analysis about the projects undertaken on behalf of the community. Eventually local media criticism subsided, although *The Ecorbyist* is still published.

Today, the "Corby Works" slogan is integrated into nearly every aspect of community life. The local soccer team — sponsored by the District Council — plays in a stadium whose seats state "Corby Works" when they are folded up and not in use.

Leveraging Capital

The group felt that if they did not use public capital, other communities would. But Corby was an intensely Labour-oriented community with a Tory national government. The group decided to make Corby the entrepreneurial capital of the world — with government help. Thatcher's ministers were impressed and saw the advantages of helping a Labour-dominated area become more directed toward the free (although subsidized) market. Philosophy of labor and economics aside, Corby was successful in obtaining government money for three reasons: it had a plan detailing what it needed; its leaders had the political will and power to implement the plan and not embarrass the central government; and the CEO and party leadership had the talent to sell anything to anyone.

The essence of their plan was as follows:

1. Demolish the old steelworks and clear the land for an industrial park. The first priority was to assemble and clear "derelict" land from the old steelworks. Several grants, one for £19 million from central government and another for £2 million from the European Economic Community (EEC), were obtained for this purpose. Within two short years, what had been an expansive steelworks — 270 hectares — loaded with reinforced concrete foundations 20 feet deep, strewn with blast furnaces 10 stories high, and steeped in asbestos had been reduced to a vacant piece of land.

The significance of the demolition and recovery of the land was twofold: first, it provided the community with a valuable piece of property to market. Second, and perhaps more important, it represented a psychological break with the days of steel production and heralded a new era of entrepreneurship. Clearing the land forced people to look ahead and provided something tangible to anticipate.

2. Market land within a designated enterprise zone. In June 1981, Corby became the first Enterprise Zone in England.[6] In the Enterprise Zone, private sector entrepreneurs were given considerable leeway in managing their affairs with minimal regulation from government and a ten-year tax and rent abatement (Butler 1981).

Other distressed urban areas in the United Kingdom received Enterprise Zone status. Nearly all have failed to meet expectations. At present, land in Corby is becoming scarce. As a result, land values have skyrocketed. A decade ago, land could not be given away. Today, the region is alive with land speculators and developers.

3. Improve the infrastructure at industrial sites, and create small business incubators and "advanced factories." The District Council secured grants to provide utilities to their new industrial sites. The central government provided an initial grant of £3 million. The New Towns Commission has spent about £12 million every year since the plant closing. And the EEC's Regional, Social, and Energy Funds contributed about £130 million. The group built flexible industrial spaces on speculation to attract businesses. Speculation on commercial sites is risky, but in this case it paid off: few vacancies are available.

4. Control vacant land for future development. Once the group had assembled initial properties, they correctly anticipated future land specula-

tion. They began purchasing all the land they could to hold until needed for development or to sell to raise public revenue. Today, they are able to get market value for public land when it is in the interest of the community to sell it. In so doing, they have created a stream of non-tax revenue to use for other projects and for community services.

5. Exploit grants and loans to offer subsidies and incentives to business. The CEO quickly learned to "wheel and deal" with central government departments offering grants and loans. Eventually, the community became a partner with government departments. Corby packaged "good" deals in a professional manner, and the government departments were confident that the deals would not return to haunt them.

In addition to exploiting U.K. programs, Corby was one of the first and the most successful communities to obtain funding for development from the European Economic Community. BSC (Industry) made this liaison possible.[7]

6. Promote community development as an economic development tool. The group realized that economic development must go hand in hand with community development. The group initiated several innovative community development projects. They were one of the first district councils to sell public housing to tenants. Units were turned over to tenants for £1,000 apiece, since housing stock in Corby was run down and would soon require demolition. After transfers of ownership, housing improved at the same time that demand shot up, increasing the value of these same units to nearly £75,000 apiece. Now, developers have constructed and sold tracts of luxurious townhouse units — further driving up land values.

Also because of the rapid growth in the community, the District Council created a large urban park with its own steel museum to recount and preserve the past glories of that industry, built its own hospital because existing national health service facilities were inadequate, and renovated an olympic-size swimming pool for local residents.

7. Enhance the image of the community. Before the steel closures, Corby was not well known because it is small and not centrally located. Corby is not on a major rail line from London. After a one-hour trip by train, travelers must venture fifteen to twenty minutes by car after leaving the station at Kettering. Feeling that this created image problems, the District Council purchased a rail spur and created its own station facility so that Corby now appears on the transit maps in the United Kingdom.

Corby wanted to get away from its image as a steel town. It succeeded by picking up industrialists, dignitaries, and public officials at the rail station in the city's new Jaguar, lodging visitors in one of the many restored historic inns, and providing private tours of famed Rockingham Castle.

The district is in the middle of fox-hunting country, which officials hasten to point out. Corby has managed to improve its image by going upscale while not forgetting the steel workers who built the community — the "Corby Works" theme.[8]

YOUNGSTOWN'S STRATEGY

Youngstown was unable to develop a unified strategy following its initial efforts to reopen the mills. Numerous groups and organizations sprang out of the reopening efforts, all vying for their share of economic development funding. As more claimants were added, the shares grew smaller and participants began to see their efforts as a zero sum game: "you win, I lose." With no clear winners in sight, claimants eventually settled into a stalemate, taking what they could get and attempting to thwart the efforts of competitors. Out of frustration, the private sector eventually attempted to create its own competitive organization to impose consensus, but this only added another competitor to the crowded field. Only by late 1990, more than a decade after the plant closing, had this deadlock begun to show signs of easing up.

A Crowded Field

Before introducing the players in the development game, it is necessary to understand the regional politics. The region is made up of two counties: Mahoning and Trumbull. Mahoning includes Youngstown, along with the cities of Campbell, Struthers, Canfield, and Lowellville, as well as three major townships: Boardman, Austintown, and Poland. Trumbull includes Warren, along with numerous villages and townships. For years, Mahoning dominated local politics and economics because the steel mills were mostly located there — ironically in Campbell, Struthers, and Lowellville, not Youngstown. When the steel industry was declining in the late 1960s, Trumbull attracted the Lordstown General Motors plant, becoming a separate economic power in the region. In addition to economic restructuring, people began moving out of the cities into the suburbs, lured by shopping malls, new housing, and low crime rates. Over the past thirty years, then, there have been continuing battles: Youngstown versus Warren, small cities and villages versus big cities, cities versus suburbs, neighborhoods versus the city versus the downtown, and Trumbull County versus Mahoning County.

Nearly every political jurisdiction has had at least one economic development organization, and the region itself boasted several organizations. Each organization was funded by a combination of local, state, and federal monies representing different agencies. Private funding was also widely distributed. On a regional level, the development effort annually consumed tens of millions of dollars, yet each participant received a relatively small share.[9]

The Players

The local economic development groups and organizations have been described in detail in other publications (Buss and Vaughan 1989). What is important to grasp is the multiplicity of the organizations that are involved in economic development. The region has its own economic development corporation — Mahoning Valley Economic Development Corporation (MVEDC) — supported by state grants and a Small Business Administration 503 revolving loan fund. It operates two industrial parks. The cities of Campbell, Struthers, Lowellville, and Poland have sponsored an economic development corporation (CASTLO) with its own state-subsidized industrial park. The region also is the only one in Ohio with a branch office of the Ohio Department of Development. Downtown Youngstown is represented by four groups: the city Department of Development, the Youngstown Revitalization Foundation (funded by the Economic Development Administration, or EDA, and Community Development Block Grants), the Board of Trade, and Youngstown Area Chamber of Commerce. Youngstown State University, located in the downtown, has a small business incubator, a small business development center, a small business technical assistance center, an entrepreneurship training program, a technology transfer office, an office to assist firms requiring engineering expertise, and several departments to conduct research on economic development issues. A regional planning body — an A-95 review agency — is funded by federal government.[10] The Youngstown Area Chamber of Commerce has created a Regional Growth Alliance, whose entire focus is to promote economic development. Two venture capital firms, one community-oriented and the other privately owned, are active in economic development affairs. Because of intense politics in the past, the region has three Private Industry Councils, whereas most communities have only one. Minority groups have their own funded organizations; one operates a technical assistance program, the other operates a revolving loan fund using Community Development

Block Grant monies. Neighborhood and merchant groups are quite powerful: there are two merchants' groups that have received a great deal of public funding, and one highly successful (in terms of funding) neighborhood group. Added to these groups in Youngstown are a comparable number of organizations representing Warren, only thirteen miles to the north.

Expertise

Traditionally, in Youngstown, economic development and planning positions have gone to people with little expertise or technical skills. These appointments are typically viewed as political patronage. Even when organizations have sought out experts, the very best have not been willing to relocate in Youngstown.[11] As a result of this continuing lack of expertise, the area not only is unable to execute the basics but lags behind others in innovation. In effect, then, the money raised by the community for economic and community development has not paid dividends. As an example, the Youngstown Revitalization Foundation failed to initiate a single development deal in its first five years in existence.

Strategies

Youngstown considered a series of strategies offered by different organizations over the decade, but community organizations could agree to none.

1. The Mahoning Valley Economic Development Corporation (MVEDC) received a grant from EDA to prepare a Comprehensive Economic Development Strategy (CEDS) for the region in 1978. MVEDC contracted with Battelle Memorial Institute in Columbus, Ohio, to prepare the plan. Battelle took a traditional approach to development and conducted a targeted industry strategy weighing the "advantages" of the community's economic base against the needs of industry. The strategy produced a list of targeted industries that the community could attract.

The strategy was never implemented because the community had neither the expertise nor the resources to pursue it. This may have been fortunate, because all the targets turned out to be declining or irrelevant industries.

2. The Ecumenical Coalition pressured EDA into funding a feasibility study for reopening the mills as an alternative to the CEDS. The plan would have employed about one-half the laid-off steelworkers and would

have required the federal government to grant $500 million in aid to initially subsidize the mill and, after reopening, to continue the subsidy by purchasing steel from the mill at above market prices.

Although a great deal of effort was expended, the reopening never materialized. The Carter administration had allocated only $500 million in assistance to other steel-makers nationwide; Youngstown had no standing for such a claim. Many steel experts doubted whether the proposed scheme was possible even with the subsidies. But anyone who opposed the plan was publicly criticized for not supporting the community. This intimidated people with legitimate proposals for recovery. Elected officials who spoke out were threatened with electoral retaliation.

3. Following these two initiatives, planning began to focus on the downtown area. The city Department of Development, the Youngstown Revitalization Foundation, the business school at Youngstown State University, Kent State University, and two architectural firms (one local, one regional) were each publicly funded to prepare separate plans. The plans had much in common, although they were intended to compete with one another. All focused on storefront renovation, historic preservation, urban design, and investment in public buildings as the keys to recovery. It was hoped that the downtown could be returned to a turn-of-the-century business district characterized by urban parks, pedestrian malls, farmers' markets, and the like. At the same time, extensive networks of overhead walkways were envisioned. Interspersed throughout would be artist lofts, student dorms, office condominiums, and apartments for the wealthy tied in with low-income housing. Vacant department stores would be replaced by small boutiques. On the public side, government would invest in a new city/county jail, federal courthouse, state government office tower, consolidation of local government offices downtown, high rises for the elderly, a historic steel museum, a convention center, and new welfare office, all linked with parking decks and skywalks.

So far, none of these schemes has come to pass, although the public sector has constructed two high rises for the elderly and a steel museum, which has yet to open for lack of funding. The welfare department has moved from the downtown. Although they have not yet been scientifically studied, most of the projects seem to have failed because they were not convincing enough to raise public or private capital.

4. Out of frustration with the lack of progress, the Youngstown Area Chamber of Commerce created the Regional Growth Alliance (RGA) to devise and implement a strategy. Youngstown State University prepared the two-part plan. The first was a comprehensive state-of-the-art development plan. Major consultants from across the country were hired to prepare separate strategies for housing, training, human services, infra-

structure, education, small business, and more.[12] The consultants were chosen because of their success in implementing innovative projects in other cities. The second report was a targeted industry strategy prepared by a top consulting firm in the field.

Neither prong of the strategy was ever implemented — even in part. The community continued to lack knowledgeable, committed civil servants and public economic development experts. Community leaders, although impressed with the plan, did not throw their weight behind it to make it work. The targeted industry strategy would have failed in any case: retrospectively, all of the targets either were bad investments (e.g., gas and oil exploration) or were trivial (e.g., detective services).

5. In 1986, Ohio Water Services, a private sector, multistate provider of municipal water, approached the development community to obtain funding for a market/feasibility study to determine if any of its lakes that supply water could be converted into a recreation area and office complex without jeopardizing water quality or supplies. If the project were feasible, then the Ohio Water Service, which has a major real estate development division, would develop the project. The Ohio Department of Development allocated $50,000 to the project. Organizations not involved in the study also lobbied to get their own funding. The state regional economic development coordinator, feeling political pressure, divided the funding provided to the Ohio Water Service project among four counties for each to develop separate strategies. These might (but did not) include the Ohio Water Service project. The four counties never produced any plan. Ohio Water Service has since lost interest in the project.

6. At present, the Youngstown Area Chamber of Commerce is attempting to raise several hundred thousand dollars in private funding for another targeted industry strategy to be conducted by Youngstown State University. Researchers are going to examine strictly national data (and only for manufacturing) to identify growing industrial sectors. Experts in these sectors will be hired to study firms that might like to relocate in Youngstown.

Marketing

Youngstown has embarked upon numerous marketing campaigns, some of which are noteworthy. The Youngstown Area Chamber of Commerce prepared a mailing in Japanese to Japanese industrialists asking them not to invade U.S. markets, but in the same breath requesting them to consider Youngstown as a place to locate. They got no responses. Another endeavor involved taking out full-page ads in *Newsweek* magazine, each featuring several local industrialists and community leaders who extolled the virtues of local markets for doing business. These were intended as vanity pieces for local consumption rather than as serious national marketing. At present, marketing focuses on preparing documents describing the demographics and economic base of the community. Videotapes touting the community's virtues were also prepared for mass mailing. These products are similar to information already available to prospects from the local utility companies.

Selected Projects

The community tried to replace steel with aviation and to promote its airport. Enormous subsidies and incentives were offered to aviation entrepreneurs. Over four years, at least five firms attempted to start projects. One company was to build intermediate propeller-driven aircraft (larger than commuter aircraft, but smaller than a DC 5) to cover short hauls. With EDA and state funding, a factory was constructed. No aircraft were ever built: there was no market and the designs were flawed. The project was mismanaged, and only after many months was the assignment of assets and debts sorted out in federal court. This was followed by numerous other prospects in aviation, the most notable being the British Airship Corporation, a manufacturer of blimps. It was felt that there was a major market for these craft. They also were never built. This should not have surprised anyone because Goodyear — the world's expert in blimps, which is located a short forty-five miles from Youngstown — has yet to sell its blimps commercially.

Another large-scale project involved constructing a canal to accommodate barge traffic — a kind of domestic Panama Canal. The local congressman was successful in obtaining more than $1 million from Congress (which was then withdrawn) for the U.S. Army Corps of Engineers to study the possibility of linking Lake Erie with the Ohio River. Many resources were expended locally.

Local development officials liked the Reagan administration's enterprise zone initiative. An enterprise zone was created out of former steel mill properties. So far, the only tenant is North Star Steel, which would have had to locate at the site regardless of the zone incentives. Plans are now under way to designate much of Trumbull County as one large enterprise zone. On a more modest level, CASTLO is seeking to have its industrial park declared a zone.

None of the large-scale projects, including a catalog of others not discussed here, ever could have succeeded. They lacked markets, they were economically infeasible even with subsidies, inexperienced people often were promoting them, and most of the projects had some hidden agenda: a developer, politician, or consultant appeared to gain even if the project failed.

These projects required a great deal of community resources. University researchers, economic development corporation staffs, city officials, private business people, organizations like the Chamber of Commerce often had to drop everything to work on some aspect of these efforts. As a result, serious flaws in the community have frequently been ignored. For example, education was deemed the first priority for economic development; yet nothing has been done in this area. Citizens have continually rejected levies to support the schools. One election saw a referendum to give operation of the schools back to the state only narrowly defeated.

Perhaps the greatest impact of the development effort has been to create a skeptical attitude on the part of the community. Once this occurs, it is difficult to marshal community support.

EXPLAINING SUCCESS AND FAILURE

It is dangerous to generalize from two cases. Analysts can never be sure whether they are observing the exception or the rule. Furthermore, in thinking about effective implementation of public policy, analysts cannot be sure whether the factors identified are necessary or sufficient to guarantee success or failure. Nevertheless, several lessons about implementation are apparent.

1. *The window of opportunity.* When plant closings, mass unemployment, or other economic shocks strike, community leaders have a rare opportunity to put into motion strategies that they would otherwise never have been able to accomplish (see Buss and Vaughan 1989). Those with a stake in the status quo are temporarily in disarray. But the opportunity to respond positively to a crisis may not last long. Eventually, existing power structures reorganize and emerging ones must be faced. Corby and Youngstown both illustrate the opportunity for change. Because opportunities for change are rare, community leaders must quickly chart some course that is likely to pay off. Corby chose correctly. Youngstown did not.

2. *Public entrepreneurs.* Just as the private sector relies upon entrepreneurs for innovation, the public sector must have comparable people to make economic development and planning responsive to change. Successful public entrepreneurs have goals in mind for a com-

munity, agency, or themselves, which they will pursue regardless of the obstacles placed before them. When faced with barriers, they tend to step outside the system and do whatever it takes to achieve their goals. They are good at raising funding for projects — or, more properly, they are good at spending other people's money to achieve their own goals. Public entrepreneurs become activated during a crisis — like mass unemployment — because they see opportunities where others only see distress. The average administrator sees unemployment as creating unwanted increases in clients demanding services, while the public entrepreneur sees the same situation as an opportunity to offer specialized services or innovative programs. Many of the successful revitalization efforts, like those undertaken in Corby, reflect consummate public entrepreneurism. Youngstown, by contrast, reflects the bureaucratic, perhaps anti-entrepreneurial approach. In times of crisis, the routine may not succeed.

3. *Rules and regulation.* Some people fear that mechanisms such as enterprise zones could weaken regulatory safeguards promulgated by the bureaucracy to protect society. Corby's experience suggests that the worst fears of deregulation may be unfounded if regulatory policy is under local control. By contrast, in Youngstown, where rules were not waived, no progress was made.

4. *Technical expertise.* Corby's strategy was conceived by public entrepreneurs, many of whom had considerable experience and knowledge. But implementation was undertaken by experts in all phases of economic development who were willing to work for these public entrepreneurs. In Youngstown, people who were not public entrepreneurs and had no development experience designed ill-conceived strategies that were carried out by amateurs, many of whom had hidden agendas. Technical expertise in carrying out economic development cannot be overvalued.

5. *Public partnerships.* Strategies that require the infusion of huge amounts of public investment into communities necessitate a close working partnership between local communities and national (or in the United States, federal and state) government. Government officials must have confidence that their investments will be well spent — that is, spent to satisfy their goals. Government officials are more likely to grant waivers or allow flexibility if they are confident that their decisions will not come back to haunt them. Government officials are very likely to reinvest heavily in communities having successful track records. Central government in England and the EEC in Brussels needed a Corby as much as Corby needed them. There have been too few success stories in Europe that involve massive public funding. In the United States and Ohio, officials needed a Corby also. In the case of Youngstown, every investment made

was controversial — and most failed. Public partnerships are essential for success. Simply leveraging money may not be.

6. *Subsidies and incentives.* Some may argue that subsidies and incentives were necessary to achieve Corby's level of success. Without subsidies, they argue, Corby would have perished. Many of the public entrepreneurs involved in revitalizing Corby feel the same way. But Corby's experience can be interpreted differently. Nearly every distressed city in all of the western democracies has had access to the same basic array of subsidies as Corby did. If subsidies were all that was necessary, then there would be more successes like Corby. What Corby illustrates is that the right public entrepreneurs can create a stampede of development activity that occurs regardless of whether there are subsidies or not. What Corby was able to do was to convince private sector entrepreneurs that Corby was a better place to make a pound than anywhere else. Corby did this by being just as entrepreneurial as the entrepreneurs it sought to attract. Youngstown, by contrast, convinced potential prospects that their investments were at risk: red tape, lack of expertise, politics, and insecurity outweighed the meager gains expected through subsidies and incentives.

NOTES

1. Competitiveness among communities and states is fueled by the annual publication of rankings, which often include the availability of subsidies as a criterion. For example, the Corporation for Economic Development issues an annual Report Card on the States, much of which is based upon subsidies and incentives. Dun and Bradstreet annually ranks cities on the basis of rates of new business incorporations.

2. Most of the conclusions reported here come from studies and continuous participant observation in Youngstown since 1977 and in Corby since 1985. Numerous federal, state, and local grants have allowed me to study nearly every aspect of economic decline and recovery in Youngstown over the past fourteen years (Buss and Redburn 1983; Buss and Vaughan 1989). In addition, I have participated in many of the revitalization projects undertaken by the city. My conclusions about Corby come largely from interviews conducted with nearly 100 people responsible for its revitalization. These interviews were conducted not only with officials from Corby but also with British Parliament members, European Parliament members, European Economic Community officials, officials of the U.K. Departments of Industry and Environment, and citizens living in Corby. In all, four separate visits to Corby were made, and Corby officials visited me in Youngstown on four occasions.

3. MacDonald Steel is an important success story. MacDonald, formerly a U.S. Steel branch plant, was started by David Houck, a manager who was laid off when the works closed. He identified a market inadequately served by major steel companies, raised venture and equity capital, and began the business anew eight years ago. Since

then the company has flourished and he has won numerous prestigious awards for entrepreneurship. He accomplished this without subsidies.

4. Both the United States and the United Kingdom have much the same development tools. Practitioners in each country tend to use them differently.

5. Corby is a New Town founded in 1939. For a description of New Towns' government and programs, see Gideon Golany (1978). British Steel Corporation (BSC) is Britain's nationalized steel industry. In the wake of mill closures in the late 1970s and 1980s, BSC formed a corporation, BSC (Industry), to help communities recover. BSC (Industry) focuses on encouraging reuse of obsolete and underutilized steel facilities, often by setting up industrial parks.

6. Originally, Corby was not assigned Enterprise Zone status. Through effective lobbying, Corby was able to acquire one of only twenty-three Enterprise Zones. The lobbying effort illustrates the public entrepreneurial capacity of the city.

7. It has yet to be established why other BSC (Industry) officials failed to successfully pursue EEC funding.

8. Resources did not permit study of the socioeconomic status of steel workers following the closing. It is unclear whether, in purely economic terms, they have been affected positively or negatively by economic growth in Corby.

9. Numerous attempts have been made to determine how much funding from all sources has been spent on economic development (including training, infrastructure, subsidies, and education). So far, no one in Ohio has succeeded in piecing the puzzle together.

10. A-95 review refers to an Executive Order of the President requiring establishment of regional organizations to review many federal grant proposals submitted to the state for funding by federal agencies. The intent of the process is to insure that the projects are in the best interest of the region.

11. Interviews with prospects who did not locate in Youngstown suggest that they were not pleased with local politics, low salaries, and lack of resources.

12. Analysts who worked on the project include the following: Marc Bendick, Jr., of Bendick and Egan Associates; Larry Ledebur of Aslan Associates; Steve Redburn of the U.S. Department of Housing and Urban Development; Hugh O'Neill of the Port Authority of New York and New Jersey; and Roger J. Vaughan of Roger Vaughan and Associates.

11

On the Possibility of Pro-Active Community Development

David Fasenfest

> Conflicts hitherto restricted to the private sphere now intrude into the public sphere. Group needs which can expect no satisfaction from a self-regulating market now tend towards a regulation by the state. The public sphere, which must now mediate these demands, becomes a field for the competition of interests.
>
> Habermas 1974:54

The economic restructuring and deindustrialization of the past two decades are now well-discussed phenomena. So is the more recent shift in the relationship between the national and local governments as each alternately ignores or tries to come to terms with the social consequences of these changes on the local economy. Policy debates raged over whether it was better for communities to (1) engage in smokestack chasing to attract businesses in order to replace lost jobs as firms moved away or shut down permanently, or (2) pursue a program of development that relied on rebuilding from within based upon the community's strengths and comparative advantages (Eisenger 1989).

These local changes occurred within a shifting national political stage. In the United States, President Reagan's "New Federalism" encouraged and enhanced the managerial function of local governments as it withdrew federal support. At the same time, fiscal retrenchment and funding cutbacks forced communities to compete with each other and rely on shrinking funds to attract and retain investment. The result was more intense and destructive local and regional rivalries (Markusen 1987).

In the United Kingdom, the victory of the Conservatives over the Labour Party heralded the era of Thatcherism dedicated to remove government from the field of business. Local government, often under the control of Labour Party members trying to promote a new urban vision (Boddy and Fudge 1984) that would address the failure of the Labour government to realize its promises (Coates 1980; Howell 1980), fell at odds with the central government. Through a series of Local Government Acts, Thatcher's government weakened the powers of the Labour authorities, replacing powers with a series of appointed quasi-governmental organizations with central government funding.

In both cases the central question was how to rebuild the local economy so that it would be competitive in the new era. The problem was defined in terms of how to get the community back to work at the lowest price. Job creation usually meant votes, so emphasis shifted quickly to incentive packages to attract or retain employers.

Underlying all these discussions was an implicit rejection by central governments of planning and managed growth in favor of a shift to the marketplace and its signaling mechanisms. Market mechanisms were assumed to be more efficient at allocating and utilizing resources. Any attempt at controlling or manipulating production outcomes through the intervention of public policy or direct control was seen as distorting otherwise optimal solutions. This ideological rationale was inconsistent with the policies implemented: provision of subsidies that were, themselves, market distortions.

Moreover, this kind of thinking begs the question of whose interest local development policies and programs were designed to satisfy and meet. Local development in a market context encompasses more than decisions on new water treatment plants or motorway extensions. Rather, local development now has come to mean using public resources and credit for the purpose of providing guarantees and co-payments and in some cases actually underwriting the cost of private adventures. In the former case, costs and benefits are caused directly by the public action. In the latter instance, profits accrue to the investors, while the public benefits depend on counterfactual and presumptive direct (job creation) and indirect (increased local tax revenue) impacts.

This chapter examines the underlying impact and logic of market-centered approaches to achieving socially desirable outcomes, and it considers the recent examples of policy implementation presented in this volume. The chapter concludes with some suggestions for refocusing local economic development by rejecting the market model and returning to processes that involve community input into deciding upon policy choices. The chapter further argues that communities must anticipate and articulate their needs as a way of helping to set and reshape the limits of the policy debate over local economic development.

THE MARKETPLACE AS THE PROVING GROUND FOR PUBLIC POLICY

The underlying premise of a capitalist society is that privately held resources will be most efficiently utilized under conditions in which each actor tries to maximize returns on investments at the expense of all others. This mutual self-interest acts as a check on any one person gaining the upper hand over all others and ensures an optimal solution in terms of resource utilization and product array.

The exceptions to this rule of market efficiency are a class of products that have generally been called public goods. Three conditions warrant public sector interventions in markets:

1. when the cost structure of producing goods deemed necessary to society (e.g., police and fire protection) shows economies of scale that warrant collective provision;

2. when the start-up costs might outweigh the value of initial provision of a good or service until the customer base is high (e.g., power generation or water treatment); and

3. when a product serves everyone in ways that cannot be adequately assessed, so a price structure is not possible or feasible (as is the case of infrastructure improvements or roadway construction).

Although provision for such goods by the state might engender some inefficiencies, the failure to intervene in markets for such goods or to provide them where no market existed was assumed to cost more than the expense of provision. Even these assumptions justifying some public action have come under siege by the "New Federalism" and Thatcherism, as they moved continuously to shrink the circle of public sector activities.

Notwithstanding the privatization push of the past decade, the reliance on the market is suspect. The classification of producer and consumer in the private sector must be distinguished from the producer and consumer of public goods. Consumer demand in the latter realm reflects political voice and participation in agenda-setting rather than direct participation in the exchange of a product. Similarly, production of public goods is less often a matter of cost-based selection criteria among alternatively priced options, but rather the direct provision of some product deemed socially necessary and broadly consumed. The cost efficiency criteria ruling private market–based decision making do not readily apply to the provision of public goods, although some have tried to measure the degree of consumer surplus inherent in public goods as a way of choosing from among alternative policy options (Gramlich 1981).

The rhetoric of the past decade has held that the public sector in general, and local government in particular, should begin to operate according to private sector–market decision-making processes. To do otherwise was deemed to encourage misdirected outcomes and to invite (if not altogether guarantee) waste and misappropriation of resources. The reality is that different measures of success undermine the possibility of such emulation.

Profits drive the private sector, and for profits products must be sold; sales and net revenues thus measure the success or failure of a private producer's activities. Social objectives drive public policy (albeit economic objectives in the case of local development policy), so issues like net increases in employment or positive improvements in the infrastructure (social or physical) inform policy makers and the public at large as to whether or not the policies have succeeded. These often incongruous criteria have, of late, become conflated in the national and local debate over the shape of local development policy. Programs, indeed the whole enterprise of local development policy, are deemed successful if they appear to have positive effects upon the business climate. (See Bartik 1991 for a recent, and very thorough, review of local policies and their effectiveness in promoting business activity.)

But will this conflation lead to progress or confusion? The social goals may become subverted by the market means when there are multiple objectives, especially when the outputs are all public goods. Social conflict arises when, as is inevitable, different public goods serve different subsets of the society. Political power, not market demand, then determines the public goods actually produced.

When social programs target the marketplace to provide public goods (in this case in the form of renewed investment in the built environment and job creation and/or retention), they hope to induce private actors to change their existing behavior through a variety of subsidies. However, when policies are defined only to permit outcomes consistent with social goals, and not profit maximization, little happens. When policy guidelines are relaxed or programs redesigned to broaden their appeal to private sector decisionmakers (i.e., to permit profit considerations to operate), then the social goals are potentially sacrificed. There is no basis for assuming that profit-maximizing and social-maximizing behavior will ever coincide.

I have argued elsewhere (Fasenfest 1988) that non-market programs can be viewed as direct social interventions on the allocation of society's resources. Through a combination of revenue-generating programs (taxes, fees, etc.) and programmatic expenditures, the public sector redirects how resources are being used and in whose benefit. In this way social problems are dealt with (perhaps less efficiently, but more directly).

Programs that rely on the marketplace, on the other hand, intervene in the resource allocation process in the hope that shifting market incentives will result in some other outcome. The social problems that arise out of one pattern of resource distribution may not emerge if another pattern is obtained as a result of market incentives. What gets ignored is the fact that the marketplace favors those with capital over those without, and decisions are made to increase and concentrate the capital stock rather than to redistribute that stock. As a result, market mechanisms will certainly reinforce existing inequities, and the degree to which social goals are realized is more a function of serendipity than design.

POLITICS AND COMMUNITY IN LOCAL DEVELOPMENT

Local development policy takes many forms and reflects competing and shifting strategies and orientations within the community (Fitzgerald and Cox 1990), between the community and region, and even between the community and the national economy. Community economic development is a contested concept both at the level of community (who is to be included?) and in the meaning of development (how will it be manifest?). Local development has a temporal and spatial dimension (Cox 1992) that changes with respect to the competing constituencies articulating expectations from the policy process. Different interests representing past practices and policies, different class positions, financial or industrial capital, established and new community residents, and even the heretofore disenfranchised all vie for a chance to direct the community development policy agenda. However, the policy process is an iterative one in which past outcomes both reflect the balance and nature of existing social and political power and constrain the range of available policy choices (Fasenfest 1986). Underlying all these conflicts is the question of the nature of the local state (as the arena of discussion and debate) in relation to the national political structure.

Before examining the consequences and impacts of turning to the marketplace for social policy goals, we must first consider how political structure and the conceptualization of community define the context in which these policies are played out. We can celebrate the uniqueness of each case study, but it is through a discussion of differences that we can also see how commonalities provide lessons from a market-centered approach to local development.

It is important to keep in mind that political processes, existing and proposed development programs, and even the language defining problems and solutions are contingent upon the larger cultural context. Politics in different countries reflects historical and social patterns that alter the impact of terms, inform the nature of alliances, and shift the policy goals. P. Meyer (1991b) and H. Wolman (1992) have both argued that even the same words have different meaning when policies in the United States and the United Kingdom are being compared. For this reason they caution against assuming that programs with apparently similar origins and surrounding rhetoric can be easily and readily transferred from one country to another.

Gerd Hennings and Klaus Kunzmann (see Chapter 3 in this volume) make this point very strongly when they discuss the experiences of one region in Germany. Pointing to the problems of directly comparing similarly labeled programs, they remind us that any discussion of local development and local policy initiatives must carefully consider that the U.S. experience is predicated on a separation between the local and the federal government on most issues pertaining to the locality, whereas in Germany that relationship is very intertwined. Although local governments have nominal independence, the social history that includes a strong labor representation in both local government and on corporate boards ensures that the federal government provides subsidies in order to ensure an accepted quality of life.

These cultural differences notwithstanding (and perhaps having more to do with drawing direct comparisons in order to inform policies in one or another country), we can still examine the nature of politics in local policy implementation. Alma Young and Robert Whelan (see Chapter 9) show how purely political bickering and jurisdictional quarrels can interfere with setting a development program. Any attempt to create and implement a program to revitalize the harbor in New Orleans raises questions of who gets to define which interests are important, what sorts of projects get promoted, and how resources with multiple claimants are to be developed. Notwithstanding the question of competing definitions of the marketplace (more on that will follow), Young and Whelan describe a system of overlapping jurisdictions and competing agendas that in one way or another retard the overall development effort.

Political conflict can result in positive outcomes as well. As Terry Buss (see Chapter 10) demonstrates, the particular mix of entrepreneurial leadership and aggressive disregard for established local legislation by a closed circle of local leaders was made possible largely due to the desire of a newly empowered Conservative national government to undermine Labour-controlled local governments. As has been mentioned, it was not just the local governments but the underlying political philosophy that Labour represented that was the target of the Thatcher government. As a result, monies and programs that might not have been otherwise forthcoming bolstered Corby's market-centered program for growth.

A shift from national to local political structures as the locus of community development has increasingly raised a tension between the often contradictory goals of job creation and cost effective strategies (Pelissero and Fasenfest 1989). William Lever (see Chapter 5) notes that local governmental agencies in the United Kingdom shift away from job goals, while in the United States job creation (albeit not always correctly applied; see Giloth 1992) becomes one of the main criteria for assessing local policies.

But whom do these policies serve? What is the meaning of community in community development? These are precisely the questions raised by Huw Thomas and Rob Imrie in their analysis of south Cardiff (see Chapter 8). Existing businesses and residential communities do not appear to be part of that definition as redevelopment policies move to transform the local economy. Improvements do not seem to be designed to improve or take into account the conditions facing those groups in the way of progress. The meaning of community is shaped by political processes and access to those processes.

Communities are not helpless in facing the challenges imposed by this shift to market-centered approaches to local development. As Robert Giloth notes in Chapter 7, market solutions are often fads in which the solutions promoted today become the source of the problems of tomorrow. The results of market solutions lack substance and an understanding of the basic needs of the community. I will return to the question of community responses shortly.

IMPLEMENTING MARKET SOLUTIONS

Market-based policies can be examined along two dimensions for the purposes of this discussion. We need to first consider what they mean as a focus of local development and then consider the outcomes and consequences of market-dominated implementation of programs.

The marketplace means different things to different people. In the case of New Orleans, Young and Whelan (Chapter 9) point to the conflict between the market represented by the port and the market representing tourism in New Orleans. Each social aggregate supporting and promoting one of these markets finds the actions and demands of the other irresponsible and possibly counterproductive. At times, the actions of one group are designed to specifically prevent the advancement of the goals of the other. It is important, therefore, to recognize that there is not one local market; rather, market policies reflect a choice to promote a particular set of interests within a multiplicity of markets. Clearly, Thomas and Imrie's study of the port in Cardiff allows the same conclusion insofar as the market that is promoted is not the one in which the existing business and community interests of those already in the port area can express demands and offer supplies.

If we are to rely on markets to drive local development, Theodore Koebel and Cara Bailey (see Chapter 2) ask if it would be better to structure local policies to maximize local advantages. To that end they propose a targeted marketing strategy for two reasons: first, so that the local mix of resources and skills are maximized; second, so that firms that do come into the area seeking these resources and skills are more likely to succeed and prosper. In this way the community does not spend limited resources retraining labor and otherwise altering the local social and physical capital. By attracting firms that will benefit from local comparative advantages, the local economy will expand as the firms grow.

Relying on the existing situation to define the marketing goals of a community, however, implicitly accepts any deficiencies in the community while it tries to maximize growth within the constraints of those problems. These strategies may well work in the short run, but if Giloth is correct, markets can change and the community can see the gains turned into dust. Marketing strategies of this sort run a risk by not directly addressing or attempting to rectify local problems.

Such long-term strategies may well be out of the range of possible policy options in the United States. Hennings and Kunzmann suggest an alternative in their German case. Unlike the United States, where marketing strategies are purely market driven, in Germany the social context of dialogue between the community, business, and government on the local and national level all contribute to creating a redevelopment plan based on local strengths. Thus, Hennings and Kunzmann — and most of the approaches they discuss — exhibit a greater concern for the overall social economy. Policies consider the needs of many different constituencies within the context of profitability rather than being driven solely by the need to maximize profits. (See Gappert and Rose 1975 for a discussion of the social economy.)

But what of the consequences of relying on the marketplace? Buss argues that there are as many benefits as there are drawbacks, and he points to the success in Corby, when compared to the failure of Youngstown, to indicate how reliance on markets may produce desired development. A market-centered policy environment allows for quick decisions and rapid growth only if the local political structure can make a transition to the kind of entrepreneurial behavior that is traditional in the private sector but very new in local government. The vision and flexibility of the political leadership in Corby, when compared to the fragmented and overly bureaucratic leadership in Youngstown, led the community out of its economic tailspin. But even Buss acknowledges that it is not altogether clear what happened to the steel workers of Corby in the city's new era of growth and prosperity. Perhaps they went the route of displacement rather than improvement.

Charles Craypo and Jerry Paar (see Chapter 4) paint an even bleaker picture of the consequences of promoting business interests over those of the community. A market-oriented local political structure will always favor profits over jobs and will not necessarily undo the problems created by the marketplace in any event. They demonstrate that throwing money into the marketplace in order to prop up profits and forestall plant closings only delays the inevitable restructuring and probable job loss in an area. They ask how low-cost financing at the public's expense can undo what the market achieves by acting on its own, and they conclude that the only function served is to intensify local competition in a zero-sum game of regional job reallocation rather than job creation. The success of Corby would perhaps be the exception that proves the rule.

CONCLUSION

In his analysis of the destruction of Buffalo Creek, K. Erikson (1976) notes that more than natural disasters can bring trauma and pain to a community. He suggests that human actions (like massive plant closings) and environmental disasters that force the dislocation of large numbers of people can be as emotionally and psychologically devastating as any flood, earthquake, or other event of nature. It is the tearing asunder of lives, homes, social networks, family relationships, and the like that causes the reaction, not the act itself. Clearly, the economic restructuring of the past two decades qualifies.

Can communities respond to these changes, or are they doomed to ride the roller coaster of economic transition? By relying on market mechanisms alone communities depend upon the very forces that led them to the current state of affairs. The experience in Corby aside, markets do not seem to meet the needs of the community in place but rather work to transform the community and its residents. Thomas and Imrie point out that communities tend to struggle (politically and economically) over terrain already defined. What is needed now is a shift to struggling over how that terrain is to be defined in the first instance.

Perhaps the answer lies in shifting the terms of discussion and debate. When the market rules, as Alan McGregor and Andrew McArthur correctly point out in Chapter 6, profits guide funding. But, they ask, from where is the funding to come if social goals rule local policy decisions? Profit-oriented strategies are not local-centered, that is, they do not target local residents, many of whom are among the long-term unemployed. McGregor and McArthur argue instead for policies that focus on place rather than on profits, for policies that seek to employ the chronically unemployed rather than efforts that import new people to fill new positions.

How is this refocusing to come to pass? Giloth argues that it can only be achieved if the community actively resists those programs and policies proffered by local governments that accept the market mentality of planning initiatives. It is in the resistance and organizing that communities can achieve some role in shaping the redevelopment plan, and by extension, the social outcomes of public policy. Investors are profit maximizers and administrators are revenue maximizers. Communities, on the other hand, are use maximizers; their goals therefore come into direct conflict with investors and (most often) with administrators. Giloth's answer to Thomas and Imrie is that in order to define the terrain, the community must invoke political strategies that force the process to respond to their needs rather than worry about how to cope with the consequences of existing programs.

As the quotation at the start of this chapter indicates, we increasingly need to look to some sort of public arena, some public sphere, in order to deal with the conflicts of a modern society in which the marketplace has created inequities and resource imbalances. Communities struggling to rediscover the road to economic viability cannot rely solely on those very mechanisms that are the source of their current decline. Whether there is one public sphere or many public spheres (Fraser 1990) does not matter. Each community must do more than react to the conditions it faces by accepting the proffered cures and hoping to improve on their impacts. Rather, communities must take pro-active measures to engage in the public debates, to give voice to their public spheres, and to alter and widen the repertoire of policy responses to economic and social restructuring.

References

Adler, A. 1990. "D'Adamo Introduces Impact Fell Bill to Open up Dialogue with Developers." *Baltimore Business Journal*, 30 April–6 May.

Ahlbrandt, Roger S., Jr., and James P. DeAngelis. 1987. "Local Options for Economic Development in a Maturing Industrial Region." *Economic Development Quarterly* 1: 41–51.

Alden, J. D., M. Batty, S. Batty, and P. Longley. 1988. "An Economic and Social Profile of the Cardiff Bay Area." Cardiff: Department of Planning, University of Wales Institute of Science and Technology.

Allison, D. 1969. "The Battle Lines of Baltimore." *Innovations* 6 (July): 8–21.

Andrew, C. I. and D. H. Merriam. 1988. "Defensible Linkage." *Journal of the American Planning Association* 54, no. 2 (Spring): 199–209.

Ardagh, J. 1991. *Germany and the Germans*. 2d rev. ed. New York: Penguin Books.

Arnold and Porter (law firm). 1981. "Letter by S. Hester, Washington, D.C., to J. Smith, Assistant to the President, USWA." Pittsburgh, March 19.

Atwood, L. 1990. "Planners Reject Impact Fee Bill." *Baltimore Evening Sun*, 2 November.

Bailey, J. 1969. "How S.O.M Took on the Baltimore Road Gang." *Architectural Forum* (March): 40–45.

Barnekov T., and D. Rich. 1989. "Privatism and the Limits of Local Economic Development Policy." *Urban Affairs Quarterly* 25, no. 2: 212–238.

Barnekov, T., R. Boyle, and D. Rich. 1989. *Privatism and Urban Policy in Britain and the United States*. New York: Oxford University Press.

Baroni, G. 1983. "The Neighborhood Movement in the United States: From the 1960s to the Present." In *Neighborhood Policy and Planning*, eds. Phillip L. Clay and Robert M. Hollister, 177–191. Lexington, MA: Lexington Books.

Bartik, T. 1991. *Who Benefits from State and Local Economic Development Policies?* Kalamazoo, MI: W. E. Upjohn Institute for Employment Research.

Baumbach, Richard O., and William Borah. 1980. *Second Battle of New Orleans: A History of the Vieux Carre Riverfront Expressway Controversy*. Tuscaloosa: University of Alabama Press.

Beavon, K. S. D. 1977. *Central Place Theory: A Reinterpretation*. London: Longman Group Ltd.

Bechtel Corporation. 1970. *Master Plan for Long-Range Development of the Port of New Orleans*. Report prepared for the Dock Board. Houston, TX: Author.

Bellush, J., and M. Hausknecht, eds. 1966. *Urban Renewal: People, Politics and Planning*. Garden City, NY: Anchor Books.

Benington, J., and M. Geddes. 1990 "Local Economic Development: A Conceptual Framework for Comparative Analysis." Paper presented at the Great Lakes Economic Development Working Group, Chicago, September.

Bennett, R. J. 1983. "The Finance of Cities in West Germany." In *Progress in Planning*, vol. 21, pt. 1, eds. D. Diamond and J. B. McLoughlin. Oxford: Pergamon Press.

Bennett, R. J., G. Krebs, and H. Zimmermann, eds. 1990. *Local Economic Development in Britain and Germany*. London: Anglo-German-Foundation.

Berry, B. 1985. "Islands of Renewal in Seas of Decay." In *The New Urban Reality*, ed. Paul E. Petersen, 69–96. Washington, DC: Brookings Institute.

Berry, Brian J. L. 1967. *Geography of Market Centers and Retail Distribution*. Englewood Cliffs, NJ: Prentice-Hall.

Beyers, William B. 1981. "Alternative Spatial Linkage Structures in Multi-Regional Economic Systems." In *Industrial Location and Regional Systems*, eds. John Rees et al. Brooklyn: J. F. Bergin.

Birch, David L. 1981. "Who Creates Jobs?" *Public Interest* 65: 3–14.

Birindelli, Joseph. 1990. Telephone interview. Mobile, AL: Army Corps of Engineers.

Black, William R. 1972. "Interregional Commodity Flows: Some Experiments with the Gravity Model." *Journal of Regional Science* 12: 107–118.

Board of Commissioners of the Port of New Orleans. 1989. *Port Improvement Program (FY 1990–95)*. New Orleans: Port Planning and Engineering Division, Port of New Orleans.

———. 1990. *New Orleans Riverfront in Transition: A Citizens' Mandate for Planning*. New Orleans: Author.

Boddy, M., and C. Fudge. 1984. "Left Councils and New Left Alternatives." In *Local Socialism*, eds. M. Boddy and C. Fudge. London: Macmillan.

Bohm, Robert A., Henry W. Herzog, Jr., and Alan M. Schrottmann. 1983. "Industrial Location in the Tennessee-Tombigbee Corridor." *Review of Regional Studies* 13: 28–37.

Boulding, Peter, Ray Hudson, and David Sadler. 1988. "Consett and Corby." *Public Administration Quarterly* 13, no. 2: 235–255.

Boulis, J. R. 1979. "Letter to Roger Gilcrest, IRF Loan Committee Chairman." South Bend, IN, August 4.

———. 1985. Interview with C. Craypo. South Bend, IN, September.

Bradley, K., and A. Gelb. 1983. *Worker Capitalism: The New Industrial Relations*. Cambridge, MA: MIT Press.

Brambilla, R., and G. Longo. 1979. *Learning from Baltimore*. New York: Institute for Environmental Action.

References

Braschler, Curtis, et al. 1984. "Comparisons of Non-Survey Input-Output Estimates Using Alternative Reduction Techniques." *Review of Regional Studies* 14: 22–23.

Brinson, J. Ron. 1990. "Annual State of the Port Address." New Orleans, World Trade Center, September 18.

Brooke Associates. 1989. *Corby Works*. Corby, UK: Corby District Council.

Brooks, Jane S., Richard O. Baumbach, and Susan Drake. 1985. "The Resurgence of Urban Waterfronts: Redevelopment along the Mississippi River's Edge in New Orleans." Paper presented at the Urban Affairs Association Meeting, Norfolk, VA, April 17–20.

Bruck, C. 1988. *The Predators' Ball: The Inside Story of Drexel Burnham and the Rise of the Junk Bond Raiders*. New York: Penguin Books.

Bruckner, Sharon M., and Steven E. Hastings. 1983. "An Evaluation of Non-Survey Estimation Techniques for Regional Input-Output Models." *Review of Regional Studies* 13: 14–27.

Bruckner, Sharon M., Steven E. Hastings, and William R. Latham, III. 1987. "Regional Input-Output Analysis: A Comparison of Five 'Ready-Made' Model Systems." *Review of Regional Studies* 2: 1–15.

Bryson, John. 1985. *Strategic Planning for Public and Non-Profit Organizations*. San Francisco: Jossey-Bass.

———. 1988. *Strategic Planning Threats and Opportunities for Planners*, eds. John Bryson and Robert Einsweiler. Chicago: Planners Press, American Planning Association.

Bryson, J., and R. Einsweiler, eds. 1988. *Strategic Planning: Threats and Opportunities for Planners*. Chicago: American Planning Association Planners Press.

Buchanan, G. 1986. "Local Economic Development by Community Business." *Local Economy* (Summer).

Business Development Corporation. 1989. *Annual Report*. South Bend, IN: Author.

Buss, Terry F., and David Gemmel. 1990. *Youngstown/Warren, Ohio: A Reflection of the Boom and Bust of the Steel Industry*. New York: Kluwer Academic Publishers.

Buss, Terry F., and F. Stevens Redburn. 1983. *Shutdown at Youngstown: Public Policy for Mass Unemployment*. Albany: State University of New York Press.

———. 1988. *Hidden Unemployment: Discouraged Workers and Public Policy*. New York: Praeger.

Buss, Terry F., and Roger J. Vaughan. 1989. "Organization Responses to Economic Development in Northeast Ohio." *Economic Development Review* (Winter): 13–21.

Buss, Terry F., et al. 1990. "Putting It All Together: Financing Sovereign Circuits." In *Financing Economic Development*, ed. Richard Bingham, 285–301. Newbury Park, CA: Sage.

Butler, Stuart M. 1981. *Enterprise Zones*. New York: Universe Books.

Campbell, L. 1967. "Transport: A Concept Team for Baltimore." *City* (November): 15–26.

Cardiff Bay Development Corporation. 1988. *Cardiff Bay Regeneration Strategy*. Cardiff: The Summary CBDC.

Carlson, D. 1987. *Southeast Community Organization/Southeast Development Inc.: Discovering Baltimore's Urban Ethnics*. Berkeley: Center for Policy Development.
Cartwright, Joseph V., Richard M. Beemiller, and Richard D. Gustely. 1981. *RIMS II Regional Input-Output Modeling System*. Washington, DC: U.S. Government Printing Office.
Casale, Ellen. 1989. *Linking Development Benefits to Neighborhoods: A Manual of Community-Based Strategies*. Washington, DC: Community Information Exchange.
Cassidy, R. 1980. *Livable Cities*. New York: Holt Rinehart and Winston.
Clavel, P. 1983. *Opposition Planning in Wales and Appalachia*. Philadelphia: Temple University Press.
―――. 1986. *The Progressive City*. New Brunswick, NJ: Rutgers University Press.
Coates, D. 1980. *Labour in Power*. London: Longman.
Cohen, S., and J. Zysman. 1987. *Manufacturing Matters: The Myth of the Post-Industrial Economy*. New York: Basic Books.
Cohn, J., ed. 1970. "The Urban Affairs of Business: Special Issue." *Urban Affairs Quarterly* 6: 1.
Coopers, Lybrand. 1986. *The Investment Function of the Scottish Development Agency*. Report to the Industry Department for Scotland. London: Author.
―――. 1988. *The Evaluation of the Clydebank Enterprise Fund*. Report for the Scottish Development Agency. London: Author.
Council for Economic Action. 1982a. *Industry Growth Opportunities for Boston*. Boston: Author.
―――. 1982b. *The Right Business for You in Boston*. Boston: Author.
―――. 1983. "A Preliminary Assessment of the Success of the Urban Business Identification System." Boston: Author.
―――. 1984. *The Business Development Program*. Boston: Author.
―――. 1989a. *Small Business Development System: A Comprehensive Approach to Enterprise Development*. Boston: Author.
―――. 1989b. *Summary of the Small Business Development System*. Boston: Author.
―――. 1990. Interviews with Linda T. Lafluer, Program Director. Boston.
Cox, K. 1992. "The Concept of Local Economic Development Policy: Some Fundamental Questions." In *Community Economic Development: Policy Formation in the US and UK*, ed. D. Fasenfest. London: MacMillan.
Craypo, C. 1984. "The Deindustrialization of a Factory Town: Plant Closings and Phasedowns in South Bend, Indiana, 1954–1983." In *Labor and Reindustrialization: Workers and Corporate Change*, ed. D. Kennedy. University Park: Department of Labor Studies, Pennsylvania State University.
―――. 1988. "Industrial Restructuring following Plant Closings and Phasedowns." In *Proceedings: Spring Meeting, 1988*. Madison, WI: Industrial Relations Research Association.
Crenson, M. A. 1983. *Neighborhood Politics*, chap. 6. Cambridge, MA: Harvard University Press.
Cumbler, J. 1989. *A Social History of Economic Decline: Business, Politics, and Work in Trenton*. New Brunswick, NJ: Rutgers University Press.
Cunningham, J., and M. Kotler. 1983. *Building Neighborhood Organizations*, chap. 5. South Bend, IN: University of Notre Dame Press.

References

Department of Environment. 1987. *Managed Workspaces*. London: Her Majesty's Stationery Office.
Department of Finance, 1991. "Worksheet on Baltimore Property Tax Changes by Council District, 1976–1990." Baltimore: City of Baltimore.
Department of Planning. 1987. *Canton Guide Plan: A Cooperative Effort between the Baltimore City Department of Planning and the Neighborhood Progress Administration*. Baltimore: City of Baltimore.
Department of Social Security. 1990. *Households below Average*. London: Her Majesty's Stationery Office.
Dodson, P. 1979. "South Bend Lathe Difficulties." *South Bend Times*, 2 March.
———. 1985a. "Box Firm to Join Airport Park." *South Bend Times*, 28 September.
———. 1985b. "System Spells Success: President." *South Bend Times*, 14 July, pp. 32–33.
———. 1988a. "Company in Turmoil but Boulis Keeps Post." *South Bend Times*, 3 January, p. D-1.
———. 1988b. "Era Ends as Boulis Takes Leave of Company." *South Bend Times*, 3 April, p. F-1.
———. 1989. "South Bend Lathe Withdraws Moratorium Request." *South Bend Times*, 2 March.
———. 1991a. "Health Insurance Is Key Issue in South Bend Lathe Strike." *South Bend Times*, 1 May, p. B-4.
———. 1991b. "Lathe Company Still Besieged by Infighting." *South Bend Times*, 6 January.
———. 1991c. "Workers End Strike at South Bend Lathe." *South Bend Times*, 15 May, p. B-3.
Donnison, D., and A. Middleton. 1987. *Regenerating the Inner City: Glasgow's Experience*. London: Routledge.
Economic Development Administration. 1975. "Grant Agreement." *Adjustment Assistance Grant*. Washington, DC: U.S. Department of Commerce, May 15.
Eggler, Bruce. 1992. "N.O. Council Oks 3-Way Land Swap Involving Riverfront." *Times-Picayune*, 16 April, p. B3.
Eisenger, P. 1989. *The Rise of the Entrepreneurial State*. Madison: University of Wisconsin Press.
English, B. 1989. "Property Tax Credit Raised in Annapolis." *East Baltimore Guide*, 6 April.
Erikson, K. 1976. *Everything in Its Path: Destruction of Community in the Buffalo Creek Flood*. New York: Simon and Schuster.
Fainstein, S., and N. Fainstein. 1987. "Economic Restructuring and the Politics of Land-Use Planning in New York City." *Journal of the American Planning Association* 53, no. 2: 237–248.
Falk, N. 1980. "Finding a Place for Small Enterprises in the Inner City." In *The Inner City: Employment and Industry*, eds. A. Evans and D. Eversley, 367–388. London: Heinemann.
Fasenfest, D. 1986. "Community Politics and Urban Development." *Urban Affairs Quarterly* 22, no. 1: 101–123
———. 1988. "Urban Policies, Social Goals and Producer Incentives: Are Market Mechanisms and Policy Objectives Compatible?" In *Market Based Public Policy*, ed. R. Hula. London: Macmillan.

———, ed. 1992. *Community Economic Development: Policy Formation in the US and UK*. London: MacMillan.

Feagin, J. 1982. "Urban Real Estate Speculation in the United States." *International Journal of Urban and Regional Research* 6, no. 1: 35–69.

———. 1988. *Free Enterprise City: Houston*. New Brunswick, NJ: Rutgers University Press.

Feagin, J. R. 1990. "Are Planners Collective Capitalists? The Cases of Aberdeen and Houston." *International Journal of Urban and Regional Research* 14, no. 2: 249–273.

Field, M. 1988. "Just Say No: The Waterfront Coalition Digs In for the Battle over Canton's Gold Coast." *City Paper*, 11–17 August, pp. 14–16.

Fitzgerald, J., and K. Cox. 1990. "Urban Economic Development Strategies in the USA." *Local Economy* 4, no. 4:278–289.

Fraser, N. 1990. "Rethinking the Public Sphere: A Contribution to the Critique of Actually Existing Democracy." *Social Text* 25/26: 56–80.

Frieden, B. J., and L. B. Sagalyn. 1989. *Downtown Inc: How America Rebuilds Cities*. Cambridge, MA: MIT Press.

Galbraith, M. 1985. "Businesses Find Better Climate in Indiana." *South Bend Times*, 16 August.

Ganguly, P. 1985. *U.K. Small Business Statistics and International Comparisons*. London: Harper Row.

Gappert, G., and H. Rose. 1975. *The Social Economy of Cities*. Urban Affairs Annual Review, vol. 9. Beverly Hills, CA: Sage Publications.

Gilcrest, R. 1983. "IRF Loan Chairman, Letter to E. Jeep, Economic Development Administration, Regional Office." Chicago, July 21.

———. 1985. "C. Craypo Interview with the IRF Loan Committee Chairman." South Bend, IN, June 13.

Giloth, R. 1989. *Waterfront Development: Impacts on Housing Affordability in Canton, Fells Point, and Upper Fells Point 1985–1988*. Baltimore: Southeast Linkage Group.

———. 1990. "Beyond Common Sense: The Baltimore Renaissance." *Local Economy* 4, no. 4 (February): 290–297.

———. 1992. "Stalking Local Economic Development Benefits: A Review of Evaluation Literature." *Economic Development Quarterly* 6, no. 1: 80–90.

Giloth, R., and J. Betancur. 1988. "Where Downtown Meets Neighborhood: Industrial Displacement in Chicago 1978–1987." *Journal of the American Planning Association* 533 (Spring): 279–290.

Giloth, R., and R. Mier. 1989. "Spatial Change and Social Justice: Alternative Economic Development in Chicago." In *Economic Restructuring and Political Response*, ed. Robert A. Beauregard, 181–208. Newbury Park: Sage Publications.

Golany, Gideon, ed. 1978. *International Urban Growth Policies*. New York: John Wiley.

Goodman, R. 1979. *The Last Entrepreneurs: America's Regional Wars for Jobs and Dollars*. Boston: South End Press.

Gordon, D. 1977. *Problems in Political Economy: An Urban Perspective*. 2d ed. Lexington, MA: Heath.

Gramlich, E. 1981. *Benefit-Cost Analysis of Government Programs*. Englewood Cliffs, NJ: Prentice-Hall.

Gunts, E. 1988. "City May Require Builder to Spare Canton Building, *Baltimore Sun*, 23 September.
———. 1990. "Canton Crafts Own Plans for American Can." *Baltimore Sun*, 15 November.
Habermas, J. 1974. "The Public Sphere: An Encyclopedia Article." *New German Critique* 3: 49–55.
Harrison, B., and B. Bluestone. 1989. *The Great U-Turn*. New York: Basic Books.
Hayton, K. 1990. *Getting People into Jobs. Report to the Department of Environment: Action for Cities*. London: Her Majesty's Stationery Office.
Healey, P., P. McNamara, M. Elson, and A. Doak. 1988. *Land Use Planning and the Mediation of Urban Change*. Cambridge: Cambridge University Press.
Hennings, G., and K. R. Kunzmann. 1990. "Priority to Local Economic Development. Industrial Restructuring and Local Development Responses in the Ruhr Area — The Case of Dortmund." In *Global Challenge and Local Response: Initiatives For Economic Regeneration in Contemporary Europe*, ed. W. B. Stohr. London and New York: Mansell.
———. 1991. "Restructuring a Traditional Industrial City — The Case of Dortmund." In *Urban Regeneration in a Changing Economy*, eds. J. Fox-Przeworski, J. Goddard, M. de Jong. Oxford: Clarendon Press.
Holland, M. 1989. *When the Machine Stopped: A Cautionary Tale from Industrial America*. Boston: Harvard Business School Press.
Howell, D. 1980. *British Social Democracy*. 2d ed. London: Croon Helm.
Hughlett, Mike. 1991. "Marine Terminal Project on Again." *Times-Picayune*, 25 January, p. C1.
Hula, R. 1990. "The Two Baltimores." In *Leadership and Urban Regeneration*, eds. Dennis Judd and Michael Parkinson, 191–215. Newbury Park, CA.: Sage Publications.
Huskey, Lee. 1985. "Import Substitution: The Hidden Dynamic in the Growth of Frontier Regions." *Growth and Change* 16: 43–55.
Imrie, R., and H. Thomas. 1992. "The Wrong Side of the Tracks: A Case of Local Economic Regeneration in Britain." *Policy and Politics* 20, no. 3: 213–226.
Industrial Revolving Fund. 1975. "Trust Agreement." City of South Bend, June 10.
———. 1985. "Guidelines and Procedures." City of South Bend, October 22.
Jacobs, M. 1986. "Community Businesses: Are Their Aims Confused?" *Local Economy* (Summer).
Jacobson, J. 1990a. "The Gold Coast: Waterfront Developers Scale Back on Projects." *Baltimore Sun*, 24 October.
———. 1990b. "Upscale Housing Transforms Waterfront." *Baltimore Sun*, 25 October.
Katz, Allan. 1990. "Development Is Always a Battle on the Mississippi Riverfront." *City Business*, 8 October, p. 40.
Keating, M. 1988. "The City That Refused to Die: Glasgow." In *Politics of Urban Regeneration*. Aberdeen: Aberdeen University Press.
Keating, W. D. 1986. "Linking Downtown Development to Broader Community Goals." *Journal of the American Planning Association* 52, no. 2 (Spring): 133–141.
Keith, R. C. 1982. *Baltimore Harbor: A Pictorial History*. Baltimore: Ocean World Press.

Kelly, J. 1988a. "Canton History Is Packed in American Can Buildings." *Baltimore Evening Sun*, 27 June.
———. 1988b. "Panel Urges Saving American Can." *Baltimore Evening Sun*, 9 September.
———. 1990. "Apartments, Stores Urged for American Can Co. Site." *Baltimore Evening Sun*, 14 November.
King, Leslie J. 1984. *Central Place Theory*. Beverly Hills: Sage Publications.
Kotschenreuther, P. J. 1990. "Realtors Oppose Sprinkler and Impact Zone Bills." *Greater Baltimore Board of Realtors Newsletter* (July).
Kuttner, R. 1976. "Ethnic Renewal: How Ordinary People in East Baltimore Have Created a Model Answer to Inner-City Blight." *New York Times Magazine*, 9 May.
Lawless, P. 1988. "Urban Development Corporations and Their Alternatives." *Cities* 5, no. 3: 277–289.
Ledebur, Larry. 1986. *Youngstown's Economic Base*. Youngstown, OH: Youngstown Chamber of Commerce.
Leliaert, R. 1984. "Project Future Blitzes Neighboring States in Jobs War." *South Bend Times*, 13 May.
Lever, W. F. 1986. "Old Policies in a New Role." In *The City in Transition*, eds. W. F. Lever and C. Moore, 44–61. Oxford: Oxford University Press.
Levine, M. R. 1987. "Downtown Redevelopment as a Growth Strategy: A Critical Appraisal of the Baltimore Renaissance." *Journal of Urban Affairs* 9, no. 2: 103–123.
Levy, John M. 1990. "What Local Economic Developers Actually Do: Location Quotients versus Press Releases." *Journal of the American Planning Association* 56: 153–160.
Linares, Leonor. 1990. Telephone Interview with staff member of Chamber of Commerce and Campaign for Greater Louisville.
Llewellyn-Davies Planning. 1988. *Cardiff Bay Regeneration Strategy*. Cardiff: Cardiff Bay Development Corporation.
Logan, J. R., and H. L. Molotch. 1987. *Urban Fortunes: The Political Economy of Space*. Berkeley: University of California Press.
Louv, R. 1983. *America 2*. New York: Penguin Books.
Luttner, S. 1985. "South Bend Fishing for Cleveland Industry." *The (Cleveland) Plain Dealer*, 7 July.
McArthur, A. A. 1987. "Jobs and Incomes." In *Regenerating the Inner City: Glasgow's Experience*, eds. D. V. Donnison and A. Middleton. London: Routledge and Kegan Paul.
McArthur, A. A., and A. McGregor. 1986. "Policies for the Disadvantaged in the Labour Market." In *The City in Transition*, eds. W. F. Lever and C. Moore. Oxford: Clarendon Press.
McCrystal, S. 1990. "Galliagh Community Co-Operative Society." In *Community Enterprise in the Local Economy, TERU Research Paper No. 2*, eds. A. McGregor and A. A. McArthur. Glasgow: Training and Employment Research Unit, University of Glasgow.
McGahey, R. 1990. "Improving Economic Development Strategies." *Journal of Policy Analysis and Management* 9, no. 2: 532–535.

McGill, W. 1975. "Revolving Fund and Subsequent Beneficiaries." In *ESOP: How It Works! The South Bend Lathe Way*. Indiana University at South Bend, Conference Proceedings, November 17–18 (mimeo).

McGregor, A., A. A. McArthur, and V. Noone. 1988. *An Evaluation of Community Business in Scotland*. Edinburgh: Scottish Office.

McGregor, A., and F. Mather. 1986. "Developments in Glasgow's Labour Market." In *The City in Transition*, eds. W. F. Lever and C. Moore. Oxford: Clarendon Press.

Machiavelli, N. 1947. *The Prince*. Northbrook, IL: AHM Publishing Corp.

MacInnes, J. 1988. "The North-South Divide: Regional Employment Change in Britain 1975–87." In *CURR Discussion Paper No. 34*. Glasgow: Centre for Urban and Regional Research, University of Glasgow.

McIntosh, P., and V. Keddie. 1979. *Industry and Employment in the Inner City*. London: Department of Employment, HMSO.

Macsherry, C. 1988. "Developers, Preservationists and the City Battle out the Year." *City Paper*, 23 December, pp. 10–12.

Markusen, A. 1985. *Regions: The Economics and Politics of Territory*. Totowa, NJ: Rowman and Littlefield.

Merrifield, A. 1991. *Redeveloping American Can: Economic Restructuring, Waterfront Transformation, and Neighborhood Activism in Southeast Baltimore*. Baltimore: Institute for Policy Studies, Johns Hopkins University.

Meyer, P. B. 1991a. *Meaning and Action in Local Economic Development*. Louisville: School of Urban Policy, University of Louisville.

———. 1991b. "Meaning and Action in Local Economic Development Strategies: A Comparison of Policies in Britain and the United States." *Environment and Planning C: Government and Policy* 9, no. 4: 383–398.

———. 1992. "A Tale of Three (British) Cities: Economic Development Politics in Cardiff, Leeds and Glasgow." In *Community Economic Development: Policy Formation in the United States and United Kingdom*, ed. D. Fasenfest, 122–128. London: MacMillan Press.

Meyer, P. B., and R. Boyle, eds. 1990. "Special Issue: Lessons from the USA." *Local Economy* 4, no. 4: 271–347.

Meyer, P. B., and R. Kraushaar. 1989. "The Grass Is Always Greener: Political Structure and Economic Development in the United States." *Community Development Journal* 24, no. 2: 95–100.

Mollenkopf, J. 1981. *The Contested City*. Princeton: Princeton University Press.

Molotch, H. 1976. "The City as a Growth Machine: Towards a Political Economy of Place." *American Journal of Sociology* 82.

Moore, C., and S. Booth. 1986. "The Pragmatic Approach: Local Political Models of Regeneration." In *The City in Transition*, eds. W. F. Lever and C. Moore. Oxford: Clarendon Press.

MSWV (Minister fur Stadtentwicklung, Wohen and Verkehr des Landes Nordrhein-Westfalen), ed. 1988. *Internationale Bauausstellung EmscherPark. Werkstaff fur die Zukunft alter Industrieregionen. Memorandum zu Inhalt und Organisation*. (Memorandum on Content and Organization). Dusseldorf: Author.

MURL (Minister fur Umwelt, Raumordnung und Landwirtschaft des Landes Nordrhein-Westfalen), ed. 1989. *Umwelttechnik in Nordrhein-Westfalen*. Dusseldorf: Author.

MWMT (Minister fur Wirtschaft, Mittelstand und Technologie des Landes Nordrhein-Westfalen), ed. 1987. *Zukunftsinitiative Montanregionen. 1 Zwischenbericht*. Dusseldorf: Author.
Newton, K. 1975. "American Urban Politics: Social Class, Political Structure and Public Goods." *Urban Affairs Quarterly* 11, no. 2: 241–264.
Noble, D. 1984. *Forces of Production: A Social History of Industrial Automation*. New York: Alfred A. Knopf.
Olsen, S. 1980. *Baltimore: The Building of an American City*. Baltimore: Johns Hopkins University Press.
Owings, N. 1973. *The Spaces In Between: An Architect's Journey*. Boston: Houghton Mifflin.
PA Cambridge Economic Consultants. 1987. *An Evaluation of the Enterprise Zone Experiment*. Report to the Department of the Environment, Inner Cities Research Programme. London: Her Majesty's Stationery Office.
Park, Se-Hark, Malek Mohtadi, and Atif Kubursi. 1981. "Errors in Regional Input-Output Models: Analytical and Simulation Results." *Journal of Regional Science* 2: 321–339.
Pelissero, J., and D. Fasenfest. 1989. "A Typology of Suburban Economic Development Policy Orientations." *Economic Development Quarterly* 3, no. 4: 301–311.
Pigozzi, Bruce William, and Rene C. Hinojosa. 1985. "Regional Input-Output Inverse Coefficients Adjusted from National Tables." *Growth and Change* 16: 8–12.
Plaza Land Associates. 1988. *Development Plan for American National Plaza*. Baltimore: Author.
Pressman, J., and A. Wildavsky. 1973. *Implementation*. Berkeley: University of California Press.
Pross and Prosser (accounting firm). 1982. *City of South Bend, Indiana, Economic Development Administration, Grant No. 06-19-01251, Interim Audit for the Period May 23, 1975, through September 30, 1982, Together with Auditors' Comments*. South Bend, IN: Author.
Pulver, Glen C. 1984. "The Application of Comprehensive Community Economic Analysis." *Review of Regional Studies* 14: 24–28.
Pyke, F., G. Beattine, and W. Sengenberger. 1990. *Industrial Districts and Inter-Firm Co-operation in Italy*. Geneva, Switzerland: International Institute for Labor Studies, International Labor Organization.
Redburn, F. Stevens, and Susan Clarke. 1983. "Off-Budget Urban Policy." Paper presented to the Association for Policy Analysis and Management, Philadelphia, October.
Redburn, F. Stevens, and Terry F. Buss. 1984. "Religious Leaders and the Politics of Revitalization." In *Public Policy Formation*, ed. Robert Eyestone. Greenwich, CT: JAI Press.
Reich, L., and D. Carroll. 1980. "The Port of Baltimore." In *Urban Waterfront Lands*, ed. Committee on Urban Waterfront. Washington, DC: National Academy of Sciences.
Reps, J. W. 1972. *Tidewater Towns: City Planning in Colonial Virginia and Maryland*. Williamsburg, VA: Williamsburg Foundation.
Reutter, M. 1988. *Sparrows Point*. New York: Summit Books.
Reynolds, R. 1990. "President, USWA Local 1722, Interview by C. Craypo." South Bend, IN, June 20.

Rhoads, Steven. 1985. *An Economist's View of the World*. Cambridge: Cambridge University Press.
Rich, L. R., J. Clark Netherwood, and E. B. Cahn. 1981. *Neighborhood: A State of Mind*. Baltimore: Johns Hopkins University Press.
"Riverfront 2000: Are Things Rolling on the Riverfront?" 1990. *Gambit*, 27 March, p. 11.
Rothenberg, J. 1967. *Economic Evaluation of Urban Renewal*. Washington, DC: Brookings Institute.
Rowthorn, B. 1986. "Deindustrialisation in Britain." In *The Geography of Deindustrialisation*, eds. R. Martin and B. Rowthorn. London: Macmillan.
Ruby, M. 1989. "Impact Fees Suggested in Canton and Fells Point." *Daily Record*, 15 September.
Ryan, Timothy P. 1992. "The Economic Impact of the Port of New Orleans and the New Orleans Maritime Industry." Report to the Board of Commissioners of the Port of New Orleans, March 15.
Samuel, P. D. 1989. "Swerdlow Cancels Plans for Canton Development: Vandalism, Arson Force Bank's Withdrawal." *Daily Record*, 8 September.
———. 1990. "Swerdlow Leaves American Can in Mystery: Legal Maneuvering Holds Up Disposition of Canton Property." *Daily Record*, 16 May.
Schwarz, J. E., and T. J. Volgy. 1988. "Experiments in Employment: A British Cure." *Harvard Business Review* 88, no. 2: 104–112.
Scottish Development Agency. 1987. *Annual Report 1987*. Glasgow: Author.
Scottish Office. 1989. *New Life for Urban Scotland*. Edinburgh: Author.
Shopes, L. 1991. "Fells Point: Community and Conflict in a Working Class Neighborhood." In *The Baltimore Book: New Views of Local History*, eds. Elizabeth Fee, Linda Shopes, and Linda Zeidman, 121–154. Philadelphia: Temple University Press.
Simmons, J., and W. Mares. 1982. *Working Together: Employee Participation in Action*. New York: New York University Press.
South Bend Lathe. 1984. "Employee Stock Ownership Committee," Proxy Statement and Request for Voting Direction for Annual Shareholder Meeting to Be Held on October 18, 1984. South Bend, IN: Author.
South Bend Times. 1966. "Special Supplement: South Bend Lathe, 1906–66." 17 June.
———. 1975. "Pride Evident as Employees Take Over Lathe Plant." 8 July.
Sowell, Thomas. 1980. *Knowledge and Decisions*. New York: Basic Books.
Stevens, Benjamin H., and Glynnis A. Trainer. 1980. "Error Generation in Regional Input-Output Analysis and Its Implications for Non-Survey Models." In *Economic Impact Analysis: Methodology and Applications*, ed. Saul Pleeter. Boston: Martines Nijhoff.
Stevens, Benjamin H., George Treyz, and Michael Lahr. 1988. "On the Comparative Accuracy of RPC Estimating Techniques." In *RSRI Discussion Paper Series*, no. 131. Peace Dale, RI: Regional Science Research Institute.
Stoker, G. 1988. "Urban Development Corporations: A Review." *Regional Studies* 23, no. 2: 159–167.
Stoker, R. 1987. "Baltimore: The Self-Evaluating City." In *The Politics of Urban Development*, eds. Clarence Stone and Heywood Sanders, 244–268. Lawrence: University of Kansas Press.

Stone, C. 1987. "The Study of the Politics of Urban Development." In *The Politics of Urban Development*, eds. Clarence Stone and Heywood Sanders, 3–24. Lawrence: University of Kansas Press.
Strategic Plan for the City of New Orleans. 1986. New Orleans: Port of New Orleans. The document was developed by two consulting firms, acting jointly: Temple, Barker, and Sloane; and Cocchiara and Renner.
Strathclyde Regional Council. 1990. *Strathclyde Economic Trends No. 26*. Glasgow: Author.
Sweet, David C. 1980. "The Systematic Approach to Development." In *Industrial Location and Community Development*, ed. Barry M. Moriarity. Chapel Hill: University of North Carolina Press.
———. 1986. "The Systematic Approach to Economic Development." Cleveland: Cleveland State University, College of Urban and Public Affairs.
———. n.d. "Economic Development — Computer Software." Cleveland: Cleveland State University, College of Urban and Public Affairs.
Teitz, M. B. 1989. "Neighbourhood Economics: Local Communities and Regional Markets." *Economic Development Quarterly* 3: 111–122.
Thomas, H. 1989. "City Profile — Cardiff." *Cities* 6, no. 2: 91–101.
Thomas, H., and R. Imrie. 1989. "Urban Redevelopment, Compulsory Purchase and the Regeneration of Local Economics — The Case of Cardiff Docklands." *Planning Practice and Research* 4, no. 3: 18–27.
Thompson, Wilbur R., and Philip R. Thompson. 1985. "From Industries to Occupation: Rethinking Local Economic Development." *Economic Development Commentary* 9: 12–18.
———. 1987. "National Industries and Local Occupational Strengths: The Cross-Hairs of Targeting." *Urban Studies* 24: 547–560.
Tiebout, C. M. 1972. "A Pure Theory of Urban Expenditure." Reprinted in *Readings in Urban Economics*, eds. M. Edel and J. Rothenberg, 513–523. New York: MacMillan Press.
Times-Picayune. 1990a. "Editorial." 18 October, p. B10.
Townsend, A. R. 1987. "Regional Policy." In *Industrial Change in the United Kingdom*, ed. W. F. Lever. Harlow: Longman.
Tribune Business Weekly. 1991. "Court Gives Sibley 30-Day Reprieve." 6 February.
Truelove, L. 1977. *SECO History*. Baltimore: Southeast Community Organization.
Turok, I., and U. Wannop. 1990. *Targeting Urban Employment Initiatives*. Report for the Department of the Environment, Inner Cities Research Programme. London: Her Majesty's Stationery Office.
U.S. Department of Commerce, Economic Development Administration. 1973. *Industrial Location Determinants*. Washington, DC: U.S. Government Printing Office.
Vance, M. 1985. Memo to Jon Hunt, Director of Human Resources and Economic Development, June 5.
Vaughan, Roger J., Robert Pollard, and Barbara Dyer. 1984. *The Wealth of States*. Washington, DC: Council of State Planning Agencies.
Vogel, Ronald K. 1990. "The Local Regime and Economic Development." *Economic Development Quarterly* 4: 101–112.
Walden, Donald. 1990. Telephone interview. Columbus, MS: Tennessee-Tombigbee Waterway Development Authority.

Warner, Coleman. 1990. "Dock Board and City of New Orleans Often Compared Unfavorably," in "Study: Orleans Government Jobs Lack Competition." *Times-Picayune*, 1 October, p. B1.
Waterfront Coalition. 1990. *Listing of Waterfront Projects, 1985–1991*. Baltimore: Waterfront Coalition.
Webber, Michael J. 1984. *Industrial Location*. Beverly Hills: Sage Publications.
Weiss, M. 1986. "The Origins and Legacy of Urban Renewal." In *Urban and Regional Planning in an Age of Austerity*, eds. P. Clavel, J. Forester, and W. W. Goldsmith. Oxford: Pergamon.
White, M. J. 1980. *Urban Renewal and the Changing Residential Structure of the City*. Chicago: University of Chicago.
White, Sammis B., et al. 1990. "ES202: The Data Base for Local Employment Analysis." *Economic Development Quarterly* 4, no. 3: 240–254.
Whyte, W. F., and C. Craypo. 1988. *Evaluation Research on Federally Assisted Employee Buyouts*. EDA Project No. RED-816-G-84-13, submitted June 15. Typescript. Washington, DC: Economic Development Administration.
Whyte, W., H. Tove, C. Meek, R. Nelson, and R. Stern, eds. 1983. *Worker Participation and Ownership: Corporative Strategies for Strengthening Local Economies*. Ithaca, NY: ILR Press.
Williams, John. 1989. "CAVE: A Bolt Hole for Firms when Bay Laps the Door." *Business Wales* 10 (August/September): 20–21.
Willis, K. G. 1987. "Spatially Disaggregated Input-Output Tables: An Evaluation and Comparison of Survey and Non-Survey Results." *Environment and Planning A* 19: 107–116.
Wilson, J. Q., ed. 1966. *Urban Renewal: The Record and the Controversy*. Cambridge, MA: MIT Press.
Wolman, H. 1992. "Cross-National Comparisons of Urban Economic Programs: Is Policy Transfer Possible?" In *Community Economic Development: Policy Formation in the United States and United Kingdom*, ed. D. Fasenfest. London: Macmillan; New York: St. Martins Press.
Wolman, H., and M. Goldsmith. 1990. "Local Autonomy as a Meaningful Analytic Concept: Comparing Local Government in the United States and Great Britain." *Urban Affairs Quarterly* 26, no. 1: 3–27.
Wolman, Harold. 1988. "Local Economic Development Policy." *Journal of Urban Affairs* 10: 19–28.
Woodward, W., C. Meek, and W. F. Whyte, eds. 1985. *Industrial Democracy: Strategies for Community Revitalization*, part 2: "Forms of Community Worker Ownership." Beverly Hills, CA: Sage Publications.
Zeidman, L., and E. Hallengren. 1991. "Radicalism on the Waterfront: Seamen in the 1930s." In *The Baltimore Book: New Views of Local History*, 155–174. Philadelphia: Temple University Press.
Zwerdling, D. 1980. *Workplace Democracy*. New York: Harper and Row.

Index

Advisory Council on Historic Preservation, 107, 111
Affordable housing, 112
Allied Steel and Wire (ASW), 121, 126–27
American Association of Port Authorities (AAPA), 135
American Can, 106–17
American National Plaza, 110–11
Amsted Industries, 56–57
Association of British Credit Unions, 91
Atlantic Wharf, 122, 124, 125, 126, 127

Backward linkages, 19, 20, 23, 42
Baltimore, 12, 103–17
Baltimore Taxpayer's Coalition, 112
Barthelemy, William, 137, 144
Beyers, William, 19
Birmingham, 87
Black, William, 25, 27
Bohm, Robert, 20
Boston, 21–23
Boulis, J. Richard, 56–58, 67–68
Brinson, J. Ron, 135, 143
British Airship Corporation, 163
British Steel Corporation (BSC), 151, 153, 157, 167 n.5

British Steel (Industry) Limited, 78
Bund, 38
Business Development Corporation (BDC), 60, 66, 68
Business subsidies, 13

Cannery Row, 104, 106, 110
Canton, 104, 105, 106, 116
Canton and Fells Point Urban Renewal Amendments, 110
Capital Access, 21
Capital improvement projects, 135
Cardiff, Atlantic Wharf, 122, 124, 125, 127
Cardiff Bay Development Corporation (CBDC), 120–28
CASTLO, 159, 163
Central Business District (CBD), 132, 134
Centroport Study, 139
Clyde Workshops, 78
Clydebank, 78
Clydeside, 71
Collingdon Road, 121–27
Communes, 38–40
Community: business, 92–95; cooperatives, 90; credit unions, 91, 95–98; development, 157, 175; economic

action, 86–98; economic analysis, 18; economic development strategy, 18, 19; enterprise, 86–98
Community Development Block Grants, 159
Community Outreach, 21
Community Program, the, 95
Community-based housing associations, 91
Comprehensive Economic Development Strategy (CEDS), 160–61
Compulsory purchase orders, 122, 128
Computerized numerically controlled (CNC) lathe, 57
Consensus principle, 46
Consultative processes, 120, 126
Containerization, 132–33
Corby, England, 13–14, 150–58, 165–66
Corporation for Economic Development, 166
Council for Economic Action (CEA), 20, 21–23, 28
Cranhill Credit Union, 91
Crossnational comparison, 5, 14, 174, 175

Deindustrialization, 69–71
Department of Economic Development, 64
Department of Employment, 77
Depression, 70
Deregulation, 133, 165
Designation of development districts, 71
Diversification, 10, 13
Dock Board, 140–45
Dun's Market Identifier (DMI), 29

Economic development, 4, 8, 17, 75–82, 86, 104–14, 149, 153; programs, 4, 73, 174; research, 159; strategy, 19, 23, 43–44, 55–68, 104, 157, 159, 164

Economic Development Administration (EDA), 27, 159, 160
Economic Development Agency (EDA), 55–56, 59–67
Economic diversification, 10
Economic initiatives, community-based, 85–86
Economic regeneration, 72–82
Employee Retirement Income Security Act, 55–56
Employee stock ownership plan (ESOP), 55–68
Employment and Training Subsidies, 81
Employment Grants Scheme, 81
EmscherPark International Building Exhibition, 44, 48–51
Emscherzone, 44, 48–51
Enterprise Funds for Youth (EFY), 77
Enterprise Trusts, 74–75, 77
Enterprise Zone (EZ), 80–81, 156, 164, 165, 167 n.6
European Economic Community (EEC), 156, 165
European Social Fund (ESF), 79, 81

Fells Point, 104, 105–16
Ferguslie Park Community Holdings, 90, 92
First Source Bank, 59
Foreign trade, 132
Forward linkages, 19, 20, 42
Freie Reichstadte, 38

Galliagh Community Co-operative Society, 90, 98
Germany, 7, 11, 35–54, 174, 176; communes, 38–39; Emscherzone, IBA-EmscherPark, 44, 48–51; local tax revenues, 7; Ruhrgebiet, 5, 11, 35–54; Ruhrgebiet, Initiative for the, 44, 51–53
Glasgow, 69–83, 87, 90; Clydeside, 71; District Council, 73; unemployment, 70–71
Glasgow Eastern Area Renewal (GEAR), 82

Index

Glasgow Opportunity, 77
Gold Coast development, 103–17
Govan Workspace, 90
Grants, central government, 71
Greater Baltimore Committee, 106
Greens, the, 40
Grundgesetz, 38
Grunen, Die, 40

Habermas, Jurgen, 169
Hall, Duncan, 153
HarborPlace Festival Market, 104
Heatwise, 76
Herrhausen, Alfred, 51
High technology, 57
Historic preservation, 107–12, 161
Housing, 116–17, 152, 157, 161; allocation policies, 71; cooperatives, 91; estates, 90, 92; high-income, 102, 107–8, 110–11, 123, 157, 161; low-income, 161; trust fund, 113; public, 70, 73, 76, 91, 157
Housing and Urban Development (HUD), 110

Impact analysis, 17
Impact Zones, 113
Income tax, 39
Industrial development, 10, 44, 47, 48–51, 66, 69–71, 156; strategy, 123
Industrial revolving fund (IRF), 55–68
Industrialization strategy, 44
Industry, 10, 11, 26, 37, 55–68, 70–71, 73, 78, 122–23, 124, 157; agriculture, 132; coal, 5, 37, 41, 42–48, 73; lathes, 55–68; maritime, 134–35, 138, 139–45; oil, 133; pharmaceutical, 68; plastics, 62; regional assistance grants, 73; steel, 5, 13, 14, 35–36, 37, 41, 42–48, 70, 73, 122, 150–52, 157–58, 161, 166 n.3; transportation, 133
Industry identification, 21
Industry tax, 39

Initiative for the Future of Coal and Steel Regions, 44–48
Initiative for the Ruhrgebiet (IR), 44, 51–53
Inner Harbor Navigation Canal (IHNC), 132
Innovation principle, 45
Input-output methodologies, 17–18, 20, 23
Intercommunal equalization of tax potential, 39
Interindustry linkages, 19–20, 23
International Rivercenter Corporation (IRC), 140
Internationale Bauausstellung Emscher-Park (IBA-EmscherPark), 44, 48–51
Ireland, Northern, 91

Job creation, 63–68, 92–98, 154, 170, 172, 175
Joint Industrial Development Committee (JIDC), 153–54
Joint Tax Committee of Canton and Upper Fells Point, 112–13

Kleinstaaten, 38
Kommunale Selbstvenwaltung, 38
Kommunaler Finanzausgleich, 39
Kommunalverband Ruhrgebiet, 51

Labor force participation: division of labor, 70; employment, 41, 42, 44, 48, 55, 70–72, 75–76, 79, 81, 85, 87, 92–98, 113, 124, 150–52; outmigration of labor, 41; and youth, 77, 81
Labour Party, and control of local government, 72, 74, 170, 175
Laender, 38
Land Authority for Wales (LAW), 126
Land taxes, 39, 43
Land use planning policies, 70
Legislation, 71–72, 105, 109, 112–13, 137–38, 175
Liberal/Democratic Alliance, 72
Linkage: backward linkages, 19, 20, 23, 41; forward linkages, 19, 20,

41; interindustry, 19–20, 23; policies, 113–14
Llewellyn-Davies Planning, 122
Local development policy, 170–76
Local enterprise development, 10
Local taxation, 7
Location quotient method, 22
Louisiana Transportation Trust Fund amendment, 136
Louisville, Kentucky, 24–25

MacDonald Steel, 166 n.3
Machiavelli, Niccolo, 3, 9, 15
Macro-economic development, 36
Mahoning Valley Economic Development Corporation (MVEDC), 159, 160
Management Education, 21
Manufacturing, 10, 11, 26, 37, 55, 70–71, 73, 87, 122–23
Maritime industry, 134–35, 138, 139–45
Market Identification, 21–23
Marketing targets, 18–21, 23–24
Merchant groups, 160
Metropolitan statistical area (MSA), 21
Mintz, Donald, 137
Mississippi River Gulf Outlet (MRGO), 132, 134, 135
Movement Against Destruction (MAD), 107
Municipal self-reliance, 6

National Loan Fund, 81
National Training Agency, 76
National Urban Program, 79
Neighborhood organizations, 105–16, 159–60
Neighborhood regeneration, 85–98, 110–16
New Energy Corporation, 61
New Enterprise Workshops (NEW), 78–79
New Federalism, 169–70, 171
New Orleans, 13, 132–45
New Orleans Exhibition Hall Authority, 143
New Towns, 71–72

Nine-dimensional policy space, 8–10
Non-local business recruitment, 10
North Docklands Industrial Improvement Area, 122
Northrhine Westphalia, 44–49

O'Donnell, Captain John, 106
Ohio Water Service, 162

Politico-rational processes, 120, 126
Port Improvement Program (PIP), 136
Practical Training for Business, 79–80
Prince's Business Youth Trust, 77
Product life cycle theory, 20
Profit cycle, 20
Project Future, 60
Public goods, 171–72
Public housing, 70, 73, 76, 91, 157
Public incentives, 10
Public investment, 10
Public-private partnership, 48, 52, 111; principle, 46
Public sector economic participation, 72
Public versus private housing, 71, 73
Pulver, Glen, 17

Quasi-autonomous non-governmental organizations (quangos), 121, 125, 127
Queens Cross Housing Association, 91

Recession, British, 87
Regeneration strategy, 122
Regional assistance grants, 72–73
Regional Growth Alliance (RGA), 161
Regional Growth Potential (RGP) model, 20, 23–26, 28
Regional restructuring, 44–53
Research and development, 46
Revitalization, 150–66, 175
Riverfront 2000, 141, 144
Riverfront Economic Development Agreement, 144
Rivergate, 134, 139, 142–44
Roemer, Buddy, 136, 137, 138
Rouse, James, 104

Index

Rowthorn, Brian, 70
Ruhrgebiet, 5, 11, 35–54

Schaefer, William Donald, 108, 109
Schmoke, Kurt L., 109–10
Scotland, 11–12, 69–83; Clydebank, 78; Clydeside, 71; Edinburgh, 76; Ferguslie Park, 90, 93; Glasgow, 69–83, 87, 90; local government politics in west central Scotland, 72; Scottish Cooperative Development Committee, 80; Scottish Development Agency (SDA), 74, 76, 77, 78, 79, 80; social polarization, 72; Scottish Development Finance, 81–82; Scottish Nationalist Party, 72; Strathclyde, 74, 79; West Central Scotland Plan, 83
Scottish Development Agency (SDA), 74, 76, 77, 79, 80; Small Business Division, 77
Scottish Development Finance, 81–82
Scottish Nationalist Party, 72
Sectoral specialization, 10
Semi-judicial processes, 120, 126, 128
Shipbuilding, 70, 90, 106
Single European Market, 35
Small Business Administration (SBA), 60, 66, 68
Small business and urban renewal, 124–29, 156–57
Small Business Development System (SBDS) model, 20, 21–23, 28
Small business incubators, 156–57, 159
Social cushioning, 41
Social Democrats, 40
Social polarization, 70–72
Socially oriented market economy, 36
South Bend, Indiana, 55–68
South Bend Industrial Revolving Fund (IRF), 58
South Bend Lathe Company (SBL), 11, 55–68
South Cardiff, Wales, 12–13, 119–29
South East Community Organization (SECO), 107, 111, 112, 113

South Glamorgan, Wales, 122–24
Southeast Council Against the Road (SCAR), 106
Southeast Linkage Group (SLG), 109, 113–14
Soziale Marktwirtschaft, 36
Sozialplan, 41
Spatial linkages, 19
Standard Industrial Classification (SIC), 18
Steel, 150–52, 157–58, 161, 167 n.3
Strategic planning, 131–45
Strathclyde Community Business, 79
Strathclyde Region, 73–74
Subsidiarity, 38–40
Subsidies, 149–66, 170, 172, 174
Supply-side economics, 72
Supra-local state, 11, 12
Sweet, David, 18, 20

Target community, 22
Targeted marketing, 18–29
Taxes, 109–10, 112–13, 151, 170, 173; abatement, 149, 156; income tax, 39; industry tax, 39; land tax, 39; tax reforms, 40; tax revenues, 65, 66, 136, 152, 170, 173
Tchoupitoulas Corridor, 136–38
Technical assistance, 21
Techno-rational policy, 120, 126
Tenn-Tom model, 20, 25–26, 27, 28
Tenn-Tom Waterway Development Authority, 25–26, 27
Tennessee-Tombigbee waterway, 25
Thatcher, Margaret, 152, 155–56, 175
Thatcherism, 170, 171
Three-tier system, 38–40
Tiebout hypothesis, 6
Tourism, 102, 138, 141, 145
Training and Employment Grants Scheme, 81
Transportation, 132, 137, 158, 163; Trust Fund, 137
Triangle Industries, 110–11

Unemployment Insurance Administration, 27

Unions, 40–41, 56–67
United Kingdom, 5, 85–98, 150–58; approach to unemployment, 71–72; central government grants, 7; Enterprise Trusts, 74; local economic development, 4, 85–98; local economic policy choices, 9; North-South divide, 72; recession, 87; as unitary state, 6
United States, 5; adoption of SBDA model, 22; domestic comparative case studies, 14; federal system, 6; and Germany, 174; local economic development, 4
Upper Mississippi River, master plan, 136, 139
Upriver Facilities, 137
Urban Design Concept Team, 107
Urban development, 42, 104–14, 161
Urban Development Action Grants (UDAGs), 108, 110
Urban Development Corporations (UDCs), 120
Urban renewal, 85–98, 106–17, 119–29, 161; amendments, 110, 113
U.S. Army Corps of Engineers, 20, 25, 163
U.S. Commerce Department's Economic Development Agency (EDA), 55–56, 59–67

Vocational training, 46; Enterprise Funds for Youth (EFY), 77; National Training Agency, 77; Practical Training for Business, 79–80; Training and Employment Grants Scheme, 81; Workwise, 76–77, Youth Employment and Training Institute, 81; Youth Training Scheme, 76–77

Wales: Atlantic Wharf, 122, 124, 125, 127; Cardiff, 121–28; Land Authority for Wales (LAW), 126; South Cardiff, 12–13, 119–29; South Glamorgan, 122–24
Waterfront Coalition, 109–12
Waterfront development, 12, 13, 14, 102, 103–17, 123, 133, 134
West Central Scotland Plan, 83
Worker cooperatives, 80
Workwise, 76–77
World War I, and trade disruption, 70

Youngstown, Ohio, 13–14, 149–52, 158–65
Youngstown Revitalization Foundation, 159, 160, 161
Youth Employment and Training Institute, 81
Youth Training Scheme, 76–77

Zukunftsinitiative Montanregionen (ZIM), 44–48
Zuweisungen, 39

About the Editor and Contributors

CARA L. BAILEY recently completed a Master of Urban Affairs degree at Virginia Polytechnic Institute and State University. She was previously an associate with a Berkeley-based consulting firm, where she gained broad experience conducting economic impact studies of proposed development projects and land-use plans. Ms. Bailey plans to focus her career on making affordable housing development a central component of community development planning efforts.

TERRY F. BUSS is Professor of Urban Studies at the University of Akron. He has published nearly two hundred articles and books on public policy issues as diverse as economic development, plant closings, health care, entrepreneurship, and geriatrics. His most recent book, *On the Rebound* (co-authored with Roger Vaughn), details a strategy to help communities respond to plant closings.

CHARLES CRAYPO is Professor and Chair of the Economics Department at the University of Notre Dame. He also has been a faculty member at Michigan State University, The Pennsylvania State University, and Cornell University. He is the author of books and articles on unions and collective bargaining, regional deindustrialization and revitalization, and the economics of low-wage employment.

DAVID FASENFEST is on the faculty of the Department of Sociology and Anthropology at Purdue University and has held other positions, most recently as Director of Urban and Economic Development Research in the Urban Research Institute of the University of Louisville. He has published widely on community development, community power, and local economic change. He is the editor of *Community Economic Development: Policy Formation in the United States and United Kingdom* and author of *Income Stories: The Changing Structure of Family Income in the 1980s*.

ROBERT P. GILOTH is Executive Director of South East Community Organization and Southeast Development Inc. in Baltimore, Maryland. He was Deputy Commissioner for Economic Development in Chicago under Mayor Harold Washington, directing research and evaluation studies of economic development programs. He has taught at the University of Maryland and Tufts University, and he has written widely on community development and urban policy issues.

GERD HENNINGS is Professor and Director of the Local Economic Policy Unit at the Fachbereich Raumplanung (Department of Spatial Planning), University of Dortmund, and occasional lecturer at the European Business School in Oestrich-Winkel near Frankfurt. He is the author of numerous publications on regional and local economic policy, and he continuously advises local economic development agencies in Germany, particularly cities in traditional industrial regions.

ROB F. IMRIE is Lecturer in Geography at the University of London. He is co-author of *Transforming Buyer-Supplier Relations* and co-editor (with Huw Thomas) of *Urban Policy and City Regeneration*.

C. THEODORE KOEBEL is Director of the Virginia Center for Housing Research and Associate Professor of Housing, Urban Affairs, and Planning at the Virginia Polytechnic Institute and State University. Prior to joining Virginia Tech in 1991, he was on the faculty of the University of Louisville and served as Associate Director of that university's Urban Research Institute.

KLAUS R. KUNZMANN is University-Professor and Director of the Institut fuer Raumplanung at the Fachbereich Raumplanung (Institute of Spatial Planning, Department of Spatial Planning), University of Dortmund, since 1974. He taught urban planning at the Technical University of Vienna, Austria, from 1967 to 1971. He was the founding president of the Association of European Schools of Planning (AESOP). In 1989 he was Visiting Professor at the Institut d'Urbanisme of the

About the Editor and Contributors

University of Paris (Paris VIII), and in 1992 he was granted the EEC–Jean Monnet Chair of European Spatial Planning. His main research interests include European spatial planning and innovative policies of spatial development and of restructuring traditional industrial regions.

WILLIAM F. LEVER is Professor of Urban Studies in the Department of Social and Economic Research at the University of Glasgow. His fields of interest include employment change and urban policy; his current research is largely focused on shifts in urban and regional systems in Europe. He has written books on industrial change, policies for urban economic regeneration, and European cities. He has worked as a consultant to the Organization for Economic Cooperation and Development, the British government, the European Community, and other bodies. He is also the editor of *Urban Studies*.

ANDREW A. McARTHUR is Lecturer in Urban Studies at the University of Glasgow. He specializes in the evaluation of local economic development policies and has a particular interest in community-based initiatives. In addition to his long-standing interest in community business, he has researched the impact of neighborhood credit unions and is currently working on strategies to involve residents in urban regeneration projects.

ALAN McGREGOR is Director of the Training and Employment Research Unit at the University of Glasgow. His research interests include urban labor market analysis, assessment of employment and training programs, and evaluation of urban regeneration projects. He has recently directed studies on housing and local economic development, community participation in neighborhood regeneration, and strategic approaches to urban regeneration.

PETER B. MEYER is Professor of Urban Policy and Economics at the University of Louisville, where he has recently become Director of the Center for Environmental Management. He previously taught at The Pennsylvania State University, where he headed the Local Economic Development Assistance Project for ten years. He is widely published in the area of economic development in both British and American journals.

JERRY PAAR is Staff Associate in the Division of Labor Studies at Indiana University–Indianapolis. He teaches and does research on the effects of plant closings, organized labor's role in regional economic development, and most recently, structural changes in production in the automobile industry.

HUW THOMAS lectures at the School of Planning, Oxford Polytechnic. He has practical and research experience in urban regeneration and local economic development, and he has published extensively in the field (often with Rob Imrie). He and Rob Imrie are currently engaged in a study of urban policy and local economic regeneration funded by the Economic and Social Research Council.

ROBERT K. WHELAN is Professor and Associate Dean in the College of Urban and Public Affairs at the University of New Orleans. He is co-author of *Urban Policy and Politics in a Bureaucratic Age* and has authored (or co-authored) numerous articles, book chapters, and papers. His current research interests center on the politics of urban economic development in New Orleans and in Canadian cities.

ALMA H. YOUNG is Professor of Urban and Public Affairs and Director of the Ph.D. Program in Urban Studies at the University of New Orleans. She formerly chaired the Board of Commissioners of the Port of New Orleans. She has written on issues of political economy and social change in the United States and the Caribbean. Her current research interests center on issues of urban development, poverty, and race in New Orleans.

Policy Studies Organization publications
issued with Greenwood Press / Quorum Books

Outdoor Recreation Policy: Pleasure and Preservation
John D. Hutcheson, Jr., Francis P. Noe, and Robert E. Snow, editors

Conflict Resolution and Public Policy
Miriam K. Mills, editor

Teaching Public Policy: Theory, Research, and Practice
Peter J. Bergerson, editor

The Reconstruction of Family Policy
Elaine A. Anderson and Richard C. Hula, editors

Gubernatorial Leadership and State Policy
Eric B. Herzik and Brent W. Brown, editors

Public Policy Issues in Wildlife Management
William R. Mangun, editor

Health Insurance and Public Policy: Risk, Allocation, and Equity
Miriam K. Mills and Robert H. Blank, editors

Public Authorities and Public Policy: The Business of Government
Jerry Mitchell, editor

Technology and U.S. Competitiveness: An Institutional Focus
W. Henry Lambright and Dianne Rahm, editors

Using Theory to Improve Program and Policy Evaluations
Huey-tysh Chen and Peter H. Rossi, editors

Comparative Judicial Review and Public Policy
Donald W. Jackson and C. Neal Tate, editors

Moving the Earth: Cooperative Federalism and Implementation of the Surface Mining Act
Uday Desai, editor

Professional Developments in Policy Studies
Stuart Nagel

International Agricultural Trade and Market Development in the 1990s
John W. Helmuth and Don F. Hadwiger, editors